T0253991

History of Computing

The *History of Computing* series publishes high-quality books which address the history of computing, with an emphasis on the 'externalist' view of this history, more accessible to a wider audience. The series examines content and history from four main quadrants: the history of relevant technologies, the history of the core science, the history of relevant business and economic developments, and the history of computing as it pertains to social history and societal developments.

Titles can span a variety of product types, including but not exclusively, themed volumes, biographies, 'profile' books (with brief biographies of a number of key people), expansions of workshop proceedings, general readers, scholarly expositions, titles used as ancillary textbooks, revivals and new editions of previous worthy titles.

These books will appeal, varyingly, to academics and students in computer science, history, mathematics, business and technology studies. Some titles will also directly appeal to professionals and practitioners of different backgrounds.

More information about this series at http://www.springer.com/series/8442

Jacqueline Léon

Automating Linguistics

 Springer

Jacqueline Léon (ID)
Laboratoire d'Histoire des Théories
Linguistiques UMR CNRS 7597
Université de Paris
Paris, France

ISSN 2190-6831   ISSN 2190-684X   (electronic)
History of Computing
ISBN 978-3-030-70644-9   ISBN 978-3-030-70642-5   (eBook)
https://doi.org/10.1007/978-3-030-70642-5

This Springer imprint is published by the registered company Springer Nature Switzerland AG
The registered company address is: Gewerbestrasse 11, 6330 Cham, Switzerland

Foreword

With the latest comeback of artificial intelligence as 'deep learning', newspapers and industry have been promising us new computer breakthroughs in linguistics and information retrieval. Building upon automatic processing of data that are massively harvested from the web, we are promised in some not too distant future near-perfect automatic translations, expert chatbots that understand and answer human queries, or even conversations with virtual assistants. However, as some reports have brought to light, much human effort, often under precarious circumstances, is tacitly injected in the machine's 'deep learning'[1] and we do not yet know how the learning curve of this enhanced technology may evolve.

But it is not the first time that we have been promised perfect translation or improved human-computer interaction, rather, as history teaches us, the industry's self-advertising through the projection of a futuristic utopia is a recurrent phenomenon of our computer age. Already in the 1950s, formalisations of language were proposed that would supposedly make automatic translation possible. They turned out to be performing poorly. And already in the 1960s we saw the first usage of computing facilities for corpus linguistics prefiguring later big data or digital humanities. But, tempered by the limited resources of the time, this was without the (over)ambitious high hopes pinned on today's big data. This goes to show that it is now more timely than ever to go back in time and reflect upon past developments in computer linguistics. Both the successes and the limits of earlier efforts can help to historically inform us and to critically assess our current situation.

The present book is a history of how the digital computer encountered the field of linguistics in the wake of the Second World War and slowly but lastingly changed the very field of linguistics, creating new (sub)fields such as Automatic Translation, Natural Language Processing or Computational Linguistics. Two important turns are described in this book. The first one, which may be called the 'automatic turn', is the automation of language, enabled through the formalisation and

---

[1] Julia Carrie Wong, 'A white-collar sweatshop: Google Assistant contractors allege wage theft', *Guardian*, May 25, 2019.

mathematisation of language that took place roughly between 1949 and 1966. The second turn, the 'corpus turn', is the emergence of natural language processing in the 1990s, continuing and enlarging earlier research in documentation systems and corpus linguistics with the help of microcomputers.

Though efforts to formalise language and automate linguistics antedate this fateful encounter, the advent of the digital computer accelerated and heavily influenced the automation of language. It enabled, both theoretically and practically (and also financially), the use of mathematical methods in language, and, later, the systematic and automatic exploitation of large corpora in linguistics. But this encounter was also a two-way process. Linguistics also contributed to the newly developing field of computing. It motivated the development of some early programming languages, documentation systems and query languages, and, most conspicuously, provided some of the important theoretical tools for computing and programming such as indexing and parsing algorithms or the Chomsky hierarchy.

The main trigger for the encounter between linguistics and computing was the Second World War. Linguistics took part in the war effort as much as the other sciences, a fact that is often overlooked (cf. Chap. 3). Apart from the more obvious connection to cryptography, linguistics was also essential for developing effective language training courses for the army, and for translating foreign texts. During the Cold War that followed the World War, it was especially the feeling that quick translation of Russian research and intelligence into English was badly needed that prompted military investments into automatic translation. Warren Weaver's 1949 report on mechanical translation started off a decade of intensive work on automatic translation.

Though digital computing had its origins mainly in solving scientific and business computing, its redefinition in the late 1940s as 'information processing' had broadened the ambitions and the agenda of digital computing. Linguistic computing now became definitely a part of this enlarged vision. Even more, it has been contended that, as automatic translation was on the agenda, it contributed to spreading the use of the words 'translation' and 'language' among the communities of people that programmed and coded the early digital computers.[2] In any case, there was some convergence between the formal methods developed in automatic translation and those developed for automatic programming; in addition, one of the first string-processing languages, COMIT, was developed by Victor Yngve's team at M.I.T.

Research groups in automatic translation did not necessarily rely on already existing linguistic models and theories. Although the so-called neo-Bloomfieldians in U.S. linguistics had already developed a particular taste for formal and/or mathematical approaches to language (cf. Chap. 4), laying the foundations for what is now called 'immediate constituent analysis', their concepts did not transfer immediately to this new context. In many cases, ad hoc procedures were developed, often more determined by practical constraints and pragmatism than by insight into

---

[2] David Nofre, Mark Priestley, Gerard Alberts, 2014, 'When technology became language: The origins of the linguistic conception of computer programming, 1950–1960', Technology and Culture, Vol. 55, Nr. 1, p. 40–75.

language itself. For instance, ideas were borrowed from cybernetics and information theory and this transfer of concepts led to many discussions within linguistics itself, thereby changing the reference framework in which linguistics operated (cf. Chap. 5). One of the recurrent themes of debate was whether a mathematical approach to language was able to capture essential features of language, such as grammar or perhaps even meaning? And also, what kind of mathematics was best suited for formalising language: an algebraic, an analytical or probabilistic approach, or perhaps a combination of those?

One of the most important developments in modern linguistics, Noam Chomsky's generative grammars, grew out of this context. Chomsky came from neo-Bloomfieldian linguistics and was influenced in particular by Zellig S. Harris's work, he also worked for a while at the Mechanical Translation unit of M.I.T.'s Research Laboratory of Electronics. Though Chomsky systematically underplays the importance of this context, the encounter with computer people and mathematicians at M.I.T. and the discussions with other linguists around automatic translation and the mechanisation of language set the scene for his work. Furthermore, the mathematical precision that the French mathematician M.P. Schützenberger brought to Chomsky's models for language and the adoption of these models for computer-theoretical work on automata and programming were quite crucial in securing and augmenting the intellectual credibility and legitimation of his linguistic models. From 1962 onwards, Chomsky's theory would start its triumphant march in modern linguistics marking the success of the formalisation of language. Around the same time, though completely independently, disappointment about the poor results of automatic translation set in during the early 1960s. The very idea of automatic translation even got discredited as witnessed by the negative reports by Bar-Hillel (1960) and Automatic Language Processing Advisory Committee (ALPAC, 1964) (cf. Chap. 2).

Linguistics was also at the forefront of research in computerised information retrieval. Though the focus of much work in automatic translation was on the formal (syntactic) structure of language rather than the lexical structure, automatic translation's need for indexing and retrieving entries in a large, structured database such a dictionary or thesaurus stimulated research on automatic documentation and information retrieval (cf. Chap. 7). In the *Proceedings of the International Conference on Scientific Information. Washington DC November 16–21 1958* that brought various people from this emergent field together for the first time, researchers in automatic translation such as Victor Yngve, Anthony Oettinger, Margaret Masterman, or Zellig S. Harris figure alongside patent offices and (bio)chemists, who also had keen interest in automating large databases for storing, indexing and comparing their patents or (bio)chemical compounds. Automatic documentation together with automatic syntactic analysis would eventually be incorporated into the field of Natural Language Processing (NLP) in the 1990s (cf. Chap. 6).

Corpus linguistics, which had a long tradition in the empiricist English linguistics (Firth, Halliday), also invested itself slowly in the computerisation of linguistics. Though the first experiments were hampered by the limited computing and memory resources available at the time, the main concepts were refined over the years and gradually bigger corpora were constituted and made amenable to automatic syntactic and lexical analysis. Matching the limited possibilities of the 1980s, some linguists shifted their focus to the study of 'specialised' languages, also called restricted languages (Firth, Halliday) or sublanguages (Harris). By the 1990s, powered by cheaper and faster computing and memory systems (namely, the revolution of the microcomputer), the integration of these tools and ideas led to today's Natural Language Processing (cf. Chap. 10).

* * *

This book is the outcome of a lifelong research interest in the history of the automation of language in the age of the digital computer. Jacqueline Léon, probably the world's foremost expert on this topic, moved from being a practitioner of the field to writing the history of the field. She worked as a CNRS researcher at the research institute for the history of linguistics, the Centre pour l'Histoire des Théories Linguistiques (UMR 7597, Paris). For her habilitation in 2010, she selected and reworked a number of her articles and also added some chapters to arrive at a quite complete, detailed history of the early automation of language, covering the latter half of the twentieth century. Her habilitation resulted into a book that was published as *Histoire de l'automatisation des sciences du langage* in 2015.[3] In her work much attention is paid to the context in which this encounter between linguistics and computing took place, and to the ensuing institutionalisation. While much of the important, and better-known, work was done in the United States, Léon's book also brings into focus equally important work that was done in Europe, notably in the United Kingdom. (Chaps. 7 and 10), France (Chaps. 8 and 9) and the Soviet Union (Chap. 7). Apart from some minor changes and additions, the present English translation is essentially faithful to the French original. However, the order of chapters has been changed to reinforce the chronological and logical structure of the book and a general conclusion has been added.

Université Paris 8   Maarten Bullynck,
Saint-Denis, France

---

[3] Jacqueline Léon, *Histoire de l'automatisation des sciences du langage*, ENS Éditions: Lyon, 2015. The book was reviewed in a number of journals:

- Ycard Bernard, 2015, Historiographia Linguistica 42 2–3: 457-460.
- Galazzi Enrica, 2016, L'analisi linguistica e litteraria 2016-1, p.173
- François Jacques, 2017, Bulletin de la Société de Linguistique 112-2: 1–9
- Bertrand Emanuel, 2018, 'Mathématisations et automatisations des sciences du langage : des tournants conceptuels ou technologiques?', Revue d'Histoire des Sciences Humaines, 32, pp.288–292.

Acknowledgements

I would like to express my sincere thanks to Maarten Bullynck for his help at several steps of the translation of the text, for his suggestion of modifying the order of the chapters, of adding footnotes to make the text more readable to non-linguists, and for the final edition of the manuscript.

Many thanks also to John DeWitt and Nick Riemer for their precious help with the English version.

Contents

Chapter 1
Introduction

The automation of the language sciences started with the first experiments on machine translation undertaken just after the end of World War II in 1948–1949 in the USA and in Great Britain. I will call it "the computational turn".[1] This turn, which defines how linguists adopted and integrated the concepts and the methods of the computer sciences and mathematics, involves very specific features. It is characterised by the sudden appearance of a set of completely new concepts, methods and practices which did not belong to the "horizon of retrospection" of linguists and the language sciences.

As it is affected by temporality, scientific activity refers to its past and its future. It refers to a body of knowledge which has been developed previously (concepts, works, results) and sets itself various projects for the future. Auroux (1987, 2007) names these two types of references "horizon of retrospection" and "horizon of projection", respectively. One of the tasks of the historian of sciences is to identify the structure of the horizon(s) of retrospection.

The horizon of retrospection is transmitted through tradition. As a body of previous knowledge, it can be common to a group and an area or specific to a researcher. The horizon of retrospection can be subject to contradictory moves. For a given domain, it can be subject to oblivion: some pieces of knowledge are regularly removed from the horizon of retrospection depending on the research interests of the moment. Alternatively, it can be subject to cumulation so that new knowledge can be aggregated with previous results. When emerging, a discipline reinvents its past renegotiating its horizon of retrospection by using these contradictory moves.

The horizon of retrospection initiated by machine translation is characterised by the intertwining of engineering with fundamental sciences such as mathematics, logic, physics, the neurosciences, acoustics and recently developed sciences like cybernetics and information theory. Developed primarily at MIT, this intertwining,

---

[1] See Rorty's *The Linguistic Turn* (1967) on the attention paid to the importance of language in the formulation of philosophical questions.

© The Author(s), under exclusive license to Springer Nature
Switzerland AG 2021
J. Léon, *Automating Linguistics*, History of Computing,
https://doi.org/10.1007/978-3-030-70642-5_1

named the war sciences by Dahan and Pestre (2004), led to cutting-edge technologies like radar, anti-aircraft defense systems and computers and later, after World War II, to machine translation.

In this context, the computerisation of the language sciences constitutes an interesting case because two horizons of retrospection confront one another: that of machine translation, namely, the horizon of retrospection of the war sciences in which linguistics has no place, and that of the linguists which, most of the time, does not involve the war sciences. Actually, the computational turn is marked at the beginning by a paradox, namely, that, although machine translation implies the (automatic) treatment of languages, linguistics does not belong to the war sciences.[2] Thus, for the language sciences, the new horizon was entirely new and set up by external way. However, because machine translation, and afterwards computational linguistics, deals with natural languages, the new field is essential to the language sciences, so that they have to integrate it.

The issues raised by the computerisation of the language sciences can be addressed by the following questions: how can the horizon of retrospection of machine translation be integrated by the linguists in their own horizon(s) of retrospection? Will this new knowledge cumulate with linguists' knowledge or will it replace the former horizon of retrospection, causing its cancellation or even its oblivion? Can it be renegotiated? What is claimed in this book, is that, in order to integrate a new horizon of retrospection (the body of knowledge common to machine translation pioneers), the linguists will tap into their own scientific and intellectual tradition in order to integrate this new set of knowledge. Knowing that, facing that issue, each tradition will operate differently.

Linguistics' computational turn happened in two steps. The first step, machine translation, while instituting a new horizon of retrospection, projected a future, a horizon of projection, for the language sciences. The second step, computational linguistics and the Chomskyan program, becomes the horizon of projection anticipating the future of the computational mathematisation of language. That period of 15 years (1948–1966), from the beginning of early machine translation experiments to the establishment of computational linguistics, can be regarded as constituting the computational turn.

The computational turn is anchored in "the first mathematisation of language" of the 1930s which can be defined by the rise of formalisation promoted by the Vienna School, in particular Carnap, as a common objective for every science, setting up mathematics as one language among others. The first mathematisation of language is characterised by the setting in interaction of algorithms and formal languages resulting from mathematical logic. The domain that rose at the junction of syntactic analysis, formal languages and computer programming can be called "the second mathematisation". Algorithms which were only an abstraction for logicians in the

---

[2] Martin Joos, an acoustic engineer and a phonetist, was an exception. He was probably the only linguist to have an activity in the war sciences (see Sect. 4.2.1).

first mathematisation came to be implemented in space and time. This is why it can be called the computational mathematisation of language.

The second mathematisation of language started with the implementation of syntactic analysis methods for machine translation which led to computational linguistics as an autonomous and institutionalised field of research. It can be claimed that it is thanks to machine translation, i.e. thanks to the strategic need for producing mass translations, that the formal languages, anchored in mathematical logic in the 1930–1940s, became involved in algorithms for syntactic analysis. This move determined the rise of formal grammars, in particular Chomsky's generative grammar.

A second key moment of the automation of the language sciences can be identified in the 1990s, when the rising power of computers and software would make much computerised textual data available. The appearance of microcomputers would lead linguists to use computerised data and new linguistic tools. This second turn which I call the "corpus turn" has characteristics quite different from the first turn. Actually, the use of large computerised corpora did not constitute a real departure from linguistic traditions. It allowed linguists to implement some assumptions belonging to earlier linguistic approaches, anterior to the first turn, making a link with earlier methods, like probabilistic methods resulting from information theory.

In this book, I will focus less on the social consequences of the automation of language (Auroux 1996) than on the various modes of integration (of the new horizon of retrospection) by the language sciences. I will tackle this issue through the following questions:

(i) Has only one form of mathematisation, i.e. logico-mathematics, prevailed in the automation of the language sciences, as the development of computational linguistics would suggest, or have other forms of mathematisation come into play?

(ii) The modes of integration of the new horizon of retrospection can be considered only in a comparative way. Several traditions are examined, American, British and French, and to a lesser extent, the Russian tradition from which the sources are less accessible. The choice of these traditions is not fortuitous but results from regarding machine translation as a war technology. The countries considered here are the "winners" of World War II; they were engaged in the Cold War where machine translation occupied a strategic place. Much more than others which would follow, and in a much more massive way, these states invested considerable means in machine translation. The question that remains to be answered is whether linguistic and intellectual traditions, still quite distinct at that period, determined different modes of integration, and how.[3]

(iii) I will examine how the new area opened by computational linguistics led to the emergence of natural language processing and artificial intelligence.

(iv) I will investigate to what extent the possibility of automation gave rise to new objects and new methods in the language sciences. We will see that, thanks to

---

[3] See Léon (2014).

automation, lexical semantics will be renewed starting from old questions about the "word" as a linguistic unit.

(v) We will ask whether all the concepts and methods coming from the war sciences were integrated into the language sciences or whether some of them were privileged leaving aside others, and how. One thinks in particular of information theory, a central, unifying and universalising theory, which, at the time of its integration, knew various destinies, distinct from that of computational linguistics.

(vi) Another question concerns periodisation. We will ask whether, starting from the event constituted by the computational turn, a linear periodisation of integration can be delimited with a beginning and an end; or whether, on the contrary, various modes of integration will determine various periodisations, some of them anchored in previous centuries and still in progress today.

(vii) Lastly, we can ask whether this technological revolution constitutes a third revolution of the language sciences comparable to the emergence of writing and the grammatisation of vernaculars, respectively, the first and second revolution defined by Auroux (1994).

This book aims to give an account of three movements, machine translation as the founding event of the computational turn, the integration of this turn by the language sciences and the corpus turn. These three movements will be developed in nine chapters.

Five chapters are devoted to the USA, where everything started.

Chapter 2 "Machine Translation as Technology of War" gives an account of the event constitutive of the computational turn.

Chapter 3 "The War Effort, the Technologisation of Linguistics and the Emergence of Applied Linguistics" deals with the technologisation of the language sciences. It is devoted to the war effort undertaken by the Americans in the domain of language teaching, in which most American linguists were involved. Many were also implied in cryptography, the majority as simple translators of the messages written in "exotic" languages, but some taking part in the decoding work itself. The war effort led to the emergence of applied linguistics in the USA which was characterised by an important technologisation of the methods.

Chapter 4 deals with the automation of American linguistics. Entitled "The Computational Turn and Formalisation in Neo-Bloomfieldian Distributionalism", it examines how computationability raised new challenges for American structuralist linguists concerning translation and formalisation.

Chapter 5 "Information Theory: The Transfer of Terms, Concepts and Methods" is concerned less with the automation than with the mathematisation of language. I will examine the process by which some concepts and methods of information theory, bringing together telecommunication engineering and mathematical theories, were integrated into the language sciences. Roman Jakobson's Distinctive Feature Theory presents an exemplary case of this process associating European linguistics and engineering and American war sciences.

Chapter 6 "From MT to Computational Linguistics and Natural Language Processing" addresses pioneering experiments in MT, the emergence of computational linguistics from syntactic analysis which condensed the results of structural linguistics, the first mathematisation and computer programming, and how it gave rise to natural language processing.

In Chaps. 7, 8 and 9, the American field, strictly speaking, is left aside, and other traditions than American linguistics will be examined.

Chapter 7 "Machine Translation of Semantics and Lexicon: New Issues and New Objects in the Long-Term History of the Language Sciences" attempts to show that the possibility of automation determined the identification of objects, which, although they pertained to diverse linguistic and intellectual traditions (British, Russian and French), renewed certain issues related to lexicon. It will be shown that a change of focal distance reveals a change of periodisation. To the very short time-frame of machine translation, early history can be opposed a long time stretching back sometimes to several centuries (see Chiss and Puech 1999).

The specific case of France will be examined in Chap. 8 "The French Linguistic Tradition and External Reception of the Computational Mathematisation of Language", and Chap. 9 will deal with "Automatic Documentation and Automatic Discourse Analysis: Specificity of Harris's Reception in France". Contrary to what happened in the USA, the new horizon of retrospection was completely foreign to the linguistic tradition in France, a fact which gave rise to a completely external reception of machine translation and computational linguistics, and the need for "frontier runners". Automation took on a special form in France associating information retrieval, automatic discourse analysis and the reception of Z.S. Harris.

Chapter 10 is devoted to "The Empiricist Turn of Automation-Mathematisation: Large Corpora, Restricted Languages and Sublanguages". Contrary to the machine translation turn, the corpus turn does not constitute any break with the linguists' horizon of retrospection. It was anchored in continuity and originated in the British tradition. It led to the emergence of new objects for natural language processing. It helped renewing a debate between empiricism and Chomskyanism which had started in the 1960s.

The "General Conclusion" (Chap. 11) deals with the issues of recent history and the dangers of presentism.

Let us add a methodological point: the corpus of texts concerning early experiments in machine translation (1948–1966) can be identified if not exhaustively, then at least easily. The relatively restricted number of published texts makes it possible to record them all: the first collective books and journals (*Machine Translation* and *La Traduction Automatique* and their successors). In addition, one of our tasks was to collect grey literature and personal records from institutions and pioneers of the field. Their ranking and filing are an essential component of our research.[4]

---

[4] The creation of a fond of archives and documents on the history of machine translation and computational linguistics (1954–1975) is carried out at CNRS UMR7597 laboratory Histoire des Théories Linguistiques, in collaboration with Camille Faivre. In the bibliography the documents belonging to this fond are referred to as History of the Automatic Treatment of Language (HATL).

For this research, I largely used the items, records and digitalised texts of the Corpus de textes linguistiques fondamentaux (CTLF) http://ctlf.ens-lyon.fr/, and I would like to thank Bernard Colombat and Arnaud Pelfrêne who gave me access to these sources.

Chapter 2
Machine Translation as Technology of War

2.1 Introduction

The first phase of the automation of language comprises two stages: machine translation (MT) in the early 1950s and computational linguistics in the early 1960s. This phase was accompanied by the sudden introduction of a new horizon of retrospection for linguistics during the brief period lasting from 1948 until 1966. This was the result of the massive intervention by those institutions that had made drastic decisions about orientating and financing science in the wake of the upheaval caused by World War II. As a technology of war, machine translation was developed in the USA by government authorities, which devoted considerable resources to MT in order to respond to the strategic and political challenges in the post-war period. On the back, computational linguistics was proposed as the "new linguistics" in a quite ruthless way.

Two key personalities, Warren Weaver and Yehoshua Bar-Hillel, and the following three reports ensured the establishment of the new horizon of retrospection on the institutional level:

(i) 1949 [1955]: *Translation*, Warren Weaver
(ii) 1960: *The present status of automatic translation of languages*, Yehoshua Bar-Hillel
(iii) 1966: *Language and Machines: Computers in Translation and Linguistics*, Automatic Language Processing Advisory Committee (ALPAC) of the National Research Council

The issues at stake were how a new scientific-technical field could be imposed from outside, by institutions, and without any specific disciplinary anchoring in university centres. One can wonder whether such a field, which was thought of as a technology, could be transformed into an autonomous discipline, or whether it would be condemned to disappear if the results proved to be insufficient. In order to

© The Author(s), under exclusive license to Springer Nature
Switzerland AG 2021
J. Léon, *Automating Linguistics*, History of Computing,
https://doi.org/10.1007/978-3-030-70642-5_2

give an account of this pioneering moment, or better still, of this event, I have chosen to present a narrative of this institutional history. This event constitutes a "memory landmark" – "borne de mémoire disciplinaire" (Puech 2008) – for computational linguistics.

2.2 MT: A Short History?

Martin Joos's review (1956) of the first collective book on MT, published in 1955 (Locke and Booth 1955), shows that the first discussions on MT took place as early as 1943 at the Signal Intelligence Service cryptography centre, which was located at Arlington Hall in Virginia. Frequently and in a sustained manner, the pioneers of MT opposed two groups: those who developed and used computers to analyse "mysterious texts" and those who translated texts from one language into another. Whereas the translators recommended their method on the basis that it was more subtle and based on intuition, and thus partially unconscious, the cryptoanalysts challenged the translators to make the human process of translation understandable in order to be able to mechanise it. As Joos recalls, "it was mathematics and the machines that enjoyed the higher prestige; however [...] those transactions took place in the matrix of today's dominant culture" (Joos 1956, p. 293).

Urged by Warren Weaver, the first experiments in machine translation began only after the war, in Great Britain in 1948 and in the USA in 1949. The early history of MT, considered as an institutional history, is punctuated by three reports (Weaver's, Bar-Hillel's, ALPAC's) delimiting three distinct periods, a beginning, a middle and an end.

Warren Weaver's Memorandum *Translation* written in 1949 (Weaver 1955) called for the creation of centres for machine translation, mainly within the universities, whose mission would be to produce mass translations of scientific texts from Russian into English. Bar-Hillel was appointed the first full-time MT researcher at MIT in 1951. When MT groups started their experiments, with relatively high levels of funding, the legitimacy of MT was beset with errors, flawed translations and poorly evaluated linguistic problems. In fact, what could be regarded a "good" translation had not been thought about; there was no reflection neither on the translation process nor on how it can be simulated by humans.

Besides, there was no linguistic model general enough to describe all the languages.

Such was the conclusion of the first conference organised by Bar-Hillel at MIT in 1952, which recommended computer-assisted human translation rather than an entirely automated system (Bar-Hillel 1953a). Thus, in spite of the media success of the first demonstration by computer in 1954,[1] which was followed by the creation of

---

[1] The first public MT demonstration by computer took place in January 1954 in New York on an IBM machine. It was organised by the Georgetown University MT group under the direction of Leon Dostert and involved the translation of a few sentences from Russian into English using a

new centres of MT, the funders started to doubt the effectiveness of this new technology.

In 1958, Bar-Hillel was tasked by the National Science Foundation (NSF) to write a report on MT which led him to conduct an inquiry into the 20 MT teams that existed in the world at that time: ten centres in the USA, seven centres in the USSR, two centres in the UK and one centre in Italy.[2] In the conclusion of his survey, Bar-Hillel argued irrevocably that:

(i) MT had benefited from enormous investments, in terms of financial and human means.

(ii) "Fully Automatic High Quality Translation" (FAHQT), which was recommended by several MT groups, was an illusion and an unreasonable objective even for the translation of scientific texts.

(iii) Very few linguistic problems had been solved, while the most difficult ones remained to be solved.

(iv) The only "reasonable" objective, in terms of marketing good quality scientific translation, was computer-assisted translation, which involved human intervention at least in the machine output, i.e. in post-editing; meanwhile, "reasonable" refers to both technical and scientific feasibility, as well as financial competitiveness, as compared to human translation.

This report had a major impact at the time of its publication in 1960 (Bar-Hillel 1960). Written by such a respected personality as Bar-Hillel, it threw suspicion and discredit upon all MT groups. The institutional response was made by the Committee ALPAC in 1964 which put an end to the funding of MT.

The 1966 ALPAC report Language and Machine: Computers in Translation and Linguistics would have important consequences for the future of MT, and also on the status and reorganisation of linguistics in the USA. Three areas were examined by ALPAC, using specific tests:

(i) The translation needs of governmental agencies and the scientific community

(ii) How these needs were taken into account by translation organisations

(iii) The advantages and defects of MT in comparison with human translation, in terms of costs and quality

In conclusion, the ALPAC report made a certain number of observations. Contrary to what had been said, there was no shortage of translators in the USA; indeed, the supply of translators was greater than the demand for them. Automatic translation of scientific literature without post-editing was very difficult to read and may even have been a source of errors.

In addition, all testimonies indicated that the outputs of MT with post-editing were more expensive than human translations. The committee concluded that it was

---

Russian-English bilingual lexicon of 150 terms and an "operational syntax" including six operations regulating the parsing. Paul Garvin from Georgetown University and Peter Sheridan from IBM led the demonstration (Dostert 1955).

[2] For a detailed history of the early years of machine translation, see Hutchins (1986a, 2000a).

useless to spend considerable amounts of money to mechanise a small industry which was already in economic decline and employed a workforce of less than 5000 people.

Conversely, human-aided and machine-aided translations were highly regarded. Based on experiments undertaken in Germany and Luxembourg, where the European Union had begun to develop terminology data banks, the USA started its own work in the area. Indeed, ALPAC recommended the development of automatic glossaries, terminology databanks and automatic consultation of bilingual dictionaries, around the same time that computerised publishing was beginning to show positive results, in particular in the media.

As regards the history of linguistics, the ALPAC report contained another significant component. It confirmed the legitimacy of computational linguistics as the "new linguistics", based on Chomsky's generative and transformational grammar, to replace MT.

One could object to the claim made in this short history (1949–1966) that the ALPAC report put an end to MT. New MT centres, in particular in Europe, and most notably in France, were created after the publication of Bar-Hillel's report. Even in the USA, there were places where experiments continued after Bar-Hillel's report and even after the ALPAC report. This was certainly the case with the Bunker-Ramo Centre at Georgetown University and the IBM Company, which had industrial and commercial ambitions. Paul Garvin, who designed the grammatical rules used in the first demonstration in 1954, continued developing MT at the Bunker-Ramo Centre until 1969, when funding was cancelled due to the Vietnam War. In 1965, two of the four translation machines built by IBM (Alps and Mark II) which were based on a specific technology (photoscopic memory)[3] were still operational in American government services.

As the history of MT then continued beyond 1966, four subsequent periods can be identified:[4]

The first period (1966–1980) concerned the survival and the "brute force" of the large MT systems, the most notable being Systran. Systran was created in 1967 by Peter Toma (born in Hungary in 1925) as the result of several machine translation systems successively developed by Toma on IBM computers. In 1958, he worked at Georgetown University on the linguistic system GAT (General Analysis Technique) and on the computer program SERNA. In 1961 he created the Computer Concepts company where he developed Autotran, using Fortran, which became Systran in 1962. He continued working on Systran in Germany and in California where he created his own company Latsec Inc. in 1968. He obtained funding from NASA (National Aeronautics and Space Administration) in 1972. The European Commission, as well as Euratom, which adopted Systran as the basis for their MT

---

[3] The first translating machines, The USAF Automatic Language Translator Mark I (1958) and The USAF Automatic Language Translator Mark II (1964), were developed in the USA by Telemeter-Magnetics Inc. for the US Air Force. They used Gilbert King's photoscopic memory which combined very large storage capacity with very fast access (Léon 1992; Hutchins 2000b).

[4] For a quick survey of the history of MT techniques, see Leon 2006a, b.

operations in 1976, has never stopped using it since that time (Toma 2000). First developed as a Russian-English MT system, other language pairs had been prepared since the 1970s: Chinese-English, German-English, French-English, etc. Nowadays, about 20 languages are involved. From the methodological point of view, Systran is a "transfer system" inherited from the Georgetown "direct system".[5]

The second period (1980–1990) involved the Japanese turn and the automation of communication.

In the early 1980s, the development of micro-computers and text processing software, as well as the democratisation of their use, led to a new era for MT, the marketing era. MT was used to translate instruction manuals, product and machine specifications. The marketing turn was impelled by the Japanese eager to introduce their products into markets around the world. They aimed at equipping every micro-computer with a MT system, thus preparing the long-term future for an information-based society.

MT interactive systems were also developed at that time: computer-aided translation offering translator tools such as bilingual electronic dictionaries and terminology databases. From the 1980s on, MT has become part of language engineering and has been involved in the broader movement of the automation of communication affecting the whole of society.

The third period (1990–2003) is first characterised by the integration of artificial intelligence techniques into MT systems such as expert-systems and intelligent databases. These systems involved mixed strategies and techniques, involving artificial intelligence and syntactic-based procedures, which did not exist in the 1960s–1980s. However, these types of MT systems were still strongly challenged by computer-aided machine translation (see Nirenburg 1993 for a state-of-the-art survey).

The period is also marked by the return of empirical methods. This renewal was aroused by the success of stochastic methods in signal processing and speech recognition. Moreover, large corpora of textual data became available. Translation memory and aligned corpora became the major components of computer-assisted translation. Translation memory involved already existing aligned (or synchronised) bilingual corpora such as Canadian Hansards, the French-English corpus of Canadian parliamentary acts. Alignment, i.e. sentence matching, was performed by exclusively statistical criteria – for example, using the fact that long sentences in the Source Language are likely to be translated by long sentences into the Target Language and conversely. While AI approaches were rule-based, empirical

---

[5] Three main types of systems were developed in the pioneering years of MT: (i) direct translation, or word by word translation, is essentially based on a bilingual dictionary (see, e.g. Richens and Booth's Pidgin English in Chap. 7); (ii) transfer method is based on a bilingual dictionary and syntactic analysis translation programs. Source Language analysis and Target Language synthesis are to some extent independent of particular Source Language-Target Language pairs. These programs were developed within the framework of the constitution of automatic syntactic analysis as an autonomous field (see Chaps. 3 and 4); (iii) intermediary language method is based on semantic analysis (see Chap. 7) (for more information, see Hutchins 1986a, b).

approaches were statistics-based and showed the crucial role of lexicon, especially word collocations for solving local constraints, such as semantic ambiguities. Furthermore, online translation systems appeared, such as Babelfish, which was developed by Systran in 1998.

The fourth period (2003-present) witnesses the alternation of "rule-based" methods and "statistics" methods for MT, as well as the development of hybrid methods. Intelligent modules and probabilistic modules were now complemented by more traditional linguistic modules.

That said, after 1966, MT lost its status as a cutting-edge technology. It became part of the more general area of natural language processing (NLP) – i.e. the computerised treatment of language (see Chap. 6) – remaining overshadowed by computational linguistics and information retrieval. At the theoretical level, it was computational linguistics, in the wake and on the ashes of MT, which initiated the computational mathematisation of linguistics. Moreover, it was the 1966 ALPAC report that confirmed it as the "new linguistics".

2.3   MT as Technology of War

The early history of MT, involving the three stages mentioned earlier, underlines its role as a war technology, anchored in the sciences of war and war culture.

2.3.1   The Sciences of War

Several features characterise the sciences of war (Dahan and Pestre 2004):

(i) The interpenetration between sciences and engineering, in which the best mathematicians and engineers mingled such as John von Neumann, who helped in the design of the first digital computers. There were also engineers who theorised and created signal processing systems, such as Claude Shannon at Bell Laboratories. It is also worth mentioning the mathematician Alan Turing, who was part of the team that decoded the Enigma machine and helped design one of the first computers.

(ii) The scientific culture of war, originating in World War II and perpetuated during the Cold War, is a culture of urgency and permanent mobilisation, in which scientist-engineers are animated by the belief that science can solve every problem.

(iii) The unlimited opportunities to innovate as a consequence of war resulted in the disappearance of financial constraints on scientists.

(iv) Against the backdrop of an omnipresent state, a generalised movement of "nationalisation" of the sciences took place in the twentieth century, especially from 1945 onwards, with the creation of the great national research organisations. In the USA, it resulted in increased research funding by the military, rather than by industry. This kind of research funding would develop massively after the war under the guise of the "military-industrial-academic complex", a term created by President Eisenhower in 1961 and taken up by Senator J. William Fulbright in 1968 (Leslie 1993; Giroux 2007).

(v) The improvement of operations research (OR).[6] Following the army as a model, the scientist-engineers generalised a common operational approach that involved: defining a single objective, monitoring its progress and achievement, creating a task force that gathered all possible expertise, analysing the situation with the help of the sciences, engineering sciences and the social sciences. After the war, it was the RAND Corporation (Research and Development Corporation), the first "think tank" of the post-war period, which relayed the scientific culture of war. The RAND aimed at developing "rational life", according to which technical and human systems (transportation systems, the land army and companies) are coordinated sets, which can be optimised to common goals and criteria. Rational life involves eliminating human work by generalising automation. According to the principles of cybernetics, this automation consists in erasing the border between man and machine through algorithmisation.

(vi) MIT founded in the nineteenth century was the key institution of the war sciences. It was ahead in the process of concentrating and nationalising science, at least with respect to army funding. During the war, it was the seat of the D-2 section "fire control"[7] section in charge of anti-aircraft defense, radar and servomechanisms, which gathered important scientists at the intersection of science and engineering: Norbert Wiener, John Von Neumann, Claude Shannon, Vannevar Bush and Warren Weaver, inter alia. It is at MIT that Bar-Hillel was appointed, in 1951, to lead the MT centre of the Research Laboratory of Electronics.

(vii) The development of new concepts and tools. The interaction between scientists and engineers resulted, in return, in the development of new concepts and

---

[6] The notion of operations research was developed by the British during World War II to evaluate and increase the effectiveness of new weapons like bombers, long-range missiles, torpedoes and radars (Fortun and Schweber 1993; Abella 2008).

[7] From 1941 onwards, after the Blitz in Great Britain and the attack on Pearl Harbor, fire-control and anti-aircraft defense became priorities for the Americans. Two teams devoted themselves to it at MIT. A first device was worked out by the fusion of Vannevar Bush's work at MIT (Radiation Lab's experimental XT-1) and that of the Bell Laboratories (Bell Lab's M-9 predictor). Still at MIT, Norbert Wiener and Julian Bigelow worked on a statistical system of fire control. For this purpose, Wiener wrote a theoretical text "The Extrapolation, Interpolation and Smoothing of Stationary Time Series", immediately classified by Weaver, then the director of the D-2 section. Weaver gave the text to only a few scientists, bound to secrecy, who named it "Yellow Peril" because of its yellow binding. According to Conway and Siegelman (2005), this text would constitute the first outline of communications theory, developed later by Claude Shannon, and opened the way for various technological developments, among them automatic control systems (for more details see Conway and Siegelman 2005, p. 110–116).

new tools. Thus, the rise of new theories (cybernetics, information theory), and the interaction between more traditional disciplines (logic, mathematics, physics) and engineering (telecommunications, cryptography, electronics and anti-aircraft defense), led to the construction of new technological devices like radar and electronic computers. For our purposes, information theory, logic, statistics and probabilities, numerical computation and cryptography will be used as a horizon of retrospection for the constitution of MT as the first non-numerical application of electronic computers, i.e. dealing with string of characters.

Thus, MT did not start from scratch. It had its own horizon of retrospection, viz. the first mathematisation of language and the military technologies of the post-World War II military-industrial complex. Both Warren Weaver and Yehoshua Bar-Hillel, who instigated and led research on MT, would contribute to establishing the new horizon, which, it is worth noting, does not include linguistics.

2.3.2 Warren Weaver (1894–1978)

The role of Warren Weaver was absolutely central in the development of the scientific culture of war. A mathematician specialised in probabilities, he was also passionate about mechanical and electric engineering and taught mathematics at Caltech and at the University of Wisconsin, where he was trained. From 1931 until the end of his career, he was the director of the Division of Natural Sciences of the Rockefeller Foundation where he promoted research programs in experimental and molecular biology in the USA and in Europe.

During World War II, invited by Vannevar Bush, the inventor of the analogue differential analyser at MIT, Weaver was part of the very powerful Scientific Research and Development, which was the very centre of the military-scientific complex. He led the section D-2 "fire control" section and created the Applied Mathematics Panel (AMP, a component of the Office of Scientific Research and Development). The AMP gathered several hundred mathematicians to conduct studies required by the war effort and defense in extremely varied fields such as computers, programming, statistics, cybernetics stemming from defense systems and most of all, calculating solutions to differential equations, e.g. in ballistics.

After the war, in 1945, he returned to the Rockefeller Foundation and participated in many government institutions in charge of the organisation and funding of research. They were civil organisations like the NSF (National Science Foundation) and the American Association for the Advancement of Science, or military ones like the Naval Research Advisory Committee. Moreover, he was one of the founder members of the RAND Corporation created in 1945–1946 by the US Air Force explicitly to help win wars.[8]

---

[8] Its charter was clear: "Project RAND is a continuing program of scientific study and research on the broad subject of air warfare with the object of recommending to the Air Force preferred meth-

Weaver knew he was a facilitator and populariser of science more than a real researcher (Weaver 1970). This was the part he played in the promotion of information theory. He was asked by Chester Barnard, then president of the Rockefeller Foundation, to write a presentation on information theory for non-specialists on the work co-signed with Shannon and published in 1949. It was from this moment on that information theory, until then confined to a few telecommunication specialists, became more widely known and aroused the interest of scientists in varied disciplines.

It was Warren Weaver, a central actor of the culture of war, equipped at the same time with a comprehensive view of science and a great talent for instigating projects, who had the idea of promoting machine translation. The core issue of the postwar period was the Cold War. In the scientific and military competition with the Soviets, the translation of Russian scientific texts into English occupied a crucial place.

In his Memorandum of 1949, Weaver considered that, in the wake of war culture and the operational approach, MT corresponded to the type of objective defined by the RAND Corporation. It automated specifically human work, defined a single objective, mass produced scientific and technical translations and implemented huge human and technical means of carrying out the objective by privileging formal solutions rather than human ones.

In addition, Weaver was concerned with facilitating communication between scientists as science became internationalised. He entitled the foreword of the first collective book on MT experiments "The New Tower", in reference to the myth of Babel (Locke and Booth (eds) 1955).

Warren Weaver took drastic action to implement his MT project. On behalf of the Rockefeller Foundation, he offered to the Englishman Andrew Donald Booth (1918–2009), director of the Birkbeck College Computation Laboratory (University of London), to help the British obtain a computer, provided that they developed non numerical applications, in particular machine translation.

His Memorandum, *Translation*, under its modest appearance – Weaver says in a footnote that he is a neophyte – was in fact a powerful war machine. He sent it to approximately 200 people, about 30 of whom were very influential and could not be unaware that if they became involved with MT, institutions and funding would come after.

Consequently, in 1949, Weaver instigated research in three American universities: the Research Laboratory of Electronics at Massachusetts Institute of Technology (MIT), the University of Washington where the MT centre was directed by the sinologist Erwin Reifler (1903–1965) and UCLA. In 1958, there were a dozen MT centres, including the RAND Corporation, which would become one of the largest MT groups (directed by David Hays and Abraham Kaplan). The financing of MT came from the National Air Force, the CIA and the NSF.

---

ods, techniques and instrumentalities for this purpose" (Abella 2008, p.14).

2.4   Machine Linguistics

Within the framework of the scientific culture of war, there was no room for linguistics. The role of linguists was limited primarily to teaching foreign languages to soldiers. Few of them took part in technological developments (see Chap. 3 below). At MIT, for example, the department of linguistics was created only in 1964, such that it was at the Electrical Engineering Department that Chomsky's first doctoral student, Robert Lees, obtained his PhD in 1963.

It was not linguistics which served as a theoretical or methodological reference for MT, and when Weaver addressed some of the linguistic problems raised by MT (idiomatic expressions and compound words, polysemy, word order), it was only to dismiss them immediately. In the technical and scientific texts to which he confined MT, these problems were limited and could be neglected. MT was not a discipline; it was a technology intended to produce economically profitable mass translations.

Linguistic issues were regarded as a non-priority in view of the problems related to the architecture and the power limitation of machines: limitation of memory, speed and storage. This was the task tackled by the first experimenters, who included specialists in modern languages (Chinese, Slavic languages, Spanish), translators (Leon Dostert) and especially engineers (Victor Yngve, Anthony Oettinger). The Englishmen Andrew D. Booth and Richard H. Richens (1919–1984), who were encouraged by Weaver to undertake MT experiments, were not specialists in languages. The former was a physicist (a crystallographer) at Birkbeck College, London, and the latter a botanist, Director of the Cambridge Bureau on Plant Breeding and Genetics of the Commonwealth Agricultural Bureau. They were "inventors" freed by the machine from any history and any anchoring in the past, namely, of any horizon of retrospection (see Chap. 7).

By creating a linguistics for the machine ("machine translation linguistics"; see Reifler 1955), the engineers denied any legitimacy to linguistics in the automation of translation. Thus, contrary to the conventions of lexicography, the first automatic bilingual dictionaries were built from shortened forms and not from lemmas. The graphic constraints imposed by the digitalisation of information led experimenters to build dictionaries of roots and terminations which did not obey the functional criteria of the grammarians that reflect phonetic or historical properties. They produced "false" radicals, called "base words", and "false" endings and redefined affixes (e.g. for Russian). In their experiments of 1948, Booth and Richens (1955) defined the base as the longest common part to the various forms of an entry provided it was not ambiguous. For example, for the French verb *saisir*, they recommended the choice of the radical *saisi* rather than *sai-* because the latter has common parts with *savoir*. In its automatic dictionary (Russian-English), Oettinger (1955) proposed two false radicals for Russian *okn* and *okon*, whereas for the grammarians they are the alternatives of the same root.

Following the Americans, the researchers of the Steklov Institute of Mathematics of Moscow were led to use the same methods. Whereas English has only six endings *-ing*, *-ed*, *-er*, *-est*, *-th* and *-s*, the Russians added a "false" ending, *-e*, from *love*. The "false" ending *-e* combined with the form *lov-* stored in the dictionary allowed to identify the forms, *love-s*, *lov-ing* and *lov-ed*, to be identified from ordinary inflexions.

The same applied for morpho-syntax. Reifler (1955), followed by Micklesen (1956), defined operational form classes for MT. In structural linguistics the definition of form classes is functional. Thus, in his article determining postulates for the "Science of Language", Bloomfield (1926) defines form classes functionally. Using the examples "Richard saw John" and "The man is beating the dog", he puts forward two postulates (32, 33) defining form classes:

> "32. Def. The positions in which a form occurs are its functions. Thus, the word John and the phrase the man have the functions of 'actor', 'goal', 'predicate noun', 'goal of preposition', and so on.
>
> 33. Def. All forms having the same functions constitute a form-class. Examples of English form-classes are: noun-stems, number-affixes, object expressions, finite verb expressions." (Bloomfield 1926, p.159)

The development of form classes for MT obeys two principles, linguistic and technical, which do not apply simultaneously. The linguistic principle consists in establishing basic classes of interactive forms. Next these classes are modified according to technological requirements. These basic classes of interactive forms, potentially first level immediate constituents, are named mutual pinpointers by Reifler. He gives the example of the article *den* in German which can be either masculine accusative singular or dative plural. If it is followed by *Männern*, which is only dative plural, the ambiguity is clarified: *den* and *Männern* play the part of mutual pinpointers.

If two groups of forms are mutual pinpointers in a given construction, two separate form classes are created. That implies that, in the automatic phase, larger form classes are established if they contain mutual pinpointers, whereas in structural linguistics such a subdivision depends only on the analysis. Micklesen (1956, p. 346) gives the following example. For linguistics, forms like *doing* and *swimming* belong to the class of verbs. However, for MT, because of the function of multiple mutual pinpointing they can exert either as verbs or as substantives – for example, in *writing letters is very difficult*, it is necessary to put these deverbal *-ing* forms[9] in a separate class, an operational form class. Operational form classes do not correspond to the classes described by distributional analysis; they comprise multiple mutual pinpointing instructions and play a dynamic function in the MT process.

This distortion of morphological analysis provoked vivid discussions between structuralist linguists and MT experimenters. For the latter, morphological analysis should be completely submitted to technique, and linguistically artificial objects could be created without respecting theoretical consistency. The horizon of retrospection of the Neo-Bloomfieldians was thus denied, although they had devoted several decades to describe the morphophonology of languages. The experimenters

---

[9] A deverbal is a word or a component of a word that is derived from a verb.

left aside, without any basic criticism, the methods and the results of the linguists who argued that the current work was not adapted to the machine. They acknowledged, with some cynicism, that the criteria they used were not those of grammar, but if the criteria of the linguists did not coincide with theirs, they would do without.

This state of mind is still persisting today. Melby (1992) recalls, in reference to the advice given to him in 1972 by David Hays, one of the MT pioneers, that it is not by finding the good formal model in linguistics that MT problems would be solved, but by providing solid work based on simplified linguistics. This was also the intuition of Peter Toma, the creator of Systran, who, contrary to the scientists of the time, did not believe that linguistics could provide a solution adapted to language processing. He was convinced that language processing should be adapted to the possibilities of the computer rather than the reverse (Loffler-Laurian 1996). One can mention the indignation caused by a note published in an issue of the journal *Traitement Automatique des Langues* in 1995 reporting that F. Jelinek, when he was directing the IBM research team on speech recognition, said: "Everytime I fire a linguist, our system performance improves'" (TAL 1995: 69, note 2).[10]

2.5 MT: A Flawed Technology

2.5.1 Approximate and Rough Translation

MT was a flawed technology. From the start Weaver recognised its limits, in particular the machine's incapacity to translate literary texts involving "illogical" elements like emotions and intuition. He mentioned Norbert Wiener's view on that matter whom he had tried to convince during an exchange of letters in 1947 (Weaver 1955). Wiener was sceptical of the feasibility of MT because, he argued, translating a language into another implies moving from one culture to another, which a machine is incapable of doing.

Weaver was conscious that perfect translation was illusory and that, even for scientific and technical translations, it was impossible to guarantee a complete lack of errors. Even if scientific texts were simpler to translate, since they were less ambiguous and comprised less polysemy, their translation could not be perfect. However, they could be mass translated; furthermore, approximate and rough translations, such as word by word translations, were used for practical use. Even if the output of a word by word translation was not perfect, it was good enough for scientists to be able to select which articles deserved a human translation.

In addition, Weaver claimed that a percentage of errors was acceptable when practical use was at stake. Even today, this argument is constantly being put forward by the actors of MT and NLP, although the status of such errors is ambiguous.

---

[10] See the answer of the editorial board of TAL entitled "Effectiveness of the TALN and linguists" in issue 1996–1 (p. 162) which mentions the tensions between industrial research and linguists.

Drawing on Loffler-Laurian's arguments (1996), we can ask, what does an 80% satisfactory translation actually mean? Does it mean that 80% of the sentences look like sentences written by humans, or that 80% of the words were given a correct equivalent, or that the translation was considered acceptable by 80% of people consulted? It is a fundamental question for MT and for NLP in general.

This argument raises the question of a technique which would be irremediably fallible by definition and that could not be improved. When radar and other technologies developed within the framework of the sciences of war did not work, one tried to improve them. For the opponents to the ALPAC report, this argument was used to claim that MT did not have enough time to improve and to prove it could work (Josselson 1971).

2.5.2   Gap Between Poor Results, Proponents' Ambitions and Public Success

A third source of disappointment was added to the imperfection of the results and to the disappearance of the hope of creating a translating machine: the gap between the public success of MT and the moderate ambitions of its proponents. The enthusiasm aroused by electronic machines and the illusion of their infinite potential was already apparent in 1949 when *The New York Times* published an article on the translating machine entitled "Electric Brain Able to Translate Foreign Languages is Built" (see Hutchins 1997, p. 203). This enthusiasm had such an important echo in the public that some researchers had to contradict the fabulous promises announced in the press (see Koutsoudas' denial 1956).[11]

In 1954, the first computer demonstration revealed that gap once again: the paradox of the public success of MT, largely popularised through the media, and the vain hopes it kept alive, contrasted with the majority of actors who were convinced that the FAHQT (Fully Automatic High Quality Translation) was an illusion and that it was necessary to focus on aided-translation (computer-aided or human-aided) and on syntactic analysis. This paradox would be fatal for MT. A victim of its success and unfounded expectations, it would be severely criticised by the reports (Bar-Hillel's and the ALPAC's), which stopped the experiments.

---

[11] In order to ridicule the weakness of MT systems, some funny translations from English into Russian of quotations from the Bible were often reported: "the spirit is willing, but the flesh is weak", translated again from Russian into English gives us: "The whisky is strong, but the meat is rotten" or "The ghost is a volunteer but the meat is tender". In fact, they were human mistranslations, reported by a journalist (in 1956) and attributed to the machine (see Hutchins 1995 for a more detailed discussion).

2.6 Conclusion

Machine translation as a war technology did not start from scratch. Weaver's proposals placed MT at the centre of a cluster of disciplines (logic, mathematics, statistics and probabilities, neurology and cybernetics) that had information theory as a unifying and universal theory, leaving linguistics aside. However, the first experimenters, taking their cues from the machine, would ignore any horizon of retrospection. That all had a cost: a field of research initiated by means of a brutal decision had to be legitimated.

This is how the players of the period felt obliged to constantly celebrate their own achievements to ensure their legitimacy, as soon as the new field appeared and well before the ALPAC report. One way of coping with the deficit of legitimation was to anchor it in history. By the 1950s, the experimenters equipped themselves with allegedly "historical" introductions, which were retrospective assessments aiming to praise themselves. These texts – the first of which was published in 1955 – were introductions to conferences or collective work written by MT key players themselves (Locke and Booth 1955; Dostert 1957; Booth 1958; Delavenay 1959). They indicate that the proponents elevated the beginning of MT experiments into a "memory landmark" (Puech 2008), even if it was tainted definitively by the ALPAC report (the infamous report according to Hutchins 1996).

In addition, with a significant number of the MT centres located in the university departments of modern languages, the situation was complex. The development of machine linguistics cancelled the horizon of retrospection of the Neo-Bloomfieldians. The horizon of projection, set up by the war culture and unified by information theory, was then cut off from its past. Many MT proponents belonging to the concerned disciplines participated in the development of this new culture. The challenge for the linguists, who did not take part in this stage of initial development, was to adapt the new horizon of retrospection and transform it into a horizon of projection. Computational linguistics constituted the first phase of this appropriation.

Chapter 3
The War Effort, the Technologisation of Linguistics and the Emergence of Applied Linguistics

It may seem strange to include machine translation in applied linguistics, since it was conceived outside the domain of linguistics. Yet the first associations of applied linguistics, such as AILA (Association Internationale de Linguistique Appliquée), created in 1964; AFLA (Association Française de Linguistique Appliquée), created in 1965; BAAL (British Association for Applied Linguistics) created in 1967; and the German language society GAL (Gesellschaft für Angewandte Linguistik), created in 1968, involved an important section of machine translation among their topics. The theme of the founding Congress of AILA, which took place in Nancy in 1964, was "Semantic Information in Linguistics and in Machine Translation". At the same time, the first French MT association, created in 1959, was named ATALA (Association pour l'étude et le développement de la Traduction Automatique et de la Linguistique Appliquée), thus bringing together applied linguistics and machine translation. Finally MAK Halliday, one of the pioneers of MT, devoted an entire chapter to the field in the book he wrote with A. McIntosh in 1966 called *Patterns of Language: Papers in General, Descriptive and Applied Linguistics*.

One can attempt to explain this situation by positing the following two claims: (i) applied linguistics, from its inception as a discipline at the turn of the twentieth century, was associated with technological innovations, and (ii) it owes its growth in the 1950s and 1960s to the peculiar situation of the war context and to the huge "war machine" implemented in 1942 by the USA to develop language teaching and its specific tools. Centres, associations, courses and journals of applied linguistics were created in Europe and the USA, thus ensuring its institutionalisation. In Great Britain, the School of applied linguistics was created in 1957 at the University of Edinburgh, under the direction of Peter Strevens. It was followed by the creation of the Centre de Linguistique Appliquée in Besançon by Bernard Quemada, who founded the journal *Etudes de Linguistique Appliquée* in 1962. The Center for Applied Linguistics was founded in the USA, in Washington, D.C., in 1959, under the direction of Charles Ferguson. The creation of national and international associations would soon follow after these centres.

© The Author(s), under exclusive license to Springer Nature Switzerland AG 2021

J. Léon, *Automating Linguistics*, History of Computing, https://doi.org/10.1007/978-3-030-70642-5_3

In this chapter, after a brief overview of the prehistory of applied linguistics as a discipline mainly focused on language teaching, which may be considered to be rooted in the Anglo-Scandinavian tradition, three points will be developed: the implementation of language teaching as a war machine in the USA; the relationship between applied linguistics and the sciences and war technologies, namely, machine translation and cryptography; and the characteristics of applied linguistics as it emerged from the war context in the USA.

3.1   The Prehistory of the Institutionalisation of Applied Linguistics: The Anglo-Scandinavian Field

Since the nineteenth century, applied linguistics has taken on various forms of institutionalisation (see Linn et al. 2011). Regarding the Anglo-Scandinavian movement, from which applied linguistics, that is, language teaching, originates, the reform of language teaching was founded on spelling and phonetics reform.

In the German sphere, applied linguistics was associated, as early as the 1930s, with a reflection on terminology and technical vocabularies. In the French domain, applied linguistics was rooted in vocabulary studies and lexicology.[1] For Linn (2008), the institutionalisation of applied linguistics resulted from the development of the Anglo-Scandinavian School. This "discourse community" gathered various European scientists, including Henry Sweet from Britain, Paul Passy from France and Scandinavians like Johan Storm, Otto Jespersen, Knud Olai Brekke, Carl Knap and August Western. They founded associations and learned societies such as the IPA (International Phonetic Association) and the Scandinavian society *Quousque Tandem*, created in 1886 by Jespersen, Brekkle and Western. They also created journals such as *le Maître Phonétique* in 1889.

All of them participated in the Reform Movement, whose new approach to language teaching was based on the following three principles: the primacy of spoken language and phonetics, the oral approach to teaching foreign languages and the centrality of text, especially regarding the promotion of connected texts, rather than isolated words, for language learning. These choices broke away from the language teaching conventions of the nineteenth century, which were based on learning long, useless lists of vocabulary and grammatical rules and on the production of literary translation without any oral practice of languages.

In the British tradition more specifically (Léon 2011b), application is at the core of works on language, and since the nineteenth century it has formed part of the very program of general linguistics, while at the same time leading to technological innovations. Three linguists, Henry Sweet, John Rupert Firth and MAK Halliday, may be considered as the main theoreticians of the relationship in descriptive linguistics between theory and its applications. For Sweet, one of the leaders of the Reform

---

[1] See Coste (2012) "A propos d'un manuel français de linguistique appliquée".

Movement, writing and speech are inseparable and contribute equally to the learning of a language.

He worked out a new phonetic notation, the Broad Romic, a shorthand method and an orthographic reform on which the IPA was based (Sweet 1884). Following Jespersen and in collaboration with Daniel Jones, Firth (1957c [1936]) created a project for an international practical script based on the Latin alphabet. Such a unified system of writing had advantages for printing, teaching and also for linguistics as it provided a framework for scientific notation. He also implemented new instruments for phonetics (Firth 1957e [1950b]). Finally, he advocated the use of restricted languages for translations and for establishing the grammars of the different varieties of English and school grammars.[2]

Halliday et al. (1964) included machine translation as a field for the application of linguistics and used registers, which were a modified version of Firth's restricted languages, to promote a "practical" approach to language teaching.

3.2   Language Teaching as a "War Machine" in the USA

3.2.1   Big Programs: ILP and ASTP

It is widely agreed that the institutionalisation of applied linguistics in the USA started in 1941 with the attack on Pearl Harbor, when the Americans realised the strategic potential of foreign language teaching. This question is well documented by historians such as Murray (1993), Howatt (2004), Kaplan (2002), Linn et al. (2011), Martin-Nielsen (2010) and Velleman (2008) and by key players of the period such as J Milton Cowan (1991), Robert Hall (1991), Archibald Hill (1964), Martin Joos (1986 [1976]) and William Moulton (1961).

The periodisation of the emergence of applied linguistics can be established between 1941 and 1959, from the creation of the Intensive Language Program to that of the Center for Applied Linguistics. In 1941, Mortimer Graves (1893–1982), then president of the American Council of Learned Societies (ACLS), founded an Intensive Language Program (ILP) to train students in foreign languages. This program, which was affiliated with the LSA (Linguistic Society of America) and especially with its secretary J. Milton Cowan (1907–1993), was immediately very successful. As of the summer of 1942, it included 56 courses in 26 languages in 18 universities, with a total of 700 students (Cowan et Graves 1986 [1976]).

In the same time, Charles C. Fries (1887–1967) created the English Language Institute at the University of Michigan in 1941 with the financial support of the Rockefeller Foundation. He inaugurated an intensive course in English as a Foreign Language intended for professionals coming from South and Central America. Also

---

[2] Roughly speaking, restricted languages can be defined as reduced forms of languages used for foreign language teaching and translation (see Chap. 10 for details).

in 1941, the US State Department provided a grant to the ELI for the development of an intensive Teacher Education Program. His aim was to carry out research on teaching English as a foreign language and to test scientifically based teaching material for English teaching.

From April 1943 to April 1944, the Army Specialized Training Program (ASTP), the military counterpart of the Intensive Language Program, was created under the direction of linguist (and Army major) Henry Lee Smith. By the end of 1943, this program had trained 15,000 soldiers in 27 languages in 55 universities. The ASTP developed a wide variety of teaching materials, manuals, dictionaries and teaching courses, namely, a series of manuals called "Spoken–" ("Spoken Burmese", "Spoken Chinese", etc.) which became famous and was continued after the war (Moulton 1961).[3] The ASTP was stopped abruptly in 1944 at the end of the war.

3.2.2   The Involvement of Linguists in the War Effort

In the 1930s–1940s, language teaching at the secondary level remained poorly developed in the USA, like in many Western countries, and was limited to a few languages such as Latin, Spanish, French and German. Focused on translation and learning grammatical rules, its ultimate purpose was the ability to read literature. Therefore, the ILP project could not be entrusted to language teachers. It was to Neo-Bloomfieldian distributionalist linguists that Mortimer Graves assigned the implementation of the program. Two fascicles published in 1942 by the Linguistic Society of America, one written by Bloomfield and the other by Bloch and Trager, were used for its methodological framework. Charles C. Fries's views also played a major role in the theory and methods of language teaching.

Bloomfield, Bloch and Trager: The Reform Movement and Anthropological Linguistic Methods In his *Introduction to the Study of Language*, published in 1914, Bloomfield (1887–1949) cites Henry Sweet, Paul Passy, Eduard Sievers and Jespersen. Following the principles of the Reform Movement, he advocates that language learning should be based on the teaching of phonetics. He criticises the teaching method founded on translation and asserts the primacy of hearing over reading and writing. Finally, he promotes the use of context, especially the context of the classroom: the use of greetings, short sentences and objects in the classroom, etc.

> Translation into the pupil's native language or other explicatory use of it must be avoided, for two reasons. The terms of the native language are misleading, because the content of any word or sentence of the foreign language is always different from any approximate correspondent in the native language. [...] The second reason for the avoidance of translation is that, in the association of the foreign word with the native one, the latter will always remain the dominant feature, and the former will be forgotten. [...] Instead of translation the work

---

[3] On the history of the ASTP and of its assessment, see Velleman (2008).

with a text should consist of repeated use of its content in hearing, reading, speaking and writing. (Bloomfield 1914, p. 292)

In his 1942 booklet *An Outline Guide for the Practical Study of Foreign Languages*, Bloomfield gives several practical guidelines for foreign language teaching. The pupil should primarily learn to understand and speak. In addition to the principles of the Reform Movement, he draws on the field methods used by linguistic anthropologists to describe nonwritten American Indian languages. The basic principle was that one could understand and speak a language only by imitating a native speaker, called an informant. However, native speakers, because they were not trained as teachers, were not capable of theoretical formulations. Only linguists could do that. Therefore, pairs formed by an informant and a linguist were considered the most capable of teaching languages by privileging imitation, memorisation and drill. This method became known as the "mim-mem" method (mimicry and memorisation). The use of instruments of speech analysis and of tape recorders, still not very widespread at the time, was strongly recommended. Linguists were also in charge of providing learning material based on an exhaustive analysis of the studied languages.

Grammars and dictionaries were developed inductively. Bloch and Trager's booklet *Outline of Linguistic Analysis*, also published in 1942, played a complementary role by elucidating the techniques of language analysis. The method thus devised was named the war method or Army method (Moulton 1961).

Charles Fries' Contrastive Analysis and Structural Method   As early as 1927, Charles Carpenter Fries had written books on language teaching. In his *American English Grammar*, published in 1940, he advocated a method based on contrastive analysis, which he applied at the English Language Institute created at the University of Michigan in 1941. This method consisted in comparing the structures of both the mother tongue and the foreign language in order to predict and anticipate the differences that were likely to cause learning problems. The repetition-based exercises proposed by Bloomfield were intended to be completed by the learner's active choosing of structural patterns, hence the name of "structural method". Like Bloomfield, Fries devoted a good deal of attention to learning materials, which should be based on structural analysis done by linguists. This method was widely adopted after the publication of Fries's second book *Teaching and Learning English as a Foreign Language* in 1945. It should be noted that Fries founded a journal in 1948 called *Language Learning: A Quarterly Journal of Applied Linguistics*, thus coining the term "applied linguistics".

3.3   The Operational Method and the War Sciences

The operational method was applied to the war effort as regards language teaching. We should remember that this method consisted in defining a single objective that would be predominantly financed by the government and involved massive technical and human resources and the automatisation of human tasks.

All the American linguists were enlisted in the war effort, with a large number of them in the ILP, as shown in their autobiographies published in the series First Person Singular (Davis et O'Cain 1980; Koerner 1991). In addition to significant funding from the federal government, they also received financial support from philanthropic foundations, the Rockefeller Foundation and the Ford Foundation. The massive production of teaching material and the use of technological assistance attest to their concern to develop the equipment component of language teaching. An additional factor made the recourse to technological assistance necessary at that time, namely, the low number of linguists in the USA. It should be noted that very few linguists found themselves at the intersection of language teaching and war technologies, even if the latter would have positive effects on the technologisation of teaching.

Two major personalities should be mentioned. Martin Joos, trained as an engineer, worked as a cryptographer directly and developed an assistance device for language teaching. Leon Dostert, a translator and machine translation pioneer, played a crucial role in promoting applied linguistics.

3.3.1   Martin Joos, Cryptography, Spectrographs and Instruments as Aids to Language Teaching

According to Cowan (1991, p. 81), many linguists were involved in cryptography: "There were also the Martin Jooses, Arch Hills, Win Lehmanns, Budd Claritys, John Seamans, Bill W. S. Smiths, Al Hayses, and others working in quiet anonymity while cracking German and Japanese codes and training a generation of youngsters in the art".

Joos (1986 [1976], p. 123) recalls that "Cryptoanalysts after the Second World War would be a dime a dozen". However, the linguists in question remained discrete about this activity in their autobiographies. Besides Cowan, Martin Joos was the only one who attested to it. In particular, he reported the linguists' games that rested on coding activity:

FUNEM ? / Ef U En E Em/ Have you any ham ?/
YSIF M / Y Es I Ef Em/ Why yes, I have ham/
FUNEX ? / Ef U En E Ex/ Have you any eggs ?/
X ?OEFX /Ex O E Ef Ex/ Eggs ? Oh, we have eggs/
OKMNX !/OK Em En Ex/ OK, ham and eggs !/ (Joos 1986 [1976], p. 118)

Even Bloomfield played this kind of game, as is shown in his pseudonym as the author of a Russian textbook (Joos 1986 [1976], p. 118): "Prof Dr. Ignaius Mendeleeff Lesnin/ I.M. Lesnin / I am listening".

The linguists who worked at the headquarters of the US Army's Signal Intelligence Service (SIS) at Arlington Hall in Virginia were for most part employed as translators of exotic languages. Martin Joos (1907–1978) was the only one who participated in the creation and development of new methods and instruments for ciphering and deciphering.[4]

Martin Joos was born in Wisconsin and was bilingual in English and German. He was trained as an electric engineer and had a PhD in phonetics (Joos 1942), which qualified him for cryptanalysis and the intelligence service. While working with the Bell Laboratories, where he probably met Shannon, he sought to improve the sound spectrograph, the most cutting-edge instrument at the time in the area of speech recording and analysis. In particular, it served to decipher blurred telephone messages. The sound spectrograph led him to develop a new approach to sounds in linguistics, called acoustic phonetics, which he published in 1948 (Joos 1948).[5]

Spectrographs and phonetics played a central role in the development of technologies for language teaching, speech analysis and synthesis, and more generally for the rise of language laboratories. Thanks to his activity in both cryptoanalysis engineering and language teaching, Joos was probably the only linguist actually involved in the war sciences.

He wrote a manual for the teaching of Dutch for the ILS and the ASTP, and in 1945 he created a device, the Speech Stretcher, designed to help students improve their pronunciation (Joos 1951, p. 70).

3.3.2 Leon Dostert, Machine Translation and Applied Linguistics

The second domain that interacted with applied linguistics was machine translation. As we saw in Chap. 2, the idea of machine translation originated at Arlington Hall, during the war, within the cryptanalysis units, where mathematicians and translator linguists challenged each other to find the best way to do automatic translations. The mathematicians' and engineers' proposals were dominant and would be confirmed by the early MT experiments conducted in the 1950s. Leon Dostert (1904–1971) was an exception, as he associated language teaching with machine translation activities.[6] Dostert had been an interpreter at the Nuremberg trials. He created the

---

[4] See Martin Joos' biography in Hill (1979).

[5] On the role of Martin Joos and the development of the notion of code in telecommunications, cryptanalysis and linguistics, see Fehr (2000).

[6] It should be noted that Michael Halliday in the UK and Bernard Pottier in France were also pioneers in both applied linguistics and machine translation (Léon 2001, 2007c).

Institute of Languages and Linguistics at Georgetown University in 1949 and organised roundtables every year on the relationship between linguistics and language teaching, which were published in the Monograph Series on Languages and Linguistics. He became president of the National Federation of Modern Language Teachers Association in 1960.

In addition, Dostert played a crucial role in the early years of MT. He directed the Georgetown project which created Systran, a MT system which still exists today in the form of an online translator (see Chap. 2 §2.1). In January 1954, he organised the first computer demonstration of MT together with IBM in New York. Like Joos, Dostert invented a device for language teaching, a two-track recorder that allowed students to record and listen to themselves after listening to the model (Dostert 1954). It is not therefore surprising that the Institute of Languages and Linguistics was a pioneer in the use of cutting-edge technologies for teaching. Every roundtable report included a section on technological aids and language laboratories. The 1957 roundtable was entirely dedicated to MT, and, beginning in 1955, the Monograph Series regularly published papers on the subject.

Thus, in the USA, the close connection between technological developments, language teaching and applied linguistics should be interpreted within the framework of war culture.

3.4   The Army Method and Post-War Language Teaching

In spite of harsh criticisms and heated debates (Velleman 2008), the Army Specialized Training Program had great success with the public. After the war, linguists and language teachers were confronted with a new challenge, namely, to maintain the wartime momentum, and to transfer the methods developed within the framework of the ILP and the ASTP to secondary and university education.

Actually, despite support of the Rockefeller Foundation, which organised a congress in 1943 that gathered linguists and language teachers to explore the feasibility of such a transfer, and despite the efforts of Georgetown University to organise a roundtable in 1950 on the need for language teaching in the government,[7] the federal government remained generally uninterested in language teaching programs at the high school and university level. Only programs directly linked to the Cold War were financed, such as the Army Language School in Monterey, California, or those that had geostrategic significance, like those that taught English in Latin America, in Asia and in Africa.[8] To this end, the language teaching program of the Foreign

---

[7] During this roundtable, Mortimer Graves reasserted the strategic role of foreign languages: "Ideological world war III has started and there is no certainty that it is well won yet [...] In this war for men's minds, obviously the big guns of our armament is competence in languages and linguistics" (Graves 1951).

[8] Because it was considered outside the range of Soviet missiles, Africa became a major issue of the Cold War for the Americans.

Service Institute (FSI) was created at the State Department in Washington, under the direction of Henry Lee Smith, the former director of the ASTP. The Army method was used in this new program.

Moreover, in order to develop language teaching at the high school and university level, and to apply the Army method, which required many pairs of linguists and native speakers, more linguists were needed. However, once the constraint imposed by the war effort disappeared, American linguists had little interest in language teaching, since it was not considered an intellectual task.[9] Ferguson (1959) points out that American journals of linguistics such as *Language, Word, Studies in Linguistics, Anthropological Linguistics, General Linguistics* and the *International Journal of American Linguistics* included very few articles on the application of linguistics to language teaching.

One way to cope with the shortage of linguists was to develop technological assistance: tape recorders, spectrographs, language laboratories, etc. In accordance with the ideology of the operational method, technological tools would replace or strengthen the work of native speakers, facilitate intensive oral repetition and help the student control his/her pronunciation. We have seen that key figures such as Joos and Dostert developed their own devices. After the war, these technologies became economically affordable for teaching organisations. Lastly, the project to publish language manuals, the Spoken Language Series, was amplified and developed for new languages.

Another way to compensate for the shortage of linguists was to train language teachers in linguistics. In order to use the new technologies and the learning material, which was based on complex linguistic knowledge, teachers needed some training in the domain. At least this is what Joos advocated. Pulgram also encouraged teachers to learn linguistics: "There is no reason for non-linguist teachers of languages to sit back and wait and limit their activity to sniping complaints and bemused or hostile incredulity [...] Good teaching of languages requires not a bag of tricks but professional preparation (in linguistics, not in Education!)" (Pulgram 1954, p. 80–83).

However, this project faced many obstacles and aroused teachers' hostility. Language teaching was still associated with written language learning that used translation and whose main objective was the teaching of literature. Besides, in the same way that linguists were not interested in language teaching, language teachers were not interested in linguistics. Linguistics could not be imposed from outside. Fries (1949) identified the source of the misunderstanding between linguists and language teachers: for most teachers, what was new and valuable in the Army method was its intensity and its insistence on the oral approach; they regarded any discourse on teaching based on linguistic principles and supervised by linguists as a form of corporatism and arrogance.

---

[9]As Charles Hockett stated, "All modern foreign languages taught at Cornell are taught at the undergraduate level; at that University there is no major in languages. Learning a foreign language is not essentially an intellectual task" (Hockett 1952, p. 3). In the British tradition it was the contrary (see Chap. 7).

Several initiatives were launched with the explicit aim of favouring cooperation between linguists and teachers. In addition to the roundtables at the Georgetown Institute of Language, the National Defense Education Act (NDEA) enacted in 1958, aimed at strengthening the teaching of sciences, mathematics and foreign languages, and the Center for Applied Linguistics, along with 12 other institutes, was created to train primary and secondary schools teachers in linguistics. However, doubts remained as to the relevance of this approach. In 1962, Mildenberger from the Department of Health, Education and Welfare wondered whether linguistics could really be applied to language teaching at the school level: "Perhaps linguistics does not have an applied role in language teaching in the schools" (Mildenberger 1962, p. 161).

The Center for Applied Linguistics did not want to be limited to language teaching. Its director, Charles Ferguson, in a paper published in the centre's bulletin, *The Linguistic Reporter*, discussed the application of methods and results of the linguistic science to the practical problems of language and languages by defining four main sectors of applied linguistics: (i) language teaching; (ii) literacy; (iii) translation and interpretation; (iv) language policies. In the same issue, Raleigh Morgan Jr., associate director of the centre, listed the various domains where the cooperation between linguists, psychologists and language teachers could be reinforced. Besides language teaching, he added the diagnosis of language pathologies, stylistic analysis in literature, cultural programs and literacy programs, etc.

The predominance of linguistics marked the history of American applied linguistics. Today, the specialists as well as the historians of applied linguistics (Davies 1990; Howatt 2004) continue to refer to the domain as "linguistics-applied", or as the "linguistics-driven" or "theory-driven view of applied linguistics", implying that issues are treated from an excessively theoretical point of view that does not consider real-world problems. Since its creation, both the field and methods of applied linguistics have become international. The use of its technologies, namely, its language laboratories originating from war culture, has been widespread since the 1960s–1970s.

As regards machine translation, it became associated with applied linguistics as early as the 1950s, most notably at Georgetown University, where Leon Dostert worked on both machine translation and language teaching. Thanks to the roundtables that brought together linguists, engineers and language teachers and to their publication in the *Monograph Series on Languages and Linguistics*, Georgetown University played a crucial role in the institutionalisation of applied linguistics and natural language processing. These two groundbreaking areas supported and cooperated with each other during their early years. This was particularly the case regarding the journal of the French ATALA Association for Machine Translation, *TA Informations*, which included, from 1965 to 1970, a section entitled "Nouvelles de l'AILA. Applied linguistics News", which favoured the institutionalisation of applied linguistics.[10]

---

[10] Note that, for its 40th anniversary, the 2014 AILA Congress proposed to revisit the three main topics of its first congress in 1964, in the following order: machine translation, language teaching and cooperative research within Europe.

Chapter 4
The Computational Turn and Formalisation in Neo-Bloomfieldian Distributionalism

The computationalisation of language in the context of war culture accelerated the development and the autonomy of linguistics in American universities. Linguistics was already institutionalised before the Second World War.[1] It had its own organisations like the Linguistic Society of America, which was created in 1924, and had its own summer schools, the Linguistic Institutes, and it boasted a journal of its own, *Language*. However, it was only after the war and with the investment of linguists in the war effort that linguistics gained autonomous university departments and that its institutionalisation was strengthened.[2]

MT also played a role in this process. As we saw, it was not an academic discipline, and linguistics was neither part of its horizon of retrospection nor of the horizon of its pioneers. Nonetheless, in the USA, some of the MT centres were created in university departments of foreign languages and linguistics. The heads of MT projects were specialists in foreign languages, such as Erwin Reifler in Chinese at Washington University, K.E. Harper in Slavic languages at UCLA and C. Africa and W.E. Bull in Spanish also at UCLA. There were also specialists in historical linguistics, such as Winfred Lehmann at the University of Texas. Faced with the practical requirements of MT, they had two options: (i) to give up linguistic problems to focus on the implementation of machine linguistics, with the aim of avoiding or compensating for the practical limitations of computer storage and speed; (ii) to develop automatic methods for linguistic analysis prior to or even peripheral to MT.

The Neo-Bloomfieldian distributionalist linguists did not choose either option. Harris was the only one who led a MT team at the University of Pennsylvania actually dedicated to the syntactic analysis of English based on immediate constituent

---

[1] Contrary to what Martin-Nielsen (2010) argues

[2] Before the war, linguistics was taught in the departments of anthropology.

© The Author(s), under exclusive license to Springer Nature Switzerland AG 2021
J. Léon, *Automating Linguistics*, History of Computing,
https://doi.org/10.1007/978-3-030-70642-5_4

analysis.[3] The procedures implemented concerned information retrieval more than machine translation (see Chap. 9). Harris's team received funding from the NSF and was assessed by Bar-Hillel, who in his 1960 report harshly criticised Harris's notions of transformation and kernel sentence. At that time, it should be remembered, Bar-Hillel had opted for Chomsky's notion of transformation to improve his model of categorial grammar.

Even if they did not do any experiments in MT, the very possibility of automating translation had a great influence on Neo-Bloomfieldian distributionalist linguists. The attention given to the relationship between the transcription and translation of American Indian languages led to the creation of intermediary languages that constituted a new object for linguistics and natural language processing. Some methods, like procedures regularly used by Neo-Bloomfieldians, were made more rigorous by assimilating them to weak algorithmic forms. Visible and significant changes had been introduced in the graphic representations (diagrams and tables) of the process of immediate constituent analysis and its results.

4.1   The Computational Turn for the Neo-Bloomfieldians

4.1.1   The "Neo-Bloomfieldians"

The linguists commonly referred to as the Neo-Bloomfieldians were followers of Boas, Sapir and Bloomfield, and, above all, were linguistic anthropologists who focused on the description of American Indian languages. According to Murray (1993), who dedicates two chapters of his book *Theory Groups and the Study of Language in North America* to Bloomfield and to the Neo-Bloomfieldians, the main linguists of this group were Bernard Bloch, Robert Hall, Zellig Harris, Einar Haugen, Archibald Hill, Charles Hockett, Martin Joos, Eugene Nida, Kenneth Pike, George Trager, Charles Voegelin and Rulon Wells.[4] They all had in common an inductive approach and the use of distributional analysis inaugurated by Bloomfield, whose interest in the mathematisation of language they also shared.

   The only useful generalisations about language are inductive generalisations. Features which we think ought to be universal may be absent from the very next

---

[3] On immediate constituent analysis, see note 3 Chap. 6. Distributional analysis is a technique pioneered by structural linguists who argued that in order to arrive at a description of a language, one applies analytic procedures, sometimes called "discovery procedures" (Harris 1951a), to the various strictly separated levels of analysis (morphological, phonological, lexical, etc.). It endeavours to discover relations of units within the frame of the larger ones with the help of immediate constituent analysis. Distribution is the total of all the environments, or patterns, in which an element can occur. The goal of a distributional analysis is to try to isolate recurring patterns and try to correlate these recurring patterns with some unit of meaning.

[4] According to Murray (1993), Yuen Ren Chao, Einar Haugen and Roman Jakobson also belonged to that network but only peripherally.

language that becomes accessible. Some features, such as, for instance, the distinction of verb-like and noun-like words as separate parts of speech, are common to many languages, but lacking in others. The fact that some features are, at any rate, widespread, is worthy of notice and calls for an explanation; when we have adequate data about many languages, we have to return to the problem of general grammar and to explain these similarities and divergences, but this study, when it comes, will be not speculative but inductive (Bloomfield 1933, p. 20).

However, the group formed by the Neo-Bloomfieldians was not homogeneous; there was no real leader, and their adherence to a common methodology involving many positivist aspects was more or less loose. When Hymes and Fought (1981, p. 226) took up the eight criteria established by Wells to characterise American descriptive linguistics, we see that most of these criteria are not specific to the Neo-Bloomfieldians but describe the activity of some of their predecessors and successors as well. Only criteria – (5) juxtaposition as the main grammatical relation and (6) procedural rigor – were specific to the 1940s linguists. The authors recall that the designations "Bloomfieldian", "Post- Bloomfieldian" and "Neo-Bloomfieldian" were debated very early.

Murray (1993) justified the choice of the term "Neo-Bloomfieldian" by showing how the descriptivist linguists formed a network rather than a group to which Bloomfield himself would not like to be identified[5]: "Bloomfield was not a 'Bloomfieldian' and the group that emerged during the 1940s would better be labeled 'Neo-Bloomfieldian'" (Murray 1993, p. 135).[6]

Actually for Murray, Bloomfield was less Bloomfieldian than some of his disciples like Bloch, Trager and Smith, who were attached to the exclusion of meaning and diachrony. Others, on the contrary, diverged from this extreme position by paying attention to historical and comparative data, and even to meaning. Like Bloomfield, who dedicated a chapter (Chap. 3) of his book *Language* (1933) to speech communities, they focused on unobservable phenomena such as community norms and dialects. That notion was already a source of reflection in the early 1950s, most notably for Voegelin and Harris. Finally, some of them, like Hockett and Harris, began to focus on syntax, which had been much neglected until then (see Joseph 2002, p. 61).

Most Neo-Bloomfieldians had familiarised themselves with some aspects of the formalisation of the first mathematisation of language, especially with axioms and procedures, which seemed to be entirely compatible with distributional methods. As early as 1926, Bloomfield wrote an article putting forward a method based on axioms which he called postulates. Such a method was intended to lead linguists to

---

[5] Hymes and Fought (1981, p. 223–224) note that this also was Fries's position (1961, p. 196). Although he wrote an article on the Bloomfieldian "School", he acknowledged that Bloomfield himself would not have agreed with this labelling.

[6] Murray is referring to the group of descriptive linguists who used Bloomfield's guiding principles to develop language teaching methods during World War II (see above Sect. 4.2).

define hypotheses and categories more rigorously.[7] However, as Tomalin (2006) notes, Bloomfield did not use formal language to express these postulates, stating them instead in natural language in the form of definitions and hypotheses. For example, the following axioms can be found in Bloomfield's article "A Set of Postulates for the Science of Language" (1926, p. 164):

> definition: An act of speech is an utterance
>   assumption: within certain communities successive utterances are alike or partly alike

For Tomalin (2006), Harris was the first Neo-Bloomfieldian to introduce the idea of a formalised procedure, as early as 1946. In any case, in the early 1950s, the Neo-Bloomfieldians were ready to welcome the second mathematisation of the language sciences, which was set in motion by automation.

4.1.2   The International Journal of American Linguistics in the Early 1950s

In the 1950s, the Neo-Bloomfieldians were in a dominant position. They had taken part of the institutionalisation of linguistics in the 1930s–1940s in the USA by following Bloomfield, who was one of its major actors. Let us mention the main milestones: the creation of the Linguistic Society of America and its journal *Language* in 1925, the creation of the Linguistic Institutes, studies for the Linguistic Atlas, and the tremendous support and programs implemented for the war effort.[8] Murray (1993, p. 155) reports that, according to the testimony of some 1950s linguists, "Bloomfieldian distributional analysis was 'the only game in town'" and no rival trend existed. Their hegemony would end with the institutional rise of generative grammar at the beginning of the 1960s, when Chomsky, although he had come from their group, gained his autonomy.

One of the major pieces of the Neo-Bloomfieldian dominance was the journal *International Journal of American Linguistics* (IJAL). Created by Franz Boas in 1917 to publish works on American Indian languages, the journal declined during World War II after Boas's death in 1942, but got a second wind after the war thanks to Charles F. Voegelin. Voegelin expanded the policy of IJAL in order to include discussions on general linguistics and reviews by non-linguistic anthropologists such as Twaddell, Malkiel and Hall and to extend linguistic anthropology to other regions than America, especially to Oceania and Africa. He also published Swadesh's work on lexicostatistics and the work developed at the Summer Institute of Linguistics (chaired by Pike from 1942 to 1979).

---

[7] "The postulational method can further the study of language, because it forces us to state explicitly whatever we assume, to define our terms, and to decide what things may exist independently and what things are interdependent" (Bloomfield 1926, p. 153).

[8] See Chap. 3.

It is in this journal, under the direction of Voegelin, then chairman of the Linguistic Society of America, that the computational turn of American structural linguistics can be identified, as shown by the publication in 1953 and 1954 of two issues of IJAL dedicated to translation as a procedure.

4.2 Translation in the Description of American Indian Languages

Even if translation could not be avoided by linguistic anthropologists, it had no real status. In the first half of the twentieth century, English translations of texts in American Indian languages (texts and collections of narratives from native speakers) were intended for both culturalists and linguists. In the 1940s–1950s, translations were interlinear and literal; they were used for making morphophonemic descriptions readable by linguists who did not know the American Indian language in question. At Bloomfield's instigation, the linguists' aim was to provide a morphophonemic description[9] that followed the distributionalist approach, without any contrastive view. It consisted in developing grammatical categories from the data themselves, rather than imposing an external a priori model.

Translation is always present in description.[10] By examining one of the early works in the domain, that is Hidatsa Texts, collected by Lowie in 1911 and taken up and annotated by Harris and Voegelin 1975 [1939], it appears that the transcribed text (the narrative of a myth in Hidatsa, a Siouan language) is followed by a free translation. This translation is intended for both ethnographers and linguists. The morphophonemic description is added for each unit of analysis in a footnote. Only later would it become the main part of the analysis.[11]

Voegelin and Harris put forward a reflection on the status of translation in descriptive analysis. In two articles published in 1951 (Voegelin and Harris 1951; Voegelin 1951), they proposed to rationalise the relationship between translation and transcription and their reflection would lead, on the one hand, to the development of translation procedures published in the 1953–1954 IJAL issues, and on the other hand, to the development of methods aimed at making distinctions within the same speech community from a sociolinguistic perspective.

---

[9] For Garvin (1967), the priority given to morphophonemics by American linguists resulted from the identification of the typological properties of some families of agglutinative American languages that were unknown in Indo-European languages.

[10] For a historical view of translation and transcription in American linguistics, see Lahaussois and Léon (2015).

[11] In addition to these common works on Hidatsa, Voegelin's doctoral work was on Tübatulabal, a language from California; with his second wife, Florence Robinett Voegelin, he worked on Shawnee (an Algonquian language). Harris worked on Kota, Navaho and on Semitic languages such as Phoenician, on which he worked for his PhD, and Moroccan Arabic. His examples in IJAL 1954 concern Korean and Hebrew (cf. Sect. 4.4).

4.2.1   *Interpreter Translation and Speech Communities*

Voegelin (1951) distinguished between two types of translation:

(i) The linguistic translation involving literal translation (morpheme by morpheme translation) and free translation, and
(ii) The interpreter translation.

In their 1951 article, Harris and Voegelin specified what they meant by interpreter translation. This type of translation plays a major role in the distinction between dialects within the same family of languages. They implemented a method called the "test the informant method", which rests on the mutual intelligibility of members from various speech communities and makes it possible to determine boarders between languages and above all between communities. Harris and Voegelin described the method in the following way (1951, p. 327–328):

(i) speaker A1 from community A tells a tale in his language. The tale is recorded. The fieldworker makes speaker A1 hear his own text and asks him to translate it into English,
(ii) the linguist asks speaker B1 from community B to translate into English the tale recorded in language A (starting from what B1 understands of language A).
(iii) same process is repeated for communities B, C, D, etc.

Voegelin and Harris emphasised the fact that interpreter translation focused on the intelligibility between various dialects belonging to the same family of languages, rather than on the speakers' technical competence. What is interesting, they argue, is less the translations themselves than the differences between ways of understanding the same tale. Translations are only a means to see the differences between the intelligibility by a A speaker of a tale in language A and the intelligibility by a B speaker of the same tale in language A. The method was tested by Voegelin's students for Iroquois, Algonquian and Yuman. The results were published in IJAL (Hickerson et al. 1952; Pierce 1952 et Biggs 1957), and these studies were continued within the disciplines of ethnography of communication and sociolinguistics (Hymes 1962; Gumperz et Hymes 1972).

4.2.2   *Free Translation and Language Structure*

The second part of Voegelin's reflection on translation concerned the problems raised by free translation (1951). He argued that this kind of translation cannot really be qualified as "free". Instead, he described it as "awkward", since the linguist always attempts to force into the English version all the linguistic information he finds in the American Indian language described. Actually, this kind of translation involves pseudo-information resulting from the fact that the source and target languages, that is, the American Indian language and English, involve extremely different, sometimes incompatible structures and it is useless to try to account for every structural feature of the source language in free translation. The difficulty of dealing with properties of both languages simultaneously is precisely what Voegelin would work to resolve in the following years.

It should be noted that the early 1950s experiments on machine translation orientated the reflections on translation initiated by Harris and Voegelin and led them to systematise the implementation of translation procedures. Machine translation would require them to take into account meaning, hitherto excluded, since they had to resolve semantic ambiguities in the automatic process. Translation was thus taken seriously in all its many aspects.

4.2.3   Voegelin: Translation Procedures and Weak Algorithmisation

Already in his 1951 article, Voegelin dedicates a whole page (p. 361–362) to the implementation of coding needed for the automation of morpheme by morpheme translation. In his 1954 article, he formalised the translation process into eight stages called multiple stage translation. The translation process of Shawnee into English was undertaken, he insisted, with a view towards its programming on an electronic computer. It constituted the rationalisation of the traditional two-stage translation carried out by anthropologists: interlinear (word by word) translation and free translation. One can consider this new procedure as a real algorithm in the sense that each step of the translation process is made explicit, from the identification of "words" by the native speaker (or informant) up to a smoothed out English translation with added punctuation:

First stage: informant's identification and translation of whole words
Second stage: translator's identification of morphemes
Third stage: translation spans enclosed in brackets, with equivalences given for dilemma sequences, idioms and metaphors which are then put in braces within the brackets
Fourth stage: spurious and genuine redundancies are italicized to show that they are not to be carried beyond the bracket stage of translation
Fifth stage: translation spans are enclosed in parentheses; they differ from the corresponding brackets by following TL [Target Language] word-order and TL fullness of phrase, with all addenda shown in small caps
Sixth stage: occasional words are transferred from one translation span to a neighboring span and are then written in boldface to show they have been removed from their original translation span
Seventh stage: awkwardnesses smoothed by transposition of whole parentheses
Eighth stage: punctuation of TL derived in part from FL [From Language] by various substitutions for juncture-bounded translation spans, and in part from morphological considerations. (Voegelin 1954, p. 271)

In order to implement this translation procedure, Voegelin (1953) defined units and operations (addition, substitution, deletion, reduction) leading to a quasi-language, an intermediate stage in translation between the two languages, which he called parenthetic and bracketed English before obtaining the edited text in English, called punctuated English. Translation units are prosodic contours (in brackets). Inside the contours, morphemes are delimited by various types of junctures marked by space (+) and double-cross (#). Deletion determines what is deleted in Shawnee in the translation into English (in italics in the bracketed English); addition (in small caps) adds obligatory elements in English that do not exist in Shawnee; word re-ordering is marked by commas, semicolons and stops. Bracketed English represents word order in Shawnee, while parenthetic English word order in English. Elements moved from one unit to another are marked in bold followed or preceded by a wedge on the left or the right side showing the direction of the movement. Thus, in the following example (Voegelin 1953, p. 6):

'I' belonging to the Shawnee unit [Oklahoma I >] was moved to the right in the English unit (< I live there) [July month] = (July), as the equivalent of 'month' exists in Shawnee it has been deleted in English (16 miles east >) [<east + and>], [one-mile + plus-half]
   = (<and one and a half miles south) as south does not exist in Shawnee it has been added in English; and has been moved from left to right, from the Shawnee unit [east + and] to the English unit (<and one and a half miles south); east has been moved from right to left from English to Shawnee.

The Shawnee text has been transcribed into phonemes from the recording. Contours are marked by brackets. Junctures of various types are marked by + and #:

[Oklahooma niila] [hočilenawe] [ninyeewaapitaki kiten?θwi] [n
   + ... hinoki] [(hi)noki yaama kiiša?θwa] [meta? + ... meta? θwimaali kite nekotwa?θwi]
[heta?koθaki no?ki]   [nekotimaali kitepa?θi]   [naamin ooči]   [nita?maačilooθiya]
[laapelaawikiišaθwa] [kiiša?θwa niišwi lakimooθo] [teepee(we) kite čaakatθwi + kite
čaakatθwi ... tθwi] [tθwatikita?θoowenipii (hi)ne] [nimaačilooθi #]

Bracketed and parenthetic English:

[Oklahoma I >] = (< I live there) [I-be- forty and-three] = (I'm 43), [now >], [now-this-month]= (<now this month), [te... ten-miles + plus +six] = (16 miles east >) [
   <east + and>], [one-mile + plus-half] = (<and one and a half miles south), [Norman from] = (from Norman), [I-was-born-there] = (I was born there), [July month] = (July), [second thus-he-is-counted]
   = (second) [hundred – operator = plus-ninety-operator = zero-nine
   ... ain] = (1909), [one-figures out] = (one figures out), [I-was-born #] = (I was born),

Edited and smoothed English version (with punctuation):

Oklahoma, I live there. I'm 43, now, this month. I was born there, sixteen miles east, and one and a half miles south, from Norman. I was born, one figures out, July 2 1909

Voegelin's procedure, involving translation units and operations, is an algorithm that defines all the steps of the process from the beginning to the end result. It constitutes what could be called "weak formalisation", a type of formalisation that is relatively common among grammarians and linguists.[12] The creation of an intermediary language between the two languages as a stage in translation was a new form of formalisation involving operations directly integrable into an algorithm.

4.3   Towards a Dynamic Formalisation of Morpho-Syntactic Analysis and Translation Procedures[13]

In 1954, like most Neo-Bloomfieldians, Hockett and Harris used tables and diagrams to present their morphophonemic analysis based on the distributional method.[14] In distributionalist works, diagrams did not become trees until much later. Although the notion of hierarchical constituent had been introduced by Sapir in his analysis of the Paiute word in the 1920s (Seuren 2006), and though this structure was dominant in American structuralist works, these works did not involve any tree diagram.[15] Whether it was Sapir or Bloomfield, linguists banned the use of tree representations, which remained reserved for sciences like mathematics, physics and psychology.[16]

4.3.1   Hockett: Diagrams and Hierarchically Structured Representations

In his 1954 article, Hockett first used a hierarchical diagram named "boxes", which he said was inspired by Pike (1943). He used this type of diagram extensively in his later works, especially in his *Course in Modern Linguistics* published in 1958. For Seuren (1998), this diagram was first used by Chomsky in 1956 and only later in 1958 by Hockett. However, as can be seen in diagrams (Figs. 4.1, 4.2 and Fig. 4.3),

---

[12] According to Auroux (1998), "weak formalisation" indicates abstract forms and representations developed by linguists such as transcriptions, lists, tables, etc. It should be contrasted with "strong formalisation", that is, computable formal systems that appeared in the 1930s as part of the first mathematisation of language. The second automation-computationalisation of language, when formal languages and algorithms of the first mathematisation became directly implementable into computer programs, can be described as "dynamic formalisation".

[13] For this section, see also Léon (2020).

[14] See Joos (1957) for a complete overview of distributionalist works from 1935 to 1940.

[15] Diagrams representing sentences had existed since the beginning of the nineteenth century in American grammar. Stephen Watkins Clark (1810–1901) introduced the first comprehensive diagramming system for sentences based on agglutinated "bubbles" representing the relations between words. His *Practical Grammar* (1847), reprinted several times, is nowadays considered a precursor of immediate constituents analysis. As early as the 1960s, Hays sees it as a prefiguration of dependency grammar (see Mazziota 2016).

[16] Seuren (1998) states that Bloomfield borrowed the notion of hierarchical tree from the psychologist Wundt, without using it himself, however.

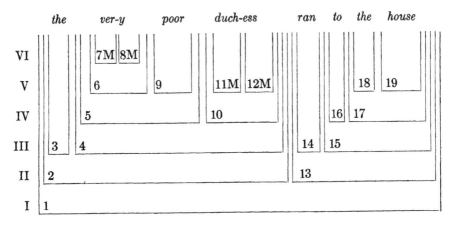

Fig. 4.1 Pike's diagram (1943, p. 70)

the	son-	-s	and	daughter-	-s	of	a	man	a-	-re	hi-	-s	child-	-ren
	sons			daughters			a man							
	sons and daughters				of a man					his		children		
	sons and daughters of a man								are		his children			
the sons and daughters of a man									are his children					
The sons and daughters of a man are his children														

Fig. 4.2 Hockett's diagram (1958, p. 152)

the man	took	the book
NP	Verb	NP
	VP	
Sentence		

Fig. 4.3 Chomsky's diagram (1956, p. 117)

it was Hockett who used it first in 1954. It is worth noting that the three versions of the diagram by Pike, Hockett and Chomsky were interpreted divergently and had three different functions.

4.3.2   Pike's Diagram (1943)

The diagram (Fig. 4.1) represents the analysis of a sentence in terms of its immediate constituents with morphological indications (M). In this hierarchical representation, levels are marked by Roman numerals, and Arabic numerals mark the order of glosses in the text.

4.3.3   Hockett's Diagram (1958)

The diagram (Fig. 4.2) represents an immediate constituent analysis of morphemes that is very close to Pike's. Hockett calls it "boxes".

4.3.4   Chomsky's Diagram (1956)

Chomsky puts forward an immediate constituent hierarchical representation (he calls it a "block"). In this case, the analysis focuses on categories instead of directly on morphemes like Hockett's. It should be noted that, in this article, which is one of Chomsky's early published articles, Chomsky is not concerned with language description. Rather, he discusses the relative power of several grammatical models. The diagram (Fig. 4.3) addresses syntagmatic grammar involving immediate constituent analysis.[17]

4.3.5   Hockett's Diagram (1954)

Let us now examine Hockett's 1954 paper published in IJAL, where he uses this type of diagram for the first time, before Chomsky. Immediate constituent analysis is here used for translation from Chinese into English. Morphological analysis of

---

[17] Chomsky comments the diagram in the following way: "Evidently, description of sentences in such terms permits considerable simplification over the word-by-word model, since the composition of a complex class of expressions such as NP can be stated just once in the grammar, and this class can be used as a building block at various points in the construction of sentences. We now ask what form of grammar corresponds to this conception of linguistics structure" (Chomsky 1956, p. 117).

Chinese, represented by immediate constituents, through successive steps, leads to the English version. Effectively, Hockett makes an immediate constituent analysis of English starting with Chinese. As in Voegelin (1954), an intermediary language is involved. Hockett shows the point, for the linguist, of keeping every intermediary step of translation between interlinear translation, morpheme by morpheme translation, and free translation. In Fig. 4.4, row 1 shows Chinese (morpheme by morpheme), row 2 shows English (morpheme by morpheme) and the last row gives a free translation: this is STILL a lot less than you owe me altogether.

Hockett considers it essential that intermediary results between morpheme by morpheme translation (row 2) and free translation (last row) be made available to the linguist. The common denominator of meaning of any possible context is given for every segment of the text. What is at stake is an option of interpretation rather than an option of translation. Hockett suggests solving semantic ambiguities with immediate constituent analysis. For example, for "I/me" and "wo" (8th column from the left), the Chinese "wo" means "I" and "me". Thanks to the context "alto-gether" located in the intermediary strata "owe me together", we can see that the gloss "I" is impossible; only "me" is possible. For Hockett that does not indicate that "wo" means either "I" or "me" but that "wo" is a common denominator of "I" and "me". Thus, he gives "wo" the meanings "I" and "me". By considering "wo" as an immediate constituent, the construction where it appears makes it possible to decide that the gloss "me" will be kept. In addition to rationalising the steps of translation, such a table takes into account morphological disambiguation and helps to solve it.

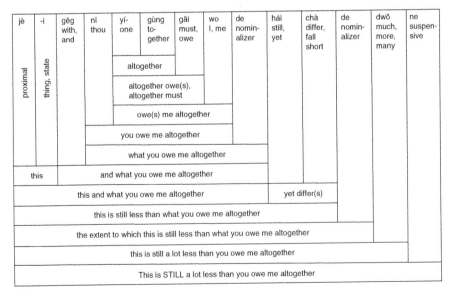

Fig. 4.4 Hockett's diagram (1954, p. 314)

4.4   Harris: Diagrams and Instructions

Harris's 1954 article published in IJAL belongs to the first phase of his work, which, according to Matthews (1999), extends over the period from 1942 to 1955 (discourse analysis and works on transformations, here excluded, belong to the second phase). The first phase is dedicated to establishing basic units from distributional patterns. In 1954, Harris had already published *Methods in Structural Linguistics* (1951a), a major text of his first period, and a copious article in *Language*, also published in 1951, in which he addresses, among other issues, the differences between linguistic systems (Harris 1951b).[18] Both texts are essential to grasping the project put forward by Harris in the 1954 article entitled "Transfer Grammar", which aims to determine whether it is possible to measure the differences between languages (Sapir's linguistics systems) with a view to translating them. It is interesting to note how the diagrammatical representation of transfer grammar, dedicated to translation, shows an evolution of formalisation.

4.4.1   Axiomatised Procedures and Early Sketches of Generative Grammar

Methods in Structural Linguistics displays a set of axiomatised procedures aiming to establish the most compact description as possible (i.e. the simplest) of every construction of the corpus of data. Harris borrows his notion of axiomatised procedure from mathematics so that he can be regarded as the first formalist linguist (Seuren 1998, p. 214 et sq.). These procedures realise an immediate constituent analysis at every level: phonemes, morphemes, words, phrases and sentences. They are represented as diagrams (Harris 1951a, p. 69). See Fig. 4.5.

	X-	Y-	Z-
a	✓		
b		✓	✓
e	✓	✓	
f			✓

$[a] + [b] = /A/$; $[e] + [f] = /E/$

Fig. 4.5 Harris (1951a, p. 69)

---

[18] Following Sapir, Harris (1962b) puts forward an international language for the sciences based on the idea that all the languages have similar structures in spite of their grammatical and lexical differences. This idea of international language led him to develop sublanguages of sciences, a project he would carry out until his death in 1992.

More generally: if segment *a* occurs in environments *X*-, and *b* in *Y*- and in *Z*- ; and if seg-ment *e* occurs in *X*- and in *Y*-, while *f* occurs in *Z*- ; we group *a* and *b* into one phoneme, say /A/, and *e* and *f* into another, say /E/. The result is that /A/ and /E/ each have identical distri-butions : each of the two phonemes occurs (is represented by some member) in *X*-, *Y*-, *Z*.

Diagram (Fig. 4.5) cannot be read alone: it should be glossed (by the small text above the table) and leads to a formula giving the result (line under the table). Units (a, b, e, f) are segments. Columns (X_, Y_, Z_) are the units' left context. The table can be read as an if-then rule (there is no else-condition) that defines phonemes A and E according to elements of the context.

At the end of the book (Harris 1951a, p. 350), there is a diagram representing the general structure of English sentences. It is an algorithm that makes it possible to derive surface sentences (actually strings of immediate constituents) from a deduc-tive axiomatic system. As Seuren (1998, p. 228) notes, this diagram is an early form of generative grammar.[19]

In (Fig. 4.6), the empty space in the top right corner shows that there is nothing at the right of V. Thanks to this diagram, the following rules can be generated:

S → N V
S → N V N
S → N V P N
S → N Vb N
S → N Vb A

This table makes it possible to generate all the possible combinations for a given language.

4.4.2   Transfer Grammar and Instructions

In his paper on Sapir, Harris (1951b) notes that it is impossible to see how two lin-guistic systems (two languages) can be distinguished from the features of their com-mon physical world; it is only possible to see how they can be distinguished on the grammatical level. Harris emphasises the formal structure of languages by stating

Fig. 4.6 Harris (1951a, p. 350)

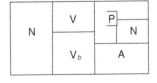

---

[19] Harwood published an article in *Language* in 1955 – thus before Chomsky's earliest publica-tions – which relies on Harris (1951a) and which puts forward the conception of grammar as a system organised by generative rules. By defining an axiomatic syntactic system that makes it possible to derive possible sequences and to distinguish them from the remainder, that is, impos-sible sequences, Harwood's aim was to determine the goodness of fit of syntactic systems.

that their fundamental mode of adequacy is less completeness, which is static, than "completability", that is, constructivity, which is dynamic and without limit. He quotes Sapir (1949, p. 153): "The outstanding fact about any language is its formal completeness. No matter what any speaker of it may desire to communicate, the language is prepared to do its work". Harris adds: "Hence what is important is not so much the distinction between grammatical form and vocabulary, as the fact that the distribution of grammatical elements, and so the grammatical structure, can change in a continuous deformation (the structure at any one moment being virtually identical with the immediately preceding structure), and that vocabulary can be added without limit (and changed in meaning). What we have, therefore, as the basic adequacy of language is not so much the static completeness of its formal structure, but rather its completability, or more exactly its constructivity without limit" (Harris 1951b, p. 296).

In his 1954 IJAL article, "Transfer Grammar", his aim is to determine how to measure and correct the differences between the two systems. Harris puts forward a method, transfer grammar, capable of measuring the differences between grammatical structures and to establishing "what is the minimum difference (or the maximum similarity) between any two language systems" (Harris 1954, p. 259). The method also has practical objectives: it can be used to work out a translation procedure that can be transformed into instructions for a computational system of machine translation.[20] The difference between two languages is defined as the number and the content of the grammatical instructions necessary to generate the utterances of language A from the utterances of language B. Harris works out transfer instructions (B-A) so that grammar B can be obtained from grammar A using (B-A) instructions. The instructions constitute an appendix, an addition to grammar A, in other words a transfer grammar of B via A. This transfer grammar is also an intermediary language designed for automatisation. See Fig. 4.7.

Other than the term "generate", the key word here is the term "instruction", which appears in Harris's work for the first time and is used 24 times in the text, which is quite significant for a twelve-page text. The term is used in the sense of instruction for a computer algorithm: "The method is also relevant to a proceduralised system of translation, and indeed can be put in the form of routine instructions for machine translations" (Harris 1954, p. 259).

The same terms, "instruction" and "generate", are used to define the grammar of a language: "A grammar may be viewed as a set of instructions which generates the sentences of a language" (Harris 1954, p. 260). However, Harris does not give details about what instructions should be, and the terms "instruction" and "generate" are not reserved for grammatical rules. Instructions are also used to generate lexicon and phonemes. In Fig. 4.7:

---

[20] The method can also be used for language teaching: Harris assumes, in a more or less hazardous way, that one can acquire a language by learning only the differences between the new language and the old one and by leaving out what they have in common. It is possible that this is an audacious interpretation of Fries's contrastive analysis for foreign language teaching (see Chap. 3).

H \ E	V +ed	will / shall V	preverbs not listed else- where + V	V to V	(may/ might/ should) + V	It's A that N (Ved /will V)	I am A/N	I will V	I Ved
V +pers	x								
pers +V		x							
(yaxol /muxrax / etc) leV			x						
Other V+le V				x					
(efsar/ naxon/etc) se pers. V					x				
Other A+se (pers V/V pers)						x			
ani (-A / -N)							x		
ani e + pers +V								x	
ani V +pers +ti									x

Fig. 4.7 Harris's (1954, p. 259) transfer instructions for verbal form in Hebrew and English

1st row: English structures
1st column: Hebrew structures Preverb: will, shall, can, could, may
V + pers.: personal suffixed elements Pers + V: personal prefixed elements

One can read Fig. 4.7 as instructions of condition then action: if there is an x in a column, then translate by the form in the corresponding row. These instructions are ordered in an algorithm and directly programmable.

If one takes the example of I in English, its translation into Hebrew is conditioned by the context. Three ordered instructions (or rules) make it possible to solve the ambiguity:

"I" (in English) is translated into Hebrew by prefix "e-" if it is followed by "will be" (in Hebrew pers +V).
"I" (in English) is translated into Hebrew by suffix "(ani) – ti" if it is followed by V + ed (V + pers).
"I" (in English) is translated into Hebrew by "ani" in any other case.

4.5   The Sources of the Generativist Program

The analysis of these works shows that immediate constituent analysis evolved progressively during several Neo-Bloomfieldian works towards a first version of generative grammar. This evolution was realised by dynamising the diagrams, that is, by transforming them into algorithms, made possible by the automation of translation. As early as 1943, with Pike, and in 1954 with Hockett, hierarchical representations appeared for the first time but remained limited to immediate constituents and to morphemes.

We saw how in 1951 Harris made this model evolve by integrating the notion of generation into diagrams, even if, in his text, "generate" is not used exclusively for grammar but also for phonemes and lexicon. The notion of instruction (condition then action), which appeared in 1954 with the possibilities of automation, transformed the model into a computable algorithm and advanced the definition of grammar. Accordingly, grammar became a set of instructions designed to generate the sentences of a language. The explication provided by Harwood in 1955 led to the definition of a grammar capable of delimiting two sets, the set of possible sentences and the set of impossible sentences, thus transforming Harris's model into a real generative grammar. All of these elements argue in favour of a continuist approach of the history of American linguistics, in opposition to the idea of a rupture, or even a revolution, between distributionalist views and the Chomskyan program.[21]

Chomsky's connections to the first mathematisation have been dealt with in historiographical works (Seuren 1998; Tomalin 2006). It is indeed strange that the view advanced in a recent book (Tomalin 2006), which focuses all its attention on the formal sources of Chomskyan theory, still gives rise to debates (Seuren 2009), since the influence of logical and mathematical theories (Church, Russell, Hilbert, Carnap, etc.), of empiricist philosophical theories (Quine, Goodman) and of theory of algorithms (Post) on Chomsky's work had arguably already been well established.

As for the Harrissian filiation, it no longer needs to be demonstrated. Moreover, Chomsky largely quotes Harris as well as Harwood in his doctoral dissertation (1955) and in *Syntactic Structures* (1957).[22]

Besides, although he always claimed he never took part in either machine translation experiments or in computer works, it nonetheless remains true that Chomsky participated in the war technology culture during the early years of MT and that his theory of grammars is also linked to the automation of syntactic analysis. Like other former pupils of Harris,[23] he was recruited in 1955 by MIT's Research Laboratory of Electronics (RLE), directed by Victor Yngve, who led the MT group and was a pioneer author of automatic syntactic analysers.[24] Already familiar with the axiomatisation of rules undertaken by Harris, he benefited from a background enabling his computational (combinatorial) conception of grammar to develop.[25] In 1956, Chomsky met Marcel-Paul Schützenberger (1920–1996) who had been invited to

---

[21] The term "model" appeared in American linguistics in the 1940s–1950s, essentially in the works of Z.S. Harris, C.F. Hockett and N. Chomsky, and took a mathematical turn gradually contributing to the mathematisation of linguistics and the development of generative grammars (see Léon 2021).

[22] It should be noted that, as John Joseph (2002) notes, since the 1970s Chomsky has always denied Harris's influence of any kind and claimed that in his own work "generative" merely means "explicative".

[23] Chomsky was recruited by Yngve with three other linguists, Joseph R. Applegate, Fred Lukoff and Betty Shefts, the first two of whom were Harris's students (*Mechanical translation* vol. 2, n° 1, 1955).

[24] Nevin (2009) notes that Chomsky's criticism of the "fuzziness" of Harrissian theories aimed at the fact that they were not reducible to an algorithm programmable on computer.

[25] According to Wildgen (2009), the fact that Harris and Chomsky chose algebra as a scientific metalanguage is consistent with the traditional conception of language as a written language, that is, discrete, linear and reducible to a spatial combinatorics. This strategical use of mathematics is

MIT (and who worked with Shannon on the semantics of formal languages). Chomsky's approach settles the relationship between computer sciences and mathematics at various levels. Chomsky owes to Post's production system his system of rewriting rules and more generally his notion of formal language. By establishing his grammar hierarchy, Chomsky (1956) claims to create an algebraic linguistics dedicated to showing the superiority of transformational grammar (see Sects. 2.4 and 2.5.1 above). However, these early works and those he undertook with Schützenberger (Chomsky and Schützenberger 1963) on pushdown automata and context-free languages would be used in compiler theory and for the definition of programming languages and algorithms of syntactic analysis.

4.6   Conclusion

For the Neo-Bloomfieldians, two technological innovations, namely, tape recorders and machine translation, fundamentally changed the task of linguistic anthropologists in the twentieth century. The automation of translation made grammar evolve towards more formalised models. However, even though translation became attractive once more among the distributionalists, MT projects themselves were not continued. Voegelin did not develop his translation method using intermediary language. Harris, although he was the only Neo-Bloomfieldian linguist who led a MT group, devoted himself to the construction of sublanguages of sciences, of which transfer grammar can be said to be the first version.[26] Thus, it was not translation that benefited from the advances of formalisation but rather the immediate constituent model, which was capable of evolution, contrary to the claims of some critics. As early as the 1950s, Bar-Hillel showed the limits of that model, which he argued only reflected structuralist linguists' attraction for constructional processes that allow for the division of complex linguistic elements into smaller elements (morphemes and phonemes): no attention was paid to logical relations, that is, to syntax. According to Bar-Hillel, another limitation of the immediate constituent model was its inability to deal with the non-adjacent elements of a sentence,[27] a deficiency that Chomsky's transformations would attempt to resolve.[28]

---

conservative as it assumes that the relevant linguistic facts are already known and that they only need to be rendered in an elegant and coherent way.

[26] It should be noted that the MT method, which was based on transfer grammar, was taken up by the Harrissian Morris Salkoff (2002), a member of Maurice Gross's research team, in order to develop an English-French MT system.

[27] This argument, often used against distributionalists, is contested by Sampson (2001, p. 145), who recalls that the notion of discontinuous constituent was introduced by Pike in 1943 and developed by Rulon Wells in 1947.

[28] As seen in Chap. 2, Bar-Hillel (1953b) himself developed an operational syntax for MT based on structural linguistic works (namely, Harris's) and logical formal languages (Ajdukiewicz). Later, he adopted Chomsky's model.

Chapter 5
Information Theory: Transfer of Terms, Concepts and Methods

Information theory is at the core of the sciences of war. Although the scientific notion of information had existed since the 1920s, it really took off with the publication of *Cybernetics* by Norbert Wiener in 1948 and with the articles by Claude Shannon in *The Bell System Technical Journal*. These articles were republished in 1949 with a preface by Warren Weaver in *The Mathematical Theory of Communication* co-authored by Shannon and Weaver. Weaver and Shannon were involved in the sciences of war. While working at both the Bell Laboratories and MIT, Shannon focused on improving cryptographic techniques and developing anti-aircraft systems. The terms used to designate information theory are various, as demonstrated in titles of its seminal works: "cybernetics", "information theory" and "(mathematical) theory of communication". As Segal (2003) points out, what is generally designated in Europe by information theory is the grouping of the theory of communication and cybernetics, whereas in the USA, cybernetics often comprises the other two. Moreover, Americans focused more on the quantitative aspect of information as it was worked out by Shannon, while the British, like Colin Cherry (with whom Jakobson worked), were more interested in the communicational side of the theory. As for France, information theory was discussed by mathematicians like Benoît Mandelbrot and Marcel-Paul Schützenberger.

This diversity echoed the huge interest aroused by information theory among scientists from all disciplines. It led to numerous and very often disparate works. Information and related notions were sometimes used metaphorically, even incorrectly. Information theory became "The Bandwagon", criticised by Shannon (1956) himself, that attracted scientists in many disciplines. Linguistics was neither present in the sciences of war nor represented at the Macy Conferences.[1] Jakobson, who was invited to the 5th Conference in 1948, and later Yuen Ren Chao and Bar-Hillel, who were invited to the 10th Conference, were the only linguists to have

---

[1] See Chap. 6. §6.5.

© The Author(s), under exclusive license to Springer Nature
Switzerland AG 2021
J. Léon, *Automating Linguistics*, History of Computing,
https://doi.org/10.1007/978-3-030-70642-5_5

participated in them. As for Claude Shannon, when invited to the 6th Conference in 1949, he gave a presentation on the redundancy of English. This was one of the linguistic issues that Shannon and Weaver addressed in their book. Other topics such as finite-state automata and Markov chains introduced the notion of probability into the study of languages.[2] Shannon also mentions Zipf's work on the frequencies of vocabulary when defining the entropy of English.[3] Information theory offered a large range of new methods and notions that tempted many linguists. While computational linguistics was partly founded by linguists within the horizon of retrospection defined by MT, information theory was imported from the outside, delivered in separate parts to meet the demand. Thus, like other sciences, the use of information theory by linguists was heterogeneous, even disparate. There was a wide variation of transfer of concepts and methods, reception and integration.

In this chapter, after a survey of the use of information as a term and notion, we will examine three modes of how information theory was integrated in linguistics: its adaptation by the Neo-Bloomfieldians, especially by Charles F. Hockett and Zellig S. Harris; the convergence of information theory, engineering and linguistics in Roman Jakobson's Distinctive Feature Theory; and its use by two French linguists, André Martinet and Jean Dubois.

5.1   Information: The Term and Notion

The term information itself is interesting because of its instability and because of the competition it fuels between its ordinary meaning, the technical meaning given by information theory and the semantic sense of "information content". Information is an ordinary word, but in linguistics it is used in various different ways. It is frequently used in the USA, in ordinary American English, to mean a piece of data or knowledge. This is the meaning used by Harris, for example, at the beginning of his work, from 1942 to 1952. In France, however, the term is hardly used by linguists in this sense.

From the 1920s onwards, it was in sciences like physics, statistics and telecommunications that information became a scientific and technical notion with a very different meaning from its common usage. Since World War II, engineers, physicists and mathematicians used information to refer to the value that characterises various modes of communication, a notion related to entropy in thermodynamics, which allows the capacity for computer storage and processing to be determined,

---

[2] Andrey Andreyevich Markov (1856–1922) studied literary texts, among them *Eugene Onegin* by Pushkin, as stochastic strings of characters. A Markov chain is a finite-state automaton whose transitions from one state to another are ruled by probabilities. In 1948, Shannon put forward a statistical model based on Markov chains to study the strings of letters in an English text.

[3] According to Segal (2003), Zipf, in his 1946 article entitled "Some determinants of the circulation of information", developed a mathematical definition of "quantity of information" close to Shannon's.

provided the semantic dimension of the term information is set aside. The mathematical notion of information remains as close as possible to its etymological meaning, that is, signal shaping. In telecommunications, like for the Bell Telephone Company, the issue was to assess the most economical means of carrying the greatest number of messages through a single wire and transmit signals with a minimum of noise. Shannon's work was developed in this context.

However, the emergence of information as a scientific term gave rise to confusion between information as content and information as signal. Hartley, one of the founders of the notion of information, introduced this confusion in 1928 by using the term "information" to mean both signal – a purely quantitative and probabilistic measure, and the actual object of information theory – as well as content (Hartley 1928). Carnap and Bar-Hillel (1952) denounced this confusion by proposing a semantic theory of information (see Bar-Hillel's presentation at the 10th Macy Conference). Bar-Hillel then put forward two terms to account for both dimensions of information, the theory of signal transmission, whose object of study was the processing of messages as sequences of signals, and the theory of information transmission for the treatment of messages that carry meaning. Curiously, it was the latter sense, the semantic sense, that the various linguistic approaches using information theory would later derive from or converge on.

In the 1950s–1960s, with the rise of information theory, altogether new terms, or old ones with new meanings, began appearing in works of linguistics. Some came from the theory of communication, such as code,[4] coding, decoding, transcoding, message, communication, transmitter, receiver, speaker, interlocutor, emission, reception, transmission and signal; others belonged to cybernetics, such as feedback and control. Finally, some terms referred more to the quantitative part of the theory, like information, quantity of information, probabilities, Markov chains, redundancy, noise, entropy, cost and ratio. These terms migrated to linguistics in different ways, thus determining various forms of reception of information theory. Reception depended on the proximity of the given terms to the notions and methods used in current linguistic approaches, and on their capacity for metaphorisation.

5.2   Information Theory and the Neo-Bloomfieldians: Integration by Adaptation

Like MT and computational linguistics, information theory appeared in the USA within a horizon of retrospection generally shared by all the American scientists, including linguists. For American linguists, the best-known works in fields of cybernetics, communication and information were Shannon's. His view on natural

---

[4]The term "code" had already been used by Saussure. Since then, the notion of code has been at the core of the linguists' reflections on the relationship between spoken and written language, between speech and writing (Fehr 2003).

language processing through quantitative properties, especially the redundancy of natural languages and the non-equiprobability of linguistic elements, was so familiar to American linguists in the 1950s that some of them neglected to cite information theory explicitly when referring to famous notions such as redundancy.[5]

Bloomfieldian linguistics had certain features that facilitated the understanding and the adoption of information theory, as well as its integration into its methods of analysis. Its behaviourist approach and its conception of language as a set of physical events (sounds and ink marks)[6] were entirely compatible with signal processing in information theory. Both approaches shared the idea that meaning was not relevant and that the use of quantitative and probabilistic methods was quite adapted to linguistic analysis.

Moreover, distributional analysis had some characteristics that made it particularly receptive to certain aspects of information theory. This is the case in particular regarding repetition, one of the central operations of discovery procedures, which echoes the notion of redundancy in information theory. Repetition is what allows the linguistic units in an utterance to be delimited and equivalent classes to be determined without recourse to meaning. Hockett (1953), in his long review of Shannon and Weaver's book in *Language*, states that the redundancy of languages is closely linked to their structure and that the linguist, contrary to the telecommunications engineer, should implement linguistic operations to "discover" units from the sound signal when starting to describe an (unwritten) language. According to him, the grouping of allophones into phonemes could be established with information theory, particularly in terms of entropy.[7]

In the examples he examines, Hockett presents the encoding of morphemes as depending on their morphemic context. For the plural "wives" of "wife", "Wife is encoded into /wayv/ if the next morpheme is the noun-plural -s and -s is encoded into /z/ rather than /s/ when the preceding morpheme is wife" (Hockett 1953, p. 87). He also discusses experiments showing that the probability of a phoneme's occurrence increases in the middle of a morpheme and diminishes at its borders. As for

---

[5] Hockett (1953) dedicated an imposing review of thirty pages to Shannon and Weaver's book in *Language*.

[6] "It [language] can be objectively studied if one considers speech and writing not as an expression of the speaker which has particular, introspectively recognised, meanings to the hearer; but rather as a set of events – sound waves or ink marks – which may be said, if we wish, to serve as tool or vehicle for communication and expression. This set of events, the many occurrences of speaking and of writing, can be described in terms of a structural model" (Harris 1959, p. 458).

[7] Phonemes are the linguistically contrastive or significant sounds (or sets of sounds) of a language: these sounds cannot be substituted for each other without a change in meaning. For example, in English /a/ /i/ /e/ /u/ /o/ are different phonemes because the words /pat/ /pit/ /pet/ /put/ /pot/ have different meanings. Allophones are the linguistically non-significant variants of each phoneme. In other words, a phoneme may be realised by more than one speech sound. Allophones can be substituted for each other without a change in meaning. For example, in French, "père" can be pronounced in three different ways: the consonant [r] can be realised as an alveolar trill, an uvular trill or a uvular fricative; they are different phonetic sounds, but their difference is not relevant from the point of view of meaning. They are interpreted as the variants of pronunciation of the same phoneme /r/.

Harris,[8] although he didn't make explicit reference to information theory until 1968, he borrowed and adapted its methods and concepts much earlier, such as the notions of redundancy and non-equiprobability of linguistic elements, the transitional probabilities at work in Markov chains, and speech and written language processing as physical events. It could even be argued that the conception of information he would develop in his last works (Harris 1988, 1991), although it may seem very different, was directly inspired by Shannon and Weaver.

In Harris's work, repetition, which is at the foundation of equivalence classes, appeared in 1952 in his article "Discourse analysis". Repetition, however, does not necessarily imply high frequency: linguistic elements are events that either occur or don't, and should be treated with probabilistic methods rather than statistical methods. In 1954, Harris put forward that languages are not equiprobable (this idea had been formulated by Shannon in 1948) and that this principle should be used as a basis for establishing equivalence classes.

Harris (1955) uses Markov chains and n-grams to determine the borders of morphemes in an utterance analysed as a series of phonemes. He works out a procedure that treats morphemes as predictable code units that can be discovered by comparing the constrained combinability of phonemes within morphemes' borders to the free combinability outside them.

In 1955, Harris implemented this method for segmenting phoneme strings. For example, the transcribed utterance /hiyzkwiker/ (he's quicker) is segmented in the following way: /hiy.z.kwik.er/. However, when he advances his use of transitional probabilities, he refers, not to Markov chains, but to Hockett's *Manual of Phonology*: "The frequency of each successor to each sound or phoneme can be studied in terms of the (transitional) probability of each phoneme in respect to its immediate neighbor alone" (Harris 1955, p. 210). In 1957, information became a semantic notion defined as the semantic invariant between two structures linked by transformation. He developed this idea throughout the 1960s.

The term "redundancy" appeared in 1959 in a text about information retrieval. Harris's objective was to reduce the complexity of sentence patterns to a few simple constructions easily usable by speakers. He intended to take into account and reduce the redundancy of languages in order to store the content (information) of scientific texts. This idea would be formalised in his 1968 book *Mathematical Structure of Language*. Information could only be represented in the sublanguage of a given science at a given time – it should be remembered that Harris devoted his last works to sublanguages. By progressively incorporating semantic information into the very heart of his theory, he gave it a new objective, which consisted in developing an information grammar for the sublanguages of sciences.[9]

While departing from the methodological aspects of Shannon's information theory (Markov chains and probabilities), which he adapted to the distributional

---

[8] For a detailed study of the significance of information theory in Harris's work, see Léon (2011a).

[9] For Harris, sublanguages of sciences are formal artificial languages, identical for a given science whatever (the natural) language (see Chap. 10).

method of identifying and classifying units, Harris advanced a semantic approach to information aiming at the development of the sublanguages of sciences. Thus, redundancy took on a new meaning. Although Shannon considered this a positive development because it improved communication in case of noise, ultimately it became a hindrance, a flaw of ordinary language, which sublanguages could remedy in order to keep information alone. However, Harris's disciples (among others) would continue using those methods for subsequent works on natural language processing, such as the use of finite-state transducers by the members of the LADL (Laboratoire d'Analyse Documentaire et Linguistique), which was directed by Maurice Gross.

5.3   Jakobson's Distinctive Feature Theory: Transfers and Convergences between Information Theory, Engineering and Linguistics

With Jakobson's Distinctive Feature Theory (hereafter DFT), we face a new type of interaction between information theory and linguistics that involves not only these two disciplines but also engineering, physics and acoustic phonetics. One might ask whether what is at stake here is a transfer of concepts and methods, or rather a convergence between the new theoretical and technological areas of research, which was made possible by the sciences of war and Jakobson's linguistic views.

DFT was implemented at the beginning of the 1950s by Jakobson in collaboration with one of his students, Morris Halle, and a Swedish acoustician, Gunnar Fant (Jakobson et al. 1952), and later with a British information theorist, Colin Cherry (Cherry et al. 1953). These works were taken over and synthesised in 1956 in Jakobson and Halle's book *Fundamentals of Language*. Later, Jakobson (1971b [1961]) commented and attempted to clarify his use of information theory. However, this reflexive movement raises some questions, as we will see.

DFT is based on the idea that ultimate linguistic units are not phonemes but features referring to speech production (the source) and the acoustics of the vocal tract (resonance and tone). The 12 distinctive features thus defined are universal and can be combined into phonemes for a given language, without any language needing to have all 12 features. This theory made significant advances in renewing phonological approaches, whether it be the Prague School's approach or the Neo-Bloomfieldian approach.

In his *Grundzüge der Phonologie*, published in 1939, Nikolai Trubetzkoy (1890–1938) uses phonetic criteria to define and identify phonological units, thus sketching out the idea of phonology as characterised by functional phonetics and as based on a continuum between phonology and phonetics (Trubetzkoy 1949 [1939]).[10]

---

[10]Phonetics is about the physical aspect of sounds. It deals with the description and classification of speech sounds, particularly how sounds are produced, transmitted and received, often without prior knowledge of the language being spoken. Phonology is about the abstract aspect of sounds.

This idea would be reinforced by DFT. Another founding principle of Prague phonology was that of opposition, which was inherited from Saussure.[11]

At the beginning of the 1930s, Trubetzkoy and Jakobson changed their definition of the phoneme. It went from being a minimal unit that was not separable into smaller units, to being a set of relevant sound properties. These properties were determined using both articulatory and perceptive phonetic criteria. While Trubetzkoy identified them on the basis of oppositions with two or more dimensions, Jakobson attempted, as early as 1938, to only use unidimensional (i.e. bilateral or binary) oppositions.[12] He advanced three types of oppositions for the localisation features: (i) sonority features: [+/- vocalic], [+/- consonantal], [+/- nasal], [+/- compact], [+/- diffuse], [+/- abrupt], [+/- strident], [+/- checked]; (ii) protensity feature: [+/- tense]; and (iii) tonality features: [+/- acute], [+/- flat], [+/- sharp]. In DFT, the opposition principle became the binary principle. Contrary to the Prague approach, DFT no longer regarded distinctive features as classifying features but as linguistic units that were both minimal and universal. Only binary and dichotomous oppositions were kept.

In Cherry et al. (1953), Jakobson states he owes the term distinctive features to Bloomfield, for whom only one constant phonetic feature exists in a phoneme beyond all its phonetic variations. This constant feature explains why the speaker interprets all the varieties as a unique phoneme. However, Bloomfield focused more on morphophonemics (phonological differences allowing morphemes to be differentiated on the syntagmatic level) than on the internal description of phonemes in terms of distinctive features, which are absent from the structural description. Lastly, Jakobson's interest in the theory of communication lies in the Moscow Circle, which he created in 1915 and which considered that the only form of natural communication was dialogue (see Romashko 2000).

5.3.1 Engineering and Acoustic Phonetics: Spectrograms

The collaboration between Jakobson and the acoustician Gunnar Fant, both of whom conceived of language as speech communication, responded to the need to base distinctive features on both acoustic and perceptive criteria. Fant was a Swedish acoustician trained in electrical engineering. His doctoral dissertation was on the relation between intelligibility and speech bandwidth reduction. He also worked on

---

It establishes what are the phonemes in a given language, i.e. those sounds that can bring a difference in meaning between two words (see note 7 above).

[11] Waugh et al. (1990) indicate the antinomies of post-Hegelian Russian dialectic tradition as being also at the source of the notion of opposition.

[12] According to Anderson (1985), it is difficult to distinguish which was specific to Trubetzkoy or to Jakobson during the Prague period. As their correspondence attests, there were very few points of disagreement between them (Sériot 2006). It was only after Trubetzkoy's death in 1938 that Jakobson's views began to really diverge.

spectrographs (like Joos and Shannon), whose development constituted a major progress for phoneticians because they provided the spectrogram (acoustic spectrum) of speech sounds (frequency, intensity, duration), which could be used to determine formants, that is, the distinctive form of sound.

The work of Fant, who was a visiting scholar at the acoustic laboratories of Harvard and MIT in 1949–1951, aroused Jakobson's interest, who saw in it a means of discovering the distinctive features common to consonants and vowels by anchoring them to sound substance derived from the use of acoustic and perceptive criteria. Morris Halle, Jakobson's student who was also trained in electrical engineering, joined them to develop an integrated theory of distinctive features. They considered that distinctive features should be based externally on the acoustic signal (substance) and also, in line with the Russian tradition of dialogue, on the speaker's articulatory and the hearer's perceptive activities, since, as Jakobson and Halle (1956, p. 34) state, we speak to be heard and we must be heard to be understood.

5.3.2   Information Theory: The Mathematics of the Continuum for Phonology

As Jakobson and Halle continued to develop DFT with the British Information theorist Colin Cherry, an advocate of a communications-based approach to information theory, they claimed that the mathematical theory of communication could provide a rigorous scientific foundation for the interpretation and analysis of phonological systems.

The mathematical theory of communication converges with DFT in several points: it provides a basis for measuring the statistical dependencies of ordered series of units, for example, the words in a text;[13] and it involves an acoustic phonetic component that deals with stochastic processes such as acoustic signals in telephone communication. For Jakobson, information theory provided an opportunity to construct a mathematisation of the continuum, that is, to formalise the transition from the continuum (the speech signals observable in production and perception) to discrete units (the phonological units of the message).

Cherry et al. (1953) adapted the five components: information source + encoder + channel + decoder + information basin from the theory of communication model. By grouping these components, one obtains sender (information source + encoder) and receiver (decoder + information basin). The authors claim that they adopt the concepts of code and message from communication theory, which were much clearer and more operational than the Saussurean dichotomy of language and

---

[13] Only Markov's works (Markov 1913; Petruszewycz 1981) prefigured that type of research. Zipf's works only set up distributions of univariate frequencies (word frequencies).

speech. They also borrowed the notion of redundancy and the binary principle, which replaced the opposition principle.

DFT strove to define a "speech code", that is, to encode phonological contrasts into binary distinctive features with a minimum of redundancy. The objective was to provide phonetics with a structure and to break down phonemes, which until then were only inventories, into distinctive features that carry information to the receiver. A distinctive feature is recognised by the receiver if it belongs to the common code he/she shares with the sender, if it is correctly transmitted and if it reaches the receiver. The authors show the importance of redundancy, which increases the reliability of speech communication by making it resistant to the various sources of distortion. Finally, they take from information theory its discrete binary analysis of communication processes based on Markov chains. The incompatibility or co-occurrence of features within a given language and a given phoneme is determined either by universally valid laws of implication or by high statistical probability. Probability enables the elimination of highly probable features and the reduction of redundancy. Jakobson (1971b [1961]) justifies the application of conditional probabilities to phonology: contrary to speech production, perception is a stochastic process. For example, in the case of homophones[14] (which only exist for the hearer), the resolution of ambiguities depends on the conditional probabilities of the context.

One could say that we are dealing with phenomena of transfer by convergence. The use of conditional probabilities that enable the resolution of ambiguities constitutes a transfer of method that leads to a mathematisation of language in interaction, which cannot be qualified as "intrinsic" "covering" even though it involves statistical methods. For Auroux (2009), "intrinsic mathematisation" enables the creation of new concepts that cannot be separated from their mathematical formulation. Intrinsic concepts in linguistics first appeared with logic, then with Boolean algebra and finally with the modern notion of calculability, which was linked to Turing machines and to the theory of formal languages. The intrinsic mathematisation of linguistics was primarily by Bloomfield and Harris with their work on axiomatisation and by the rise of formal grammars in the 1950s, like Bar-Hillel's categorial grammar (1953b) and Chomsky's transformational generative grammar (1955). Auroux gives the name "covering mathematisation" to the quantitative approaches of language that count observable elements, such as words, by assigning them a property or a number.

In DFT, redundancy operates at two levels.

First, to identity distinctive features. The phonological system of a given language can be represented by a two-dimensional matrix (phonemes and distinctive features) and three values (marked (+), non-marked (-), redundant ($\emptyset$)).[15]According

---

[14] Homophony is the linguistic phenomenon whereby two or more different written forms have the same pronunciation: bare/ bear; flour/flower.

[15] Cherry et al. (1953) give the following example, p. 39: a redundant feature helps the hearer to solve some of the ambiguities caused by signal distortion. For example, the nasal feature is marked zero for all the Russian vowels. If these zeros were changed into (+), the new symbols would not

to the authors, this matrix is a real code book designed for the identification of phonemes.

Second, to classify phonemes by reducing redundancy, that is, by lowering the number of distinctive features.

The notion of redundancy thus assumes the contradictory nature it has in information theory.[16] Even if redundancy should be reduced to improve message transmission, it must be acknowledged that it carries information and can help identifying the message when there is noise. Jakobson (1971b [1961]) insists on the fact that it is in rhetoric that the notion of redundancy first appeared and that it was linguists that discovered it: the theory of communication borrowed it and redefined it in terms of entropy, and linguistics rediscovered it by distinguishing between redundant features and distinctive features.

The binary principle no doubt constitutes one of the most interesting uses of information theory by DFT:

> The dichotomous principle underlying the whole system of distinctive features in language has gradually been disclosed by linguistics and has found corroboration in the binary digits (or to use the popular portmanteau, bits) employed as a unit of measurement by the communication engineers. (Jakobson 1971b [1961], p. 571)

The binary principle presents several advantages for DFT:

(i) It takes up and radicalises the notion of opposition. Jakobson considered the binarity of features as a principle inherent to the structure of language, which he would extend to all linguistic units.

(ii) The identification of the distinctive features of a given language is carried out as the receiver browses a dichotomous decision tree with the help of yes-no questions. It was put forward by Cherry (1957) as one of the major characteristics of information theory.

(iii) Binary decisions are easier to implement than ternary or n-ary decisions, from the logical as well as empirical point of view. Associated with the opposition marked/unmarked, where "marked" means carrying information, they are ideal for coding information.

---

mean that a Russian speaker nasalises all his/her vowels; normally he/she would not do it; even if he/she would do it, nasality would not have any phonemic signification. It is a redundant feature.

[16] "The necessity of a strict distinction between different types of redundancy is now realised in the theory of communication as well as in linguistics, where the concept of redundancy encompasses on the one hand pleonastic means as opposed to explicit conciseness (brevitas in the tradition nomenclature of rhetoric) and on the other hand explicitness in contradistinction to ellipsis. On the phonological level, linguists have been accustomed to delimit phonemic, distinctive units from contextual, combinatory, allophonic variants, but the treatment of such interconnected problems as redundancy, predictability, and conditional probabilities in communication theory furthered a clarification of the relationship between the two basic linguistic classes of sound-properties – the distinctive features and the redundant features" (Jakobson 1971b [1961], p. 571–72).

(iv) Finally, the binary principle helped initiate an explanatory approach in phonology which was absent in structuralist and distributionalist views and would be taken over by generative phonology.[17]

5.3.3 Jakobson: a Scientific Frontier Runner

One can define a frontier runner by his/her capacity to make concepts and methods circulate from one discipline to another, and in this case, from one side of the Atlantic to the other.

It should be noted that Jakobson was not the first linguist who took an interest in information theory. From the institutional point of view, it was Joshua Whatmough, a philologist and the president of the Linguistic Society of America, who officially introduced information theory into the American linguistic community by presenting Shannon's theory in his inaugural address in December 1951. In 1952, Whatmough published an article in the *Scientific American* in which he explained the evolution of languages using information quantity. Besides, it was Martin Joos, not Jakobson, who represented linguists at the Speech Communication Conference organised at MIT and Harvard in 1950 (Fehr 2000). Considering Joos's training as both an engineer and a Germanist and his contribution to the sciences of war as a cryptanalyst and acoustician, it is understandable that he was invited to this first interdisciplinary conference to gather engineers, mathematicians, physicists, phoneticians, psychologists and linguists around the issue of language as a particular case of the theory of communication. For Segal (2003), it was Joos's paper that drew Jakobson's attention to the transition from continuous to discontinuous, especially to the segmentation of the continuous flow of human language into phonemes, and the possibility of their linguistic analysis by means of discrete features.

Sometimes, Jakobson amplified the reciprocal cooperation between both disciplines: "Communication theory seems to me a good school for present-day linguists, just as structural linguistics is a useful school for communication engineering" (Jakobson 1953, p. 15).

In fact, Jakobson's references to the interaction between linguists and engineers and to cybernetics only appear in 1961 (Jakobson 1961), that is, about 10 years after DFT. As Van de Walle (2008) notes, Jakobson (1961 [1971]) claims that the elucidation in cybernetics of notions such as "goal-attainment", "goal-failure" and "negative feedback" opens new paths for linguistics, but Jakobson himself never used

---

[17] In generative theory, an explanatory model is a formal grammar based on explanatory principles, which must take into account the intuition of the native speaker. See the definition given by Chomsky in 1962: "What we seek, then, is a formalised grammar that specifies the correct structural descriptions with a fairly small number of general principles of sentence formation and that is embedded within a theory of linguistic structure that provides a justification for the choice of this grammar over alternatives. Such a grammar could properly be called an explanatory model, a theory of the linguistic intuition of a native speaker" (Chomsky 1962, p. 533).

these notions. He even gives free rein to a certain metaphorical drift by pretending to do "quantum linguistics" in two ways:

(i) By regarding distinctive features as irreducible units which can be compared to atoms: "Linguistic analysis, however, came to resolve oral speech into a finite series of elementary informational units. These ultimate discrete units, the so-called 'distinctive features,' are aligned into simultaneous bundles termed 'phonemes,' which in turn are concatenated into sequences. Thus form in language has a manifestly granular structure and is subject to a quantal description" (Jakobson 1971b [1961], p. 570).

(ii) By comparing quantum mechanics and structural linguistics, both deterministic (see Jakobson 1958) and by assigning the linguist the role of participant-observer,[18] the linguist must replace his role as a cryptanalyst, who is not the message addressee, with that of a "normal decoder", of the receiver, a member of the studied linguistic community. In 1961 he says: "The linguistic observer who possesses or acquires a command of the language he is observing is or gradually becomes a potential or actual partner in the exchange of verbal messages among the members of the speech community [...] The communication engineer is right when defending against 'some philologists' the absolutely dominant 'need to bring the Observer onto the scene' and when holding with Cherry that 'the participant-observer's description will be the more complete.' [...] Obviously 'the inseparability of objective content and observing subject,' singled out by Niels Bohr as a premise of all well-defined knowledge, must be definitely taken into account also in linguistics, and the position of the observer in relation to the language observed and described must be exactly identified" (Jakobson 1971b [1961], p. 574–575).

According to Segal (2003), the assimilation of the linguist with the participant-observer, and thus of the information theorist with the message addressee, constitutes a complete misinterpretation of Shannon's communication system. In fact, this idea belongs to Cherry, himself an information theorist, who developed it extensively in his book *On Human Communication* (1957).

Finally, it should be added that when he does not deal with phonology, Jakobson conflates the mathematical sense of information with the semantic one of content. Thus, in his 1959 article "Boas' View of Grammatical Meaning", in order to show that all the morpho-syntactic marks are marked variably in the code depending on the language in question, and that grammatical information is semantic, Jakobson uses the term information in the mathematical sense (bits of information) and in the semantic one (grammatical information and semantic information).

> The choice of a grammatical form by the speaker presents the listener with a definite number of *bits of information*. The compulsory character of this kind of *information* for any verbal exchange within a given speech community and the considerable difference between the *grammatical information* conveyed by diverse languages were fully realised by Franz

---

[18]Waugh et al. (1990) note that the theory of relativity was very attractive for Jakobson as well as every notion common to physics, mathematics and linguistics.

Boas, thanks to his astonishing grasp of the manifold semantic patterns of the linguistic world [...] It was clear to Boas that any difference of grammatical categories carries *semantic information*. (Jakobson 1971a [1959], p. 490–493, my italics)

It is certain that Jakobson inaugurated a very original form of collaboration between linguists, engineers and mathematicians by initiating and strengthening a new phonology with information theory, which led to unprecedented types of convergence and transfers of methods between linguistics, engineering and mathematics. However, it is difficult to consider him an authentic "frontier runner" (*passeur*) like Mandelbrot and Schützenberger (see Chap. 8). What is certain, in any case, is that Jakobson's use of information theory in his linguistic developments would have a significant impact on European as well as American linguistics.

5.4 Information Theory, Information and French Linguists in the 1960s

As information theory was introduced into France, its impact on French structural linguistics was disparate and transitory in varying degrees depending on its import route. It was a mathematician, Benoît Mandelbrot, who accomplished the move towards the linguists-stylisticians, which led to the renewal of traditional studies of vocabulary in the 1950s and 1960s. A second way was paved by French engineers working as cryptographers during the First Indochina War, such as René Moreau, who integrated information theory into the computational mathematical turn in France. Notably, Moreau's lectures on information theory at the Centre Favard functioned as a real "frontier space", a "transition space".

Among the linguists, Jakobson's reception by André Martinet on the one hand and by Jean Dubois on the other laid the groundwork for the introduction of information theory into French structural linguistics (see Léon 2008a). In the USA and elsewhere in the world, the cybernetics-communication-information trilogy became also unavoidable in France, and everyone, including linguists, referred to it more or less explicitly. While in 1955 several reviews of works on cybernetics were published in the *Journal de Psychologie normale et pathologique*, in 1957–1958 the *Bulletin de la Société de Linguistique* published two reviews by Martinet on information theory. The first one (Martinet 1957a), on G-A. Miller's *Language and Communication* (1951) – translated into French in 1956 – was rather negative, and the second one, on Vitold Belevitch's *Langage des machines et langage humain* (1956), which Martinet regarded as a good introduction to information theory for linguists, was more positive.

5.4.1   Martinet: The Self-Promotion of Information Theory

André Martinet (1908–1999) was probably the only French linguist who read Jakobson et al.'s *Preliminaries* (1952), which applied information theory to phonology, as soon as it was published. At that time, Martinet was living and teaching in the USA. After studying English (he passed the highly competitive French examination called the "agrégation"), he was professor (directeur d'études) at the Ecole Pratique des Hautes Etudes from 1938 to 1946, and later was appointed at Columbia University in New York where he taught for 10 years from 1946 to 1955. He was a member of the Auxiliary Language Association and was Chief Editor of the journal *Word*[19] from 1947 until his return to France in 1955. That period corresponds to the rise of information theory, during which most American linguists were tempted to jump on the bandwagon. During his stay in the USA, Martinet was initially on very friendly terms with Jakobson, who helped him settle in New York, but they soon fell out when Martinet did not want to leave the board of *Word* upon returning to France. The story of his troubled relationship with Jakobson and of their theoretical disagreements runs throughout Martinet's autobiography (1993, p. 74, p. 117 et sq., p. 125, p. 293 et sq.). In works in which he used information theory, Martinet continuously points out the discrepancies between his and Jakobson's views.

Thus, although he made significant use of information theory in his works from the 1950s and 1960s, and although he often followed the paths laid out by Jakobson, Martinet claimed he was developing his own approach to information.

In his 1955 book entitled *Économie des changements phonétiques*, which summarises his phonological works from his American years, Martinet affiliates himself with Trubetzkoy, whose views he opposes to Jakobson's. According to him, the analysis of distinctive features was already latent in Trubetzkoy's work (Martinet 1955, p.67, note 8 and 1957c, p.75); Jakobson made no new fundamental contributions to it. The universalist and binaristic apriorism developed by Jakobson et al. (1952) and Cherry et al. (1953) distorts Trubetzkoy's views. Binarism proceeds by general statements and attempts to adapt any phonological fact into pre-established frames that are identical for every language, making it incapable of accounting for diachronic changes.

> […] What makes the binaristic position absolutely unacceptable on the diachronic level is its arbitrary elimination as 'redundant' of phonic characteristics resulting from evolutions that have changed the relations within the system, which would lead to considering these changes as null and void. The diachronic point of view requires a much more vivid interest in phonetic reality than the one which is expected when one struggles to reduce the number of distinctive features to a minimum. (Martinet 1955, p. 76)
>
> […] Apriorism consists in determining distinctive features by referring to a preestablished frame whose universal value is assumed, rather than by taking into account the system of a given language. (Martinet 1957c, p. 75)

---

[19] The journal *Word* was founded in 1943 together with the Linguistic Circle of New York by linguists, some of whom were recent immigrants fleeing from the Nazis, such as Roman Jakobson.

Furthermore, Martinet disagreed with Jakobson's identification of phonemes by acoustic means, and, following Trubetzkoy, preferred articulatory means. The spectrographic analysis, which was Jakobson's favourite method, did no more than confirm the explanation immediately provided by articulatory data. Lastly, although he did not discuss Jakobson's and his collaborators' use of information theory in detail, Martinet discredited them by qualifying them as a mere physico-mathematical contrivance meant to seduce people's minds.

It should be noted that the term information, which occurs twice in *Économie* (p. 140), is linked to the notion of distinctive potential. The example given by Martinet concerns the pronunciation of double consonants. Double consonants (in French) have low frequency and thus high distinctive power, which limits uncertainty while compensating for the stronger energy expenditure sometimes required by their articulation. Information is used here in Jakobson's sense without his being mentioned at this point in the text.

> Thus I can say that, in French, /-kt-/ is richer in information than /-t-/ and that, from the point of view of the language economy, the supplementary distinction brought by /-k-/ corresponds to the extra muscular work it involves… If we now deals with /-atta-/, we can say that, when this combination is encountered five times out of a hundred, the extra work required by the pronunciation of the implosive /- t-/, which distinguishes /-atta-/ from /-ata-/, is worthwhile since it limits uncertainty to a hundred-to-five proportion. The double consonant thus has great distinctive power. In the language where /-atta-/ is encountered eighty times out of a hundred examples of /-ata-/ and ten examples of /- akta-/, /-tt-/ represents an energy expenditure of the same order as is necessary to articulate /-kt-/ but with much less information power. (Martinet 1955, p. 140)

As Verleyen and Swiggers (2006, p. 176) have pointed out, this text contains the contradictory tension that is internal to the notion of economy, between the needs of communication that require the preservation of the maximum quantity of information, i.e. a maximum number of functional oppositions, and the inertia principle, which tends to use a restricted number of frequent units.

We also see here how information contributes to the principle of least effort, which Martinet borrows from Zipf (1949). Human seeks, in all his activities, including language activities, to minimise the effort (muscular work, energy expenditure) necessary to achieve a given objective. According to Martinet, Zipf's principle realises the synthesis of communication needs and human inertia better than the principle of economy that Paul Passy developed within the frame of his functionalist theory of phonetic changes.[20]

Finally, he advocates measuring the functional significance of phonological oppositions, also called "rendement fonctionnel" (functional efficiency), using

---

[20] In his study on Martinet and the Prague School, Verleyen (2007) insists on the influence of Zipf as a psychologist rather than as a statistician. He shows that Jakobson and Trubetzkoy conceived of language in diachrony as an organic totality where the speakers' influence is rather low, while, on the contrary, Martinet thinks of the systematicity of changes in terms of the speaker's properties. This explains, Verleyen argues, why Martinet has recourse to the psychologist Zipf whose principle of the least effort attempts to account for human behaviour in general.

statistics in texts. Here again, he follows Zipf, who pioneered the foundation of a functional phonology that was not purely descriptive but also based on statistics.

His concern for the quantitative aspects of information can be found in *Éléments de linguistique générale*, published in 1960, especially in Chap. 6 "L'évolution des langues", a large part of which is dedicated to information theory (Martinet 1970 [1960]).[21] In this book, most notably in Sect. 6.9, entitled "La théorie de l'information et le linguiste", Martinet presents his own views on information theory without any reference to previous works that apply it to linguistics, not even those by Jakobson.[22] In this text, the notion of information is dissociated from that of distinctive features (thus from the Jakobsonian contribution) and appears only sporadically. Martinet's only references to information theory are Guiraud's presentations at the Société de Linguistique de Paris (SLP) in 1954, which are qualified as unsophisticated ("relativement simples"), and Belevitch's book, which Martinet reviewed in the *BSL* (Martinet 1957b).

Martinet's conception of information is rather conventional. He holds that there is a constant and inverse ratio between the frequency of a unit and the information it conveys. The more a unit is probable, the less it is informative. His distinctive contribution consists in defining information in terms of least effort. In addition to phonology, he applies the notion of information to literature and to other linguistic units such as monemes and lexical forms. Martinet uses Markov's chains to deal with these units in a very similar way to Harris's method (1955). Incidentally, Martinet reports in his *Mémoires* (Martinet 1993, p. 71) that the idea of delimiting words in an utterance by means of the probability of successive occurrences was suggested to him by a discussion with Harris in New York at the beginning of the 1950s. In this type of use, he states that information is in no way a semantic entity:

If I hear /il a p… /, /p/ has no meaning by itself, but it conveys information insofar as it excludes all sorts of possible utterances, like 'il a donné', 'il a bougé'. If /r/ is added to the truncated utterance (/il a pr… /), the uncertainty is reduced again because 'il a payé', 'il a poussé', etc. are excluded, which shows that /r/ conveys information. Consequently, information is not an attribute of meaning since insignificant units such as p/ et /r/ participate in it. (Martinet 1970 [1960], p. 177–78)

It is when he addresses the relationship between information and literature (§6–18) that Martinet uses the terms "contenu informationnel" and "densité informationnelle". An author can increase the informational content of his text, thus holding the attention of his readers, by choosing new lexical units and reducing redundancy. Whereas anticipated collocations are redundant, we expect infrequent collocations from poets.

The author need only present events, whether real or imaginary, in the most direct terms, as long as they are exceptional enough for the informational density of a narrative to retain one's attention. Through an original choice of linguistic units, he can also increase the

---

[21] We do not know whether Martinet knew the article published in the *Scientific American* in 1952 (see Sect. 5.3.3 above) by Joshua Whatmough, a Harvard philologist.

[22] In the brief bibliography of the 1970 edition, Jakobson and Halle (1956) are only mentioned in connection with their binaristic and aprioristic conceptions of phonology, which Martinet criticises.

informational content of his text and measure it exactly. This will exempt him from always needing to seek the unexpected in the events of a narrative. (Martinet 1970 [1960], p. 192)

With the term "contenu informationnel", information seems to lose its quantitative aspect in favour of a semantic dimension: "contenu informationnel" evokes contenu de sens. It may be assumed that the notion of "contenu d'information", which does not exist in Shannon and Weaver's work, comes from Guiraud, one of Martinet's cited sources. Guiraud (1954) applies Zipf's law and information theory to statistical studies of vocabulary for stylistics by assimilating frequency (of signs) and information content a little too quickly, whereas, as we have seen, information is an abstract measure that depends on choices, and is thus a probabilistic measure and not only a statistical one.

In sum, it can be said that the way Martinet uses information theory is rather complex and can take various forms. It is when he least uses the term information, in *Économie des changements phonétiques*, that his use of information as a concept is closest to Jakobson's. Although this usage is accompanied by a strong criticism of Jakobson's binaristic apriorism and his use of acoustic features, and although Martinet claims to have been influenced by Trubetzkoy rather than by Jakobson, it should be said that his notions of information power and of distinctive power involved in his definition of the concept of economy come directly from Jakobson. On the other hand, his notion of economy in diachronic phonology owes as much to Zipf's principle of least effort as to the Prague School. In his *Éléments de linguistique générale*, he develops his own elaborate view of information focused on energy and cost. Finally, two new aspects of his use of information theory should be noted: a probabilistic approach to sequences of linguistic units, which comes from Harris's works, and the notion of "contenu d'information", which is inspired by Guiraud's works in stylistics.

5.4.2 Dubois: A Harrissian-Jakobsonian Version of Information Theory

Curiously, although Jean Dubois (1922–2015) started his work as a linguist in lexicography, with his doctoral dissertation on *Le vocabulaire politique et social en France de 1869 à 1872*, which was published in 1962, he did not take any interest in the quantitative aspects of vocabulary that were very fashionable in the 1950s–1960s after they were introduced in France by Mandelbrot and Guiraud.

In his dissertation, Dubois implements Harris's distributional method (thus effectively introducing it in France) and refers to his use of it in discourse analysis.[23] His interest in information theory appeared in later work, first in his paper on tense and aspect, published in the journal *le Français Moderne* (Dubois 1964a) in 1964,

---

[23] Chevalier (2006) insists on Dubois's role of "frontier runner" by introducing American descriptive linguistics, especially Harris's work in France in the 1960s (see Chap. 9, Sect. 9.4.2.).

and then in his *Grammaire structurale du français*, published in three volumes in 1965, 1967 and 1969a, respectively. It should be noted that the term "information" appears very frequently in Volume 1 (1965) and disappears almost completely in Volumes 2 and 3. In the introduction to Volume 1, Dubois states that he aims to establish a distributional analysis of the gender and number markers of nouns and pronouns that would be complementary to Harris's distributional analysis. He intends to analyse, in terms of information, the crossed constraints between gender and number markers in order to show that in French there are rules but not exceptions. Whereas linguists mainly use the notion of cost from information theory, Dubois proposed, probably referring to Martinet's notion of "rendement fonctionnel", to implement those of redundancy and noise. The notion of information quantity used by Dubois (as well as those of conservation, lost and cost of information) is consistent with information theory. It is measured in terms of probability and inverse function: the higher the probability of the occurrence of a marker, the lower the information quantity. Thus, information quantity conveyed by written code is low since it is very redundant.

> The markers of spoken code and of written code are not equiprobable: information quantity conveyed by a redundant marker in spoken code is bigger than that carried by written code, since its probability of occurrence after the initial marker is smaller. The information quantity conveyed in written French by the second marker is very small, since it is very rare that written code comprises no redundancy (of course it is not the same with spoken code). (Dubois 1965, p. 21)

This quantitative (and Shannonian) use of information by Dubois probably comes from Mandelbrot (1954a), who appears in his bibliography along with Harris, whose use of Markov chains in the 1950s was likely influential as well.[24] Further on in the text, the term information and the collocations where it appears ("une information", "la première information", "l'information du pluriel", "l'information féminin", "l'information de genre, celle de nombre", "les /ces deux informations") are used in a very different way:

> One can wonder what happens to these two pieces of information when they are combined, that is when plural utterances convey feminine information as well... It may happen that gender information remains while number information disappears. Feminine information disappeared from both sentences. (Dubois 1965, p. 82–83)

That use of information brings the term close to content and meaning. While it previously referred to an abstract quantity that was measured in terms of probabilities and that excluded meaning, the term information now determined a grammatical signification of morpho-syntactic order, which was given by marks. To understand why Dubois made this shift in meaning, it should be recalled that he was familiar with Jakobson's *Essais de Linguistique Générale*. In fact, in a 1964 issue of the journal *le Français Moderne*, he published a review of this work of Jakobson's,

---

[24] Whereas Dubois, in his PhD, mentions G.A. Miller's *Language and Communication* (1951, French translation 1956), which constitutes an anti-behaviourist introduction to information theory for psychology students, he does not mention it in his later works.

as well as an article in which he applied Jakobson's theoretical views to tense and aspect issues (Dubois 1964a, b). Among others, Dubois borrowed from Jakobson the idea that every grammatical form (especially tense and aspect) is variously marked in the code, depending on the language. Therefore, he looked for the formal structures in which the semantic oppositions of accomplished/non-accomplished, anterior/non-anterior, and posterior/non-posterior – which define tense and aspect – are translated into a given code; it should be noted, he stated, that some languages have to translate only two of these oppositions, in cases when the third one, posterior/non-posterior, is developed at a later stage. These ideas were worked out by Jakobson in his article "Boas' View of Grammatical Meaning" (1971a [1959]), which Dubois read in his French version in *Essais de linguistique Générale*, borrowing the idea of grammatical meaning (see Sect. 3.3 above) from Boas. When he adopted Boas-Jakobson's grammatical meanings, Dubois gave a semantic meaning to information that was completely different from Shannon and Weaver's quantitative approach. It was not the only time he made use of the Jakobsonian interpretation of information theory. He adopted the way Jakobson appropriated the notion of redundancy and put it at the core of his study of markers in French. He still used it very actively in Volume 2 of his *Grammaire structurale*, contrary to the notion of information, which by then had disappeared. In Dubois's work, this use of Jakobson, which could be called a second-hand use, may seem contradictory to the distributionalist and quantitative aspects in his work. It should be recognised that information theory gained a heuristic power with Dubois that allowed him to work out the semantic dimension of linguistic categories like tense and aspect.

In conclusion, we can note the heterogeneous as well as transitory impact of information theory on linguistics. However, even if explicit references to information theory disappeared rapidly, the new approach to phonology opened by Jakobson would be continued through generative phonology, and the probabilistic way would lead to the third mathematisation of language when these methods were revived with large corpora in the 1990s (see Chap. 10).

Chapter 6
From MT to Computational Linguistics and Natural Language Processing

6.1 The Central Role of Syntactic Analysis

In Chap. 2, we examined the beginnings of machine translation, how it started as a war technology originating in the sciences of war. Apart from its military origins, there is a second strand in the development of machine translation. Its main focus was on syntactic analysis. This form of automation was perceived as less remote from linguistics than the engineers' machine translation, which had been developed under the influence of Weaver and the sciences of war.

It should be noted that the leading American linguists at the time, the Neo-Bloomfieldians, were familiar with certain aspects of the first mathematisation of language,[1] especially axioms and procedures, which had been used by Bloomfield (1933) to settle distributional method.[2] They had consulted manuals on logic and mathematics. By 1951 Harris had already implemented a formalisation of linguistic analysis in his *Methods in Structural Linguistics* (1951a).

The development of syntactic analysis in MT centres was the result of three main syntactic approaches, which interacted with each other at one point or another:

(i) The distributionalists' approach, especially that of Hockett and Harris (see Chap. 4)
(ii) Bar-Hillel's approach, directly inspired by Carnap
(iii) Chomsky's approach

---

[1] The first mathematisation of language corresponds to the rise of formalisation promoted by the School of Vienna and is characterised by the setting in interaction of algorithms and formal languages resulting from mathematical logic (see Introduction Chap. 1).

[2] The linguists commonly referred to as the Neo-Bloomfieldians were followers of Boas, Sapir and Bloomfield. They were linguistic anthropologists focused on the description of American Indian languages that had in common an inductive approach and the use of distributional analysis inaugurated by Bloomfield, whose interest in the mathematisation of language they also shared (see Chap. 4).

© The Author(s), under exclusive license to Springer Nature
Switzerland AG 2021
J. Léon, *Automating Linguistics*, History of Computing,
https://doi.org/10.1007/978-3-030-70642-5_6

Automatic syntactic analysis constituted the theoretical basis of "the new linguistics", as recommended by ALPAC, and ensured the legitimacy of computational linguistics. It also conditioned the emergence of the Chomskyan program, which actually was closely associated with the horizon of retrospection created by MT, so that it can be identified as one of its horizons of projection.

6.2   Operational Syntax for MT and Formal Grammars

For Yehoshua Bar-Hillel (1915–1975), the main issue surrounding MT was syntax. Bar-Hillel was a philosopher of language who had written his doctoral dissertation on Carnap's logical syntax. He was a proponent of the first mathematisation, introduced the notion of recursion in linguistics and designed an "operational syntax" for MT in his article "A Quasi-Arithmetical Notation for Syntactic Description". In this article, he combined different American distributionalist methods, most notably that of Harris, as presented in his book *Methods in Structural Linguistics* (1951a), and Ajdukiewicz's notation (Bar-Hillel 1953b).

Operational syntax allowed for a machine to automatically discover the syntactic structure of strings belonging to a given source natural language. It also paved the way for the development of algorithms that could translate the syntactic description of the language into a series of digital computer instructions. Programmers of these algorithms sought to automatically test the syntactic connectivity of a given sequence and find the immediate constituents[3] of any syntactically related sequence.[4]

---

[3] The notion of constituent structure was first made explicit by Bloomfield (1933), Harris (1946) and Wells (1947). A constituent is any word or group of words which enter into some larger constructions (i.e. group of words). Immediate constituents are the constituents of which any given construction is directly formed. For example, there are two immediate constituents "the old man who lives there" and "has gone to his son's house" in the utterance "The old man who lives there has gone to his son's house". "Old man" is an IC of "old man who lives there", but not of the whole utterance. However, "there has" or "man who" is not a constituent. The ICs of a given construction are its constituents on the next lower level. Those on any still lower level are constituents but not immediate constituents (from Gleason 1969, pp.128–148).

IC-analysis is a syntactic method; as such its goal is to find the best possible organisation of any given utterance. The end result of IC-analysis is often presented in a visual diagrammatic form that reveals the hierarchical immediate constituent structure of the sentence at hand, for example, (Fig. 6.1).

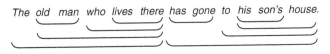

Fig. 6.1 Immediate Constituents Analysis (from Gleason 1969)

[4] For a formal definition of syntactic connexity, see Ajdukiewicz (1935).

According to Bar-Hillel, who adopted the Neo-Bloomfieldian distributionalists'
immediate constituent model, "every sentence is the result of the operation of one
continuous part of it upon the remainder, these two parts being the immediate constituents of the sentence, such that these constituent parts [...] are again the product
of the operation of some continuous part upon the remainder, etc., until one arrives
at the final constituents, say words or morphemes" (Bar-Hillel 1960, Appendix
II, p.147).

Bar-Hillel shows that, in order to find out whether a sentence is a well-formed (or
connex) expression, and what its constituent structure is, a mechanical procedure
can be applied. He presents, as an example, the analysis of the sentence "Little John
sleeps soundly". A category is associated to each word (n for noun, n/n for adjective,
n\s for verb, n\s\\n\s for adverb). Two types of cancellation rules are applicable:

$$a, a \backslash b \rightarrow b \text{ and } a / b, b \rightarrow a$$

Each application of a cancellation rule is called a derivation. The last line of a derivation is its exponent. If the exponent consists of a single symbol (here s), the sentence, and the constituent structure given by the derivation, is well-formed.

Little John sleeps sound.

(1)	n/n,	n,	n\s,	n\s\\n\s
(2)	n,	n\s,	n\s\\n\s	
(3)	n,	n\s		
(4)	s			

Later on in the article, Bar-Hillel shows that this method, while effective for
simple sentences, does not, however, work for complex sentences.

Bar-Hillel's work on operational syntax, which lay at the intersection of formal
languages, syntax and algorithms, was dedicated to the automatic treatment of languages and designed for economic and military purposes. Although he first presented his project of operational syntax at a conference for linguists (i.e. the 7th
International Congress of Linguists, which took place in London in 1952), he was
also a researcher in machine translation at MIT's Research Laboratory of Electronics,
and supported the idea of MT as a technology of war.

In a 1955 article, Bar-Hillel claimed that the main issue with MT was related to
speed, capacity and cost – the "time-cost-capacity" triangle that ALPAC would later
regard as a standard for MT evaluation (Bar-Hillel 1955). He occupied a strategic
position as a pioneer of MT at MIT and was the first expert commissioned by the
National Science Foundation (in 1958) to conduct a survey on linguistic data processing, which included assessing MT projects. He thus played a crucial role in the
consolidation of this new domain. Specifically, he:

(i) Imposed the primacy of syntactic analysis in the automatic treatment of
    languages

(ii) Institutionalised automatic syntactic analysis as an autonomous field (which was recognised by established linguists and became a breeding ground of "new" linguists)
(iii) Started the debate on natural language understanding, which would become one of the main areas of artificial intelligence

6.3   The Constitution of Automatic Syntactic Analysis as an Autonomous Field

By the end of the first conference on MT at MIT in 1952, organised by Bar-Hillel, the latter had succeeded in convincing participants that syntactic analysis was to play a crucial role in MT. Everyone agreed to define two preliminary stages of MT:

1. Creating an automatic dictionary of forms without lemmatisation[5]
2. Developing a programmable operational syntactic analysis (thereby postponing the treatment of grammatical problems)

Bar-Hillel thus succeeded in imparting the idea that syntactic analysis was a priority in itself apart from the problems of grammar, i.e. of morpho-syntax.

In the early 1950s, the first attempts at automatic syntactic analysis used the word classes established by distributionalists, finite-state automata (Markov's chains), which derived from information theory and which had already been applied by Harris and Hockett, and a bottom-up parsing strategy adapted to the recognition of word classes in a given text (see Locke and Booth 1955).[6] One of the first analysers was that of Yngve (1955), a left-to-right bottom-up procedure. It was designed to build the syntactic structure level by level, starting from sentences that were reduced to word classes, which, in turn, comprised grammatical and syntactic information.

From the late 1950s onwards, using the hierarchy of grammars established by Chomsky in 1956, analysers were based on formal grammars, and more particularly on context-free grammars (type 2). Parsers adopted a top-down strategy, which was more suitable to the implementation of rewriting rules. Significant progress had thus been made.

In "Three models for the description of language", Chomsky (1956) aimed at comparing various types of formal grammars in order to determine their capacity to generate English sentences. He established a three-classes hierarchy by showing

---

[5] Lemmatisation is the process of grouping together the inflected forms of a word so they can be analysed as a single item, identified by the word's lemma, or dictionary form. For example, the verb "to buy" may appear as "buy", "buys", "bought" or "buying". The lemma "buy" corresponds to the dictionary form.

[6] "Parsing" comes from Latin *pars orationis* (parts of speech). To *parse* means to break something down into its parts. A syntactic parser is a program that scans a sequence (generally a sentence) and analyses it into its syntactic components according to the rules of a grammar.

that neither Markov chains (finite-state automata, type 0) nor context-sensitive grammars (type 1) can generate all the English sentences and only English sentences. This can only be done by phrase-structure grammars (context-free grammars, type 2) that include a transformational component.

Type 0 grammars are the most elementary grammars. Based on a finite-state Markov process, they are unable to generate the whole set of grammatical sentences as they generate non-sentences as well. Unlike phrase-structure grammar (syntagmatic) and transformational grammars, finite-state grammars are unable to deal with recursivity:

> If a grammar has no recursive steps [...] it will be prohibitively complex – it will, in fact, turn out to be little better than a list of strings or of morpheme class sequences in the case of natural languages. If it does have recursive devices, it will produce infinitely many sentences (Chomsky 1956: 115–116).

> If a grammar of this type produces all English sentences, it will produce many non-sentences as well. If it produces only English sentences, we can be sure that there will be an infinite number of true sentences, false sentences, reasonable questions, etc., which it simply will not produce. (Chomsky 1957 p. 24)

Context-free rules expand a single category into an ordered series of categories without needing to specify a context for their application. Context-sensitive rules expand a single category into an ordered series of categories by specifying a context for their application. Context-sensitive and context-free grammars are both syntagmatic grammars whose defining trait is their adherence to the constituency relation as opposed to the dependency relation (see below Hays', Lecerf's and Lamb's dependency grammars). The generative capacity of context-sensitive grammars is stronger than that of context-free grammars, as only the former can generate structural descriptions.

However, phrase-structure grammars are limited. For example, they cannot account for discontinuous constituents and long-range relations (for example "switch the light on"); they cannot give distinct status to active and to passive sentences, etc. To account for complex structures, such as passive sentences, transformations are needed. They apply recursively to the results of syntagmatic rules.

From the computational point of view (Chomsky and Schützenberger 1963), languages defined by Type-0 grammars are accepted by Turing machines. Languages defined by Type-1 grammars (context-sensitive) are accepted by linear-bounded automata. Languages defined by Type-2 grammars (context-free) are accepted by push-down automata. Natural language is almost entirely definable by Type-2 tree structures. The syntax of most programming languages is context-free (see, e.g. ALGOL60).

Until then, MT programming had been a real challenge because of the intricacies between programming and grammar, which prevented any linguistic evaluation of systems and any progress. The use of formal languages, by contrast, allowed problems to be thought out declaratively, namely, by distinguishing between grammar (linguistic description), formal languages (which make linguistic information manageable by the machine) and parsing strategies.

Here, once again, Yngve was a pioneer. In 1960, he worked out a predictive model of syntactic analysis founded on phrase-structure grammar (i.e. a Type-2 context-free grammar), and on psycholinguistic hypotheses about short-term memory, borrowed from George A. Miller, to determine the depth of trees representing sentences (Yngve 1960). Whereas in 1955 he had used finite-state automata, in 1960 he referred to Chomsky's 1957 model (*Syntactic Structures*) without using transformations. This analyser was programmed in the COMIT language, developed for manipulating strings of characters (Yngve 1959).

Thus, MT served as a testing ground for the power of formal grammars. In the 1960s, other formalisms devoted to syntactic analysis for MT appeared, including Hays's dependency grammar (1964), inspired by Tesnière.[7]

David Glenn Hays (1928–1995) was a linguist, social scientist and computer scientist. He played a pioneering role in machine translation and computational linguistics. He worked at the RAND Corporation from 1955 till 1968, and then he joined the faculty of the State University of New York at Buffalo. At RAND, he worked on a machine translation system whose syntactic component was based on Tesnière's grammar so that he developed his own parsing system based on dependency grammar. "The insight formalised by dependency theory is that particular occurrences of minimal units are directly related to one another. Occurrence of an adjective before a noun, for example, is more closely related to the noun occurrence than to anything else" (Hays 1964). Hays played an important role in the professional organisation of computational linguistics. He was one of the founders of the Association for Computational Linguistics created in 1962 and was chief editor of the *American Journal of Computational Linguistics* from 1974 to 1978. Finally, he was one of the members of the ALPAC that put an end to MT and promoted computational linguistics as the "new linguistics" (Hutchins 1986a; Cori and Léon 2002).

Here is an example with the treatment of an ambiguous sentence "they are flying planes" with two immediate constituents diagrams and two dependency trees. Structures (a) and (c) take "are flying" as a compound verb; structures (b) and (d) take "flying planes" as a noun phrase. Yet structure (c) corresponds relationally to both (a) and (b) (see Fig. 6.2.).

Lecerf's Model of Conflicts Yves Lecerf (1932–1995) was an engineer (from the Polytechnique School) and an anthropologist. He was a pioneer of MT in France and developed the "conflict model" ("modèle des conflits") providing two syntactic representations for a given sentence, Tesnière-Hays's graph and Chomsky's graph. This double representation worked as a filter to resolve syntactic ambiguities in MT process. While Tesnière-Hays's graph rests on words and dependencies between

---

[7] Lucien Tesnière (1893–1954), a French linguist and specialist in Slavic languages, is the author of two books: *Esquisse d'une syntaxe structurale* (1953) and *Elements de syntaxe structurale* (1959). Certain concepts advanced in these works, like valence and dependency structure, inspired several models of formal linguistics and of MT in France, in the USA, and in the countries of the Soviet Bloc.

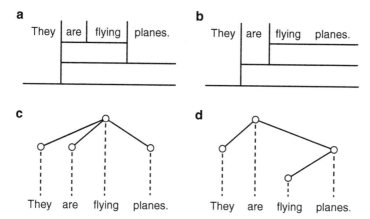

Fig. 6.2 Ambiguous sentence (from Hays 1964, p.24–25)

words without any intermediary categories, Chomsky's one rests on strings of words (immediate constituents) and categories (N, V, NP, VP, etc.). It should be noted that Lecerf retains from Chomsky's grammar only the immediate constituent structure related to phrase structure grammar and not the whole generative grammar model (see Lecerf 1960).

Sidney Lamb Stratificational Grammar Sidney M. Lamb (1929-) is an American linguist whose early works concerned the description of North American Indian languages under the supervision of Mary Haas, one of Boas's students. He led the MT Centre at Berkeley from 1958 to 1964. He developed a stratificational model of grammar for MT based upon the idea that every language comprises a restricted number of structural layers or strata, hierarchically related in such a way that units or combinations of units on one stratum realise units or combinations of units of the next higher stratum (see Lamb 1962). His view was that linguistic structure is a network, thus initiating the first steps of neurocognitive linguistics.

The use of phrase-structure grammars renewed the debate on bottom-up and top-down parsing strategies. Other approaches using heuristic methods, like Garvin's predictive analysis (1968), appeared at the same time as other methods that were purely algorithmic and deterministic, such as Yngve's transfer-based MT system (1964).[8]

In later years, syntactic parsers would rely on context-free models. More generally, in his article "The equivalences of models of language used in the fields of mechanical translation and information retrieval" (1964), Maurice Gross showed

---

[8] Garvin contrasted the heuristic method with the algorithmic method. The algorithmic method is deterministic and complete. It takes into account all the instructions necessary to get from one point to another and leads necessarily to the result. On the contrary, Garvin recommended a heuristic method, which is more of an assistance to discover the result than a direct way to reach it, for example, by resorting to arbitrary choices or learning based on trial and error.

that every language model used in machine translation and information retrieval was equivalent to a context-free grammar.[9] Context-free grammars were considered better adapted than transformational models, which had only been formalised to a limited extent anyway. This separation became even more apparent as soon as the formal limits of the transformational model were recognised (Peters and Ritchie 1973)[10] and new context-free models appeared (see Savitch et al. 1987).

Other models inspired by context-free grammars were introduced in the 1980s, such as indexed grammars, tree-adjoining Grammars, head-driven phrase structure Grammars, lexical functional grammar, unification grammars, etc. The objective of these grammars was less to formalise "natural language" as a whole than to represent fragments of a language. This move was coherent with the capacities and limitations of natural language processing. In particular, natural language processing cannot actually process a natural language exhaustively, its degree of coverage being much more limited than that of theoretical linguistics. Linguistic theory only accounts for potential language, and linguists do not need for all the rules of their theory to be available simultaneously. It functions as a stock of knowledge. Computational linguistics focuses on running (functioning, working) language. It may only implement the rules necessary for a given application, but it needs to have taken all of them into account.

6.4   Computational Linguistics

6.4.1   Syntactic Parsers

After having convinced MT pioneers to prioritise syntactic analysis, and after having proposed a model of "operational syntax", Bar-Hillel continued his "institutional" action in favour of parsers.

In his 1960 report Bar-Hillel declared that MT work had at least had the merit of bringing to light two theoretical problems worthy of further investigation, the fact that:

---

[9] Maurice Gross (1934–2001) was a pioneer in MT in France. He also worked with Chomsky at MIT and Harris at the University of Pennsylvania during the early 1960s. He played an important role in disseminating information on formal grammars in France and largely contributed to spreading Harris's works and integrating them into French linguistics (see Chaps. 8 and 9).

[10] Peters and Ritchie argue that transformational grammars are too powerful, insofar as they generate all kinds of languages, including nonrecursive languages. The problem originates in the fact that these grammars apply their derivation rules an unlimited number of times, in particular for short sentences. One result of this study is to show that the linguists' intuition, according to which natural languages are recursive, is empirically founded.

(i) Automation gave rise to unsolved formal problems like Post's canonical system theory,[11] and automata theory (finite-state automata and Turing's automata)
(ii) Techniques of syntactic analysis and programming languages were developed for MT

He devoted several pages to reviewing the various methods adopted by MT groups. These techniques constituted a truly new field, which derived from the algorithmisation of syntax and which raised the question of how linguistic models (i.e. the power of grammars) were related to automatic analysis.

One of the main questions concerning the automatic syntactic analysis of a sentence was to determine "where to start" in the sentence. The programming language COMIT, developed by Yngve in 1959, was the first language for non-digital symbols. Based on pattern matching, it enabled the manipulation of tree structures representing sentences.

The interaction between programming languages and linguistics was one of the points that ALPAC examined in detail a few years later. Most notably, it pointed out that, starting from ALGOL60, programming languages borrowed many elements from mathematical linguistics. ALGOL60 was the first programming language to use a formal system, the Backus Normal Form. In 1962, Ginsburg and Rice showed that the Backus notation was equivalent to context-free grammars, and although it was observed early on that ALGOL was not "completely" context-free (because of the semantic conditions), context-free grammars continued to be used for manipulating programming languages.[12]

Conversely, regarding the impact of programming on linguistics, the existence of a body of programming techniques led to the development of programming languages that were specialised in the resolution of linguistic problems, such as SNOBOL (1964) and a later version of COMIT (1962). Specialised programming languages and syntactic parsers testified to the emergence of a new field that lay at the intersection of logico-mathematical formalisation, syntactic theory, algorithms theory, automata theory and compilation theory.[13]

---

[11] Post's canonical systems (1943) belong to research from the 1930s and 1940s, which attempted to characterise the concept of algorithm, as applied to mathematics, in a formal way. Thus Turing machines and Post's production systems led to the same calculable functions. Devised as systems for manipulating strings of character, they comprised a triplet:

- A finite alphabet, strings set up from this alphabet, or words
- A set of initial words
- A set of rules to manipulate character strings (or production rules)

Chomsky's rewriting rules are directly inspired by Post's systems although, as Pullum and Scholz (2007) remarked, Chomsky never cites Post's key technical papers. See Partee (1978, p.167–168) referring to Chomsky and Miller (1963 section 4) for a presentation of the formalisation of these rewriting systems.

[12] See Marcus (1988) on this point.

[13] See Cori and Marandin (2001) on reciprocal borrowing between data processing and formal grammars, in particular generative grammar.

6.4.2 The Institutionalisation of Computational Linguistics

Computational linguistics was institutionalised with the creation of the Association for Machine Translation and Computational Linguistics (AMTCL) in 1962 under the presidency of Yngve and the vice-presidency of Hays.[14] The first conference, entitled "International Conference on Computational Linguistics", took place in New York in May 1965, gathering 150 participants. It was organised by several associations, including AMCTL, French ATALA and Scandinavian, Japanese and South American associations.

Thus, the widely accepted claim that the institutionalisation of computational linguistics was solely due to ALPAC proves unfounded, since in 1966 its institutionalisation was already quite advanced. ALPAC, established in 1964 – that is, 4 years after the publication of Bar-Hillel's report – played a key role in reconfiguring the field of linguistics around computational linguistics on the one hand and in saving the emerging field of language automation from MT on the other hand.

Appendices 18 and 19 of the ALPAC report deal with computational linguistics. Their authors are most likely David Hays and Anthony Oettinger, i.e. two engineers, former heads of MT groups and members of the ALPAC committee, who in the meantime had become institutional leaders of computational linguistics at large. In the appendices, they defined the principal tasks of computational linguistics, namely, to:

1. Explore the reciprocal relations between formal grammars and programming languages
2. Develop parsers as evaluation methods and testing grounds for linguistic models
3. Work out tools for language processing, in order to help linguists (called "linguistic scientists") to establish their generalisations and to test these generalisations on data

The report quotes Igor A. Mel'čuk who considered that computational linguistics was not just a subfield of linguistics limited to linguists who liked computing, but an essential technique that all linguists would need to use (Akhmanova et al. 1963).[15]

---

[14] In 1973, AMTCL was renamed Association for Computational Linguistics (ACL) thus dropping the reference to MT. A bulletin, *The Finite String*, was created in 1964, and the association started to organise conferences that took place every 2 years. The first one took place in Denver, Colorado, in August 1963. The journal *Mechanical Translation*, from 1965 until 1974 (when Yngve gave up its direction), was called *Mechanical Translation and Computational Linguistics*. From 1974 to 1983, it was called *American Journal of Computational Linguistics*, and finally from 1984 onwards *Computational Linguistics*.

[15] In that period of Cold War, American works on MT were well known by Russian researchers who started their first experiments in the wake of the first demonstration of MT on an IBM computer in New York in 1954. Some Russian works were based on American phrase-structure grammars and syntactic parsers, while other methods, more original and anchored in the Russian tradition, were founded on semantic grounds (see Chap. 7 §7.1.3). Conversely, the Americans started translating Soviet works from 1957 within the Joint Publications Research Service. The Slavist Kenneth E. Harper from UCLA established a state-of-the-art survey of Soviet works, conferences and jour-

From this perspective, MT was seen as an experimental field for testing theoretical hypotheses.

The project was ambitious. The computer was considered the "third human revolution", in reference to an article written by Hockett, who had belonged to the ALPAC committee in its early stages (Hockett and Ascher 1964). After the advent of speech and the use of tools (the lever), its arrival was seen as the third major human revolution. Perceived as the first manipulator of symbols external to the human brain, the computer was likely to modify the analysis of languages just as the microscope had changed biology. Thanks to the computer, linguistics could claim to be a consequential mathematisation, like physics. Moreover, it would allow for new interactions between theory, empirical studies and practical applications.

At the behest of the Academy of Science, ALPAC deprived MT of its role as a state-of-the-art technology used to produce mass translations and redirected funding towards a new discipline: computational linguistics. In order to legitimatise computational linguistics as the "new linguistics", the ALPAC attempted to recruit Chomsky, the rising star of linguistics in the early 1960s, by severely criticising the Neo-Bloomfieldians. This argument, likely to attract Chomsky, had the effect of canceling the dominant horizon of retrospection of the current language sciences.

The report specifically quotes the proceedings of the 9th Congress of Linguists of 1962. As is well known (see Murray 1993), during this congress the Chomskyans took control by force, pushing aside the Neo-Bloomfieldians.[16] The penultimate paragraph of the report testifies to their exclusion:

If ever a machine-aided simulation of total linguistic analysis-synthesis (or voice-to-ear-to-voice translation) becomes possible it will not be because of adherence to the type of linguistic theory widely current around 1950. (ALPAC 1966, p. 123)

The report demonstrates that, although the Chomskyan revolution did not directly concern computers, it brought fundamental changes to what constituted scientific theory itself and to the relation between empiricism and science. Some linguists rallied for Chomsky's views, which turned out to be a strategically crucial move: Bar-Hillel accepted Chomsky's transformations in 1960, giving up Harris's, and Hockett supported Chomsky in his 1968 work *The State of the Art* (Hockett 1968).

In addition to the reconfiguration of linguistics involving formal languages and computation, the promotion of computational linguistics had a second objective: to save growing language technologies from the disaster of MT. This aspect, however,

---

nals in 1961 (Harper 1961). However, American MT researchers did not draw inspiration from Soviet methods contrary to the French who used both American and Russian methods (see Chap. 8 §8.6). The other European countries of the Soviet bloc only started work on MT in the mid-1960s and did not develop original methods.

[16] According to Murray (1993), the Congress organising committee, made up of Morris Halle, William Locke, Horace Hunt and Edward Klima reserved a plenary session for Chomsky, although he was a generation younger than the four other invited speakers. Besides he was allotted four times more space in the proceedings. As for the Neo-Bloomfieldians, they boycotted the congress, acknowledging their defeat. According to Barsky (2011), Chomsky's and Harris' biographer, Harris gave up his plenary session to Chomsky.

was rather confusing. Under the name of "new computational linguistics", the report recommended subsidising all kinds of research: computerised methods for the treatment of language and heuristic methods enabling linguists to generalise and validate their theories, methods allowing linguists to test grammatical and semantic theories, automatic documentation, information retrieval, terminology data banks and computer-aided translation and even MT itself.

6.5   MT, Natural Language Understanding and Artificial Intelligence

The history of artificial intelligence (AI) has several aspects in common with the history of natural language processing. Turing's universal machine, conceived in 1936 as a thinking machine that could manipulate discrete symbols and use rules to operate calculations, was also the first finite-state automaton. It was anchored in the first mathematisation of language.

Cybernetics and information theory, which had appeared immediately after World War II, were also at the junction of both fields: IA and MT. The institutionalisation of artificial intelligence followed a parallel path to MT, and, even though they cannot be regarded as entirely independent from one another, they should not be conflated. The ten Macy conferences, organised between 1946 and 1953, marked its beginnings,[17] especially the 5th conference of March 1948, which marked the emergence of Wiener's cybernetics (see Segal 2003).

The term "first cybernetics" designates the works that were developed by the main instigators of these conferences, in particular McCulloch and Pitts, for whom logic was the proper discipline for the study of brain functioning. In the context of the Macy Conferences and first cybernetics, "first connectionism" questioned the prevalence of logic as the main approach to the study of thinking: in the brain, one finds neither rules nor a logical processor, and information is not stored in specific addresses. According to first connectionism, the brain functions with massive interconnections between neurons along a distributed diagram which testifies to an aptitude for self-organisation. The Perceptron, developed by Rosenblatt in 1958, was the first attempt at creating a device equipped with such capacities. Using the cognitivist model, which was first institutionalised at the Dartmouth conference in 1956, this approach was swept aside for 20 years, only to reappear in the late 1970s. Later, with the beginning of the neo-connectionist approach in the 1980s, some cybernetic views reappeared as well.

Rumelhart and McClelland put forward parallel distributed processing models in opposition to the symbolic processing systems of cognitivism (Rumelhart et al.

---

[17] The Macy Conferences were organised by the pioneers of cybernetics, among them McCulloch and Rosenblueth, to support interdisciplinary meetings under the aegis of the Josiah Macy Jr. Foundation, which was created in 1930 and was specialised in medical research. Only the last five conferences have been published.

1986). Self-organisational models of the 1950s were taken over in the 1980s by the neurophysiologists Humberto Maturana and Francisco Varela (Varela 1989), who founded what was called "second cybernetics". Cognitivism claims that intentionality (beliefs, desires, intentions) corresponds to the physical and mechanical reality of intelligence and that thinking is carried out by the physical computation of symbols. These symbols are a reality, both physically and semantically, and cannot be reduced to the mere physical level (see Dupuy 1994).

Without delving further into the history of artificial intelligence, it is worth noting that AI topics were not directly related to the treatment of language, and even less so to the treatment of languages. Artificial intelligence put the simulation of human intelligence at the forefront. This was accounted for by historical and epistemological works, already numerous in the 1980–1990s, which include artificial intelligence in the history of the cognitive sciences (Pratt 1987; Dupuy 1994; Heims 1993; Pélissier and Tête 1995, among others). It is worth noting that this issue is rarely mentioned in the beginnings of MT. There was no project on the computer simulation of human translation (one of the reasons probably being the weak participation of human translators in MT experiments). Conversely, very few linguists took part in the Conferences.

It would be difficult to argue that MT is a derivative of cybernetics. Of course, Shannon and Weaver were not indifferent to the issues raised by the simulation of human thinking by the machine. Shannon, in his article on the chess-playing machine (Shannon 1950), explicitly raised the question of non-human thinking and gave machine translation as an example of the capacity for machines to reason and work symbolically on conceptual elements, words or propositions. The proximity between the chess-playing machine and MT was taken up by Weaver in his contribution to *The Mathematical Theory of Communication* (Shannon and Weaver 1949), in which he mentioned the automatic translation of a language into another as an example of the generalisation of information theory and put forward the idea of "strong simulation".

However, in spite of this claim and the fact that Shannon's machine could be regarded as a "weak" AI model,[18] Weaver's hypotheses were much less ambitious than those advanced by Alan Turing (1912–1954) in his article on the imitation game (Turing's test), published in 1950. For Shannon, the machine could not go beyond the objectives for which it was devised. It was a pure algorithm which, although equipped with heuristic methods designed to limit the combinatorial explosion of the number of strokes, did not have any training capabilities, contrary to Turing's recommendation. As for Weaver, he evoked the logical hypotheses of first cybernetics. MacCulloch and Pitts's theorem (1943), he said, specifies "that a

---

[18] This term refers to the traditional opposition between "strong AI", which holds that the machine is capable of reproducing a cognitive behaviour or simulating an organism and its relationships of adaptation to an environment, and "weak AI" which holds that the machine can simulate a fragment of "synthetic" intelligence whose composition is completely different from human intelligence, but whose result, i.e. the production of representations, is identical to what human intelligence would produce.

robot (or a computer) constructed with regenerative loops of a certain formal character is capable of deducing any legitimate conclusion from a finite set of premises" (Weaver 1955, p. 22).[19]

Furthermore, the term "translation machine", used very early on by every MT experimenter, referred more to a set of technologies, machine architectures, algorithms and specialised programming languages, than to an intelligent machine capable of translation.

As for Natural Language Understanding, which became an important area of artificial intelligence in the 1970s, Bar-Hillel was the only key player of MT to reflect on this topic. In Appendix 3 of his 1960 report, which he devoted to criticising the thesaurus method of resolving semantic ambiguities (developed by members of the Cambridge Language Research Unit[20]), he discussed the importance of extra-linguistic context for the parts of MT involving Natural Language Understanding.

More specifically, Bar-Hillel argued against the feasibility of a FAHQT (Fully Automatic High Quality Translation) with the following example: "the box was in the pen". According to Bar-Hillel, this sentence implies the following linguistic context: "Little John was looking for his toy box. Finally, he found it. The box was in the pen. John was very happy". The correct meaning of "pen" in this context, which is "playpen" and not "writing tool", cannot be selected by the machine, because it is incapable of using common-sense knowledge needed to identify this meaning.

For Bar-Hillel, the resolution of the aforementioned semantic ambiguity cannot use the text context, whatever it is, whether it be found in a single paragraph or a whole book. Common-sense knowledge is needed, and machines do not have access to that kind of extra-linguistic knowledge. Machines are incapable of making inferences and solving semantic ambiguities and problems of words with several meanings (polysemy).

6.6   The Institutionalisation of Natural Language Processing

This is, of course, precisely the kind of problem that artificial intelligence addresses. Yorick Wilks's work on lexical semantics and artificial intelligence came directly from the MT work of the British Cambridge group (see Chap. 7). His work preceded the first computerised systems on Natural Language Understanding founded on a computo-representational model, such as SHRDLU, which was worked out by Terry Winograd in 1972. Lastly, the use of "second cybernetics" methods by the language sciences is relatively recent; the first connectionist networks used to solve

---

[19] It should be noted that, in 1951, Kleene showed this part of McCullough and Pitts does not hold up mathematically. Thanks to Maarten Bullynck for this remark.

[20] See Chap. 7 below for a full presentation of this group of MT.

problems of ambiguity in syntactic analysis date from the 1980s (Waltz and Pollack 1985).

Coming back to computational linguistics, it is worth emphasising that it was not limited to theoretical research at the intersection of syntax, logic, algorithmic, formal grammars and programming languages. The call for papers for the first international conference, which took place in New York in 1965, stipulated that computational linguistics include any computer application that deals with natural or artificial language processing. Paper proposals for two main types of research were accepted: fundamental research, with a linguistic or mathematising orientation, as well as research involving purely practical objectives capable of tolerating a certain margin of error, so that they could produce concrete results within a limited timeframe.

Computational linguistics thus included all the ambiguities found in MT and which NLP would later inherit. NLP is located at the intersection of somewhat contradictory objectives, such as providing tools directly dependent on social demand and industrial profitability, proposing dynamic devices of representation for linguistic knowledge and, finally, constituting testing grounds for the validation of linguistic theories. However, from the first MT projects, it must be noted that these three approaches were often intertwined.

Eager to bring together all the applications under the same label, ALPAC reinforced the internal ambiguities and contradictions of the field such as it was promoted. Current Natural Language Processing still suffers and will continue to suffer from the lack of legitimacy resulting from these ambiguities. The ALPAC report is now presented like a permanent blot, a curse which has affected Natural Language Processing until this day.

This problem was acknowledged in June 2009, for example, at the 50th anniversary celebration of the French Association ATALA (Association for the automatic processing of language), when the representative of the European program DG13, Pierre-Paul Sondag, spoke about NLP's lack of credibility in the eyes of funding donors. According to him, the ALPAC report is the cause of this situation. It still influences decision-makers and continues to discredit NLP. Such a posture is largely a myth, however, insofar as NLP has gradually succeeded in establishing itself as an autonomous discipline. In the mid-1980s, it was integrated as such in university courses, albeit with some hesitations about how to define the training of "computer linguists". Nowadays, it appears as a full-fledged topic at linguistics conferences.

In summary, the establishment of the new horizon of retrospection took place in several phases. Initially, there was a new technology originating in the war sciences that was designed to produce mass translations for economic and strategic purposes. Although this technology dealt with the treatment of languages and was partly developed by linguists in university departments that were directed by linguists, it did not actually count linguistics among its reference sciences. The need to translate texts would result in the implementation of algorithms for syntactic analysis in order to automate language processing, bringing together several different fields. These fields, i.e. logical mathematics, automata theory, theory of compilation and logical syntax, on which the war sciences conferred a homogeneous scientific status, contributed to a new turning point for the mathematisation of linguistics. This mathematisation rests on a new conception of the calculability of language. Bar-Hillel's and Chomsky's early grammars had been conceived within this framework.

Several steps were necessary to establish automation-mathematisation within the language sciences:

1. To clear the new field of its practical objectives, i.e. MT, which was discredited as an imperfect, unreliable and non-profitable technology
2. To institute the new field as a new discipline, i.e. as computational linguistics
3. To annul the horizon of retrospection of American structural linguistics, in particular the distributionalists, even though it was rooted in the first mathematisation and gave rise to Chomskyan linguistics, and thus was an integral part of the theoretical foundations of the "new linguistics"
4. To maintain coherence between theoretical requirements and technological imperfections, in order to avoid being discredited

Chapter 7
Machine Translation of Semantics and Lexicon: New Issues and New Objects in the Long-Term History of the Language Sciences

Moving on, we are leaving the American scene to examine how MT and the automation of language were carried out in other linguistic traditions. American structural linguistics integrated computational mathematisation by adaptation since distributionalist methods already shared part of the knowledge at work in computational linguistics. Soviet linguistics, British linguistics and French structuralist linguistics, by contrast, used quite different modes of integration. Each benefited from the automation of translation without, however, integrating the whole set of underlying theoretical conceptions.

Automation of languages was not always associated with mathematisation. Some groups of MT gave priority to semantics and lexicon in working out MT methods. Even if algorithm studies were necessarily involved when the automation of translation procedures was at stake, these groups were unlike those in the USA in that they did not give priority to logico-mathematical syntactic analysis. The automation of translation, based on lexicon and semantics and anchored in specific linguistic and cultural traditions, gave rise to new issues, or revived old ones, allowing new objects to emerge from the language sciences. Thus, the mathematisation of syntax was integrated in the language sciences in the wake of new issues occurring within the tradition rather than abruptly and out of the blue. Rather than be obliged to integrate a new horizon of retrospection imposed on them from outside, within a short period of time these approaches inscribed the automation of language in long-term history. Part 1 discusses the English and Russian cases, both using intermediary language, whereas part 2 studies the French case that is built around lexis.

J. Léon, *Automating Linguistics*, History of Computing,
https://doi.org/10.1007/978-3-030-70642-5_7

7.1   Semantics and Machine Translation Methods Using Intermediary Languages

In the horizon of retrospection of MT, semantic questions did not exist. Excluded from the Neo-Bloomfieldian behaviourist approach, they had been addressed from logic, especially from Carnap and Bar-Hillel's works. In fact, semantic MT approaches evolved from traditions where meaning was an issue.

Early MT experiments in Great Britain and in the USSR had several similarities. As major actors of the Cold War, the British and the Russians were the first, in the wake of the USA and the first computer demonstration of MT in 1954, to get involved in MT experiments. Even if Russian and British groups simultaneously experimented on MT, often ignoring each other's work, they both gave priority to the transfer of meaning in the translation process, and developed MT methods using semantic intermediary languages.[1]

What draws a distinction between both approaches, in addition to the political context, is their familiarity with the first mathematisation of language. With Russell's, Turing's and Wittgenstein's works (among others), the British were well aware of the first mathematisation which formed the central part of Weaver and MT's horizon of retrospection. Besides, they had their own school of information theory with Colin Cherry, Dennis Gabor and David McKay.

The Soviets tackled these issues through debates on cybernetics from the 1950s. Even if Wiener (1948) acknowledged the significance of early Russian works on statistics and dynamic systems – he mentioned Kolmogorov (1903–1987), Nicolai Krylov (1879–1955) and Nicolai Bogolioubov (1909–1992)[2] – it is difficult to determine the actual anchorage of the Russian mathematical works in the first mathematisation.[3]

7.1.1   The Pioneers: Esperanto as an Intermediary Language

Among the early MT pioneers using intermediary languages there was one Russian and two British, none of whom were linguists. They were inventors who, albeit at different times, relied on Esperanto as an intermediary language to imagine a translation machine.

---

[1] It should be noted that the Russians were aware of the British writings (Mel'čuk 1961; Žolkovskij 1961), but the British did not know about the Russian ones.

[2] "Let it be remarked parenthetically that some of my speculations in this direction attach themselves to the earlier work of Kolmogoroff in Russia, although a considerable part of my work was done before my attention was called to the work of the Russian school. [Kolmogoroff A.N. 1941 "Interpolation und extrapolation von stationären Zufälligen Folgen" Bull. Ac. Sciences USSR ser. maths 5 3–14]" (Wiener 1948, p.11).

[3] This point, addressed by Mindell et al. (2003), merits closer examination.

Trojanskij's Machine (1931, 1947) The project of translation machine thought out by engineer Smirnov-Trojanskij (1894–1950) in 1931 was only written down in 1947 in a text with the title "De la machine à traduire, construite sur la base d'une méthode monolingue". It was published in 1959 by early Soviet researchers on MT, Panov and Korolev (1959).[4] By taking up this 1930–1940 project, the Soviet researchers' aim was to attempt to establish the Russians as the real MT pioneers before the Americans, as was the case with the launch of the Sputnik in 1957.

The following table (Fig. 7.1) illustrates Smirnov-Trojanskij's translation method (see Archaimbault and Léon 1997, p. 115).

The underpinning of Trojanskij's conception of the automation of translation is the idea of a structure common to all the languages beyond their diversity; Trojanskij suggested using an intermediary text between the source and the target languages which he termed logical, which consists in a series of words in their basic grammatical forms used as dictionary entries. In Trojanskij's system, from a text in source language A, the translator obtains a text in logical language A1 which the machine will translate into logical language B1, with the help of a dictionary translating the entries automatically. The text B1 will be edited manually by a human editor into target language B.

Some of the logical language forms, such as form + verb mark ("as") and noun mark ("o"), are clearly borrowed from Esperanto.[5]

For Trojanskij, the crux of his translation method is that it is a monolingual method, as each translator can know only one language. Thus he made translation accessible to everyone since it can be related to school exercises where a text is divided into parts of propositions and parts of speech. Besides, there are many economical benefits provided by the method, such as the possibility of having recourse to unqualified translators.

A	A1	(B1 + C1)		(B + C)	
das Bild	das Bild-o	картина-о	le tableau	картина	le tableau
der Welt	die Welt de -o	Мир de -o	le monde de -o	мира	du monde
zeigt	zeigen-as	Показывать-as	montrer-as	показывает	montre
wie	wie	как	comment	как	comment
die Materie	die Materie-o	материя-о	la matière-o	материя	la matière
sich bewegt	sich bewegen-as	двигаться-as	se mouvoir-as	движется	se meut
wie	wie	как	comment	как	comment
die Materie	die Materie-o	материя-о	la matière-o	материя	la matière
denkt	denken-as	Мыслить-as	penser-as	мыслит	pense

Fig. 7.1 Trojanskij's table

---

[4] Trojanskij's patent and his algorithm can already be found in facsimile in Panov, Liapunov and Mukhin's article of 1956 (p.27–34).

[5] In Esperanto, "o" is the noun morpheme and "–as" is the mark of present tense for verbs.

Richens and Booth's Pidgin English (1955) For Andrew D. Booth (1918–2009) and Richard H. Richens (1919–1984), a language is a series of symbols representing ideas. Translation is the operation which substitutes a language with another while expressing the same set of ideas. The procedure consists in decomposing words of a source text into semantic units (roots and affixes separated by *), each of them representing an idea (1), and to effect word by word translation by applying a bilingual dictionary. The result is a series of words and grammatical directives looking like a stereotypical form of Pidgin English (2) comprising grammatical directives coming from the analysis of the source language (3). The asterisk indicates the sequence where morphological decomposition resulting from post-editing has taken place. This sequence should be rewritten in standard English (4).

1. *French text (source)*

    Il n'est pas étonn*ant de constat*er que les hormone*s de croissance ag*issent sur certain*es espèce*s, alors qu'elles sont in*opér*antes sur d'autre*s, si l'on song*e à la grand*e spécificité de ces substance*s.

2. *Pidgin English (output)*

    v not is not / step astonish v of establish v that / which ? v hormone m of growth act m on certain m species m, then that / which ? v not operate m on of other m if v one dream / consider z to v great v specificity of those substance m.

3. *Grammatical directives used in the example*

    m: plural (multiple, plural or dual) v empty field

    z unspecified

4. *Post-editing result*

It is not surprising to learn that growth hormones may act on certain species while having no effect on others, when one remembers the narrow specificity of these substances.

In the Russian case, as in the British one, those approaches, which may seem naive to linguists and semanticists, show the importance of artificial languages in their respective horizons of retrospection. But the similarities end there. The models of intermediary language which were achieved were very different. The contexts also were different. Trojanskij designed his machine long before computers appeared, in the context of 1930s multilingual planning which aimed at translating all the languages of the Union. Note that the leading figure of this movement was Drezen (Archaimbault 2001).

MT in Great Britain started with the encounter in 1946 between Warren Weaver and Andrew D. Booth, the director of the computer centre of Birkbeck College in London. Weaver committed himself to equip Birkbeck College with an electronic computer provided that non-numerical experimentations would be carried out on it, namely, MT. As was said before, neither Booth nor Richens was a linguist, nor even mathematicians. The former was a crystallographer and the latter was a biologist, a specialist in plant genetics. They were "inventors" without any anchoring in the war sciences or in the first mathematisation of language.

7.1.2 Lexis, Context and Thesaurus: The Experiments of the Cambridge Language Research Unit (1955–1968)[6]

The British MT group, the Cambridge Language Research Unit (CLRU), did not comprise engineers and, unlike the Americans, did not feel the strategic-economic pressure to furnish economically profitable mass translation. The group was led by a philosopher, Margaret Masterman (1910–1986), one of Wittgenstein's pupils, and included linguists (Martin Kay and M.A.K. Halliday) and mathematicians (the statistician A.F. Parker-Rhodes and the computer scientists Yorick Wilks and Karen Spark-Jones). The participation in the group by Richard Richens, who, as we saw, started MT experiments as soon as 1948, probably contributed to the early acknowledgement of the group by the Americans. In particular, Richens co-signed with Booth a chapter of the first collective MT book published at MIT (Locke and Booth 1955). As early as 1956, CLRU participated in a congress organised by MIT and, in the same year, received funding from the NSF.

In spite of their proximity with the Americans, the members of the CLRU did not adopt a logico-syntactical approach. They worked out an intermediary language based on semantics, which lays at the crossroad of two trends in the British tradition: seventeenth-century universal language schemes and contextual theories of meaning of the 1930s (Malinowski and the second Wittgenstein). One can distinguish three successive universal language projects which had been developed by the members of the CLRU between 1955 and 1968: Nude, Nude II, and templates.

Intermediary Language Nude Richens (1955) built his intermediary language upon seventeenth-century universal language schemes, especially Dalgarno's *Ars Signorum* (1661) and Wilkins' *Essay towards a real character and a philosophical language* (1668). Note that one of Wilkins's intellectual descendants is the botanist Linné. Richens, as a plant specialist, probably knew Wilkins's work.

Richens's language was conceived of as a semantic network of fifty "naked ideas" where the structural (and especially morphological) particularities of the source language had been removed, hence its name Nude. The semantic network, Richens explained, is what is invariant during translation. Naked ideas are structured into chunks (semantic units). These are formulas composed of semantic primitives and syntactic operators. For example, (Fig. 7.2).

Six primitives are used in this example (Fig. 7.3).

as well as two syntactic operators:

Dot [.] marks a monadic relation: an adjective or an intransitive verb is marked by the expectation of a relation with a noun.[7]

Apostrophes ['] are used as parentheses within a word.

---

[6] See Léon 2007a for a detailed presentation of the CLRU works.

[7] Operator [:] marks a dyadic relation, for example, a transitive verb is marked by the expectation of a subject or an object. Nude has a syntax which can be considered the prefiguration of case grammar: a transitive verb is marked for a subject and an object.

Fig. 7.2 Richens' Nude
formulas

.Pz	One
Xp'CL	Seed
Xp'CL.Pz	one seed

p	Plant	X	part, component
z	negation, opposite, contrary	C	causation, influence
P	plurality, group, number	L	living, alive

Fig. 7.3 Richens' Nude primitives

Richens' "algebraic" interlingua, conceived of as a network of semantic primitives is very close to a universal characteristic. Like Wilkins, Richens addressed the issue of compositionality. The meaning of a word is the composition of meaning elements:

seed = Xp'CL [X part + p plant / C cause L life].

However, they did not succeed in designing an automatic procedure to extract semantic networks from basic texts using Nude. Hence, it was not really exploited for MT.

Nude II: A Thesaurus Intermediary Language From Nude, Margaret Masterman developed a second intermediary language project which was based all at once on Nude, on the notion of thesaurus and on the Wittgensteinian theories on the definition of word meaning by its contexts of use. However, contradictory that might seem, this attempt to link an a priori conception of meaning – carried out by any universal language project – with the conception of meaning as use, had interesting implications. One of the components of the new intermediary language was Roget's thesaurus, published in 1852, rightly regarded by historians of linguistics as one of Wilkins's continuers (Cram 1985; Salmon 1979). Margaret Masterman replaced the fifty Nude primitives with the thesaurus head words and improved the syntax.

Primitives are English words. The syntax of Nude II consists in two connectors and a bracketing convention.

[:] two elements are linked by addition to the main element.
[/] is a verbal connector, non-commutative, representing the relation of subject to verb or of verb to object.
() parentheses. They replace Richens's apostrophes and group primitives into pairs.

The primitives of Nude II (Masterman et al. 1959, p. 62) used in the previous example are the following (Fig. 7.4).

Heads are organised as semantic networks with non-hierarchical structure (leading to lattice formalisation). Heads should have meaning but do not need to be words of a given language. Masterman, as Wittgenstein's pupil, adopted his views

	NUDE ELEMENT	APPROXIMATING AREA OF MEANING	EXAMPLE
6	CAUSE	Causative actions	Cause/(have/sign) (say)
13	HAVE	Pertain "of"	Cause/(nothave/life) (kill)
33	MAN	Human Kingdom	(part: folk): man (member of family)
41	SIGN	Symbol (any sort)	Cause/(have/sign)(speak)

speak	*he says*	*speaker*
cause / (have /sign)	man/(cause / (have /sign))	man:(cause/ (have /sign))

Fig. 7.4 Masterman's Nude II primitives

on word meaning as usage and refused to regard Nude II primitives as a priori universal concepts as did Richens in his Nude version.

Masterman also rejected any cognitive hypothesis which would regard primitives as the elements of a language of thought, such as Fodor's Mentalese. For Masterman, the thesaurus is what links two contradictory conceptions of meaning, that is, universal language opposed to usage.

According to Masterman, the method of intermediary language using a thesaurus directly originates from Wittgenstein's intuitions (1961 [1953]) according to which the meaning of a word is defined from its contexts of use. The main hypothesis bolstering the feasibility of a thesaurus – and therefore that of an intermediary language using a thesaurus – is that, although the set of the possible uses of words is infinite in a given language, extralinguistic primary situations of communication are finite.

This hypothesis has a big impact on MT. Translation, like communication, is only possible if both populations and cultures related to the languages concerned by translation share a common stock of extralinguistic concepts, even if they are different. This view implies that translation between two languages involves translation between two cultures.

Wilks's Templates The third project was worked out by Yorick Wilks (born in 1939), one of the youngest members of the CLRU and one of Masterman's pupils. He adapted the Nude language in order to solve semantic ambiguities in a text (Wilks 1968).

The conception of ambiguities accepted by any MT experimenter – and later by NLP in general – consists in assimilating the notions of semantically ambiguous word with that of polysemic word, that is, in considering that all the possible meanings of a word can be given by a dictionary. In the wake of Wittgenstein, Firth and Masterman, Wilkes, by contrast, defined semantic ambiguities from their context of use, that is, a text. In order to solve these ambiguities, he worked out a system of semantic representation of texts using templates. The system was able to capture the most essential part of the information in texts. Templates, as patterns representing the meaning of a proposition or a sentence, are produced by formulas which are very close to Nude formulas.

These formulas encode the various meanings of a word by means of 53 primitives, 45 of which are shared with the archiheads pertaining to the thesaurus method.

Thanks to a pattern matching procedure, the various representations of a word are contrasted with those of the text. Like in the thesaurus, if the representations of two different words comprise the same primitives, they allow ambiguity to be resolved, or, better, to suggest a preferred meaning. Wilks would later call this "preferential semantics".

Wilks's works clearly opened the way to studies on semantic primitives, worked out within the framework of MT, in the new debates of the late 1960s on non-referential semantics and artificial intelligence. They constitute part of the horizon of projection of early MT attempts, opening the way to internationalised developments of linguistics. Simultaneously, they maintained a British specificity inherited from Sweet, Wittgenstein and Firth and characterised by work on texts rather than on isolated sentences.

7.1.3   MT in the USSR: Comparatism, Language Planning and Intermediary Languages

Cybernetics and MT in the Soviet Union in the 1950s While in the USA, MT was clearly a product of cybernetics and information theory, the link with these topics was less apparent in the USSR. It should be said that the prosperity of cybernetics in USSR varied greatly (Mindell et al. 2003). Wiener's book *Cybernetics*, published in 1948, was the subject of a hostile campaign, as cybernetics was considered a "bourgeois" science. After Stalin's death in 1953, a change of attitude in the Soviet scientific community could be observed. In November 1954, Arnost Kolman's talk « Qu'est-ce que la cybernétique ? » to the Academy of Social Sciences of the Central Committee of the Communist Party was published in the German Democratic Republic (GDR) and later in the journals *La Pensée* and *Behavioral Science*.

This change can also be attributed to the fact that by 1953, because of his critical works on American society, Wiener was no longer considered an "imperialist scientist"; especially, in the second edition of his book *The Human Use of Human Being* (Wiener 1950), Wiener attacked Maccarthyism and campaigned against the use of the atomic bomb. Finally, cybernetics and feedback, at work in anti-aircraft control systems devised during World War II, became necessary for the Soviet army. A confidential report written by Vice-Admiral Aksel Berg seemed to have played a crucial role. In 1958, Wiener's book was translated into Russian. From 1961, cybernetics was no longer a "bourgeois" science but a theory which had to be promoted. Khrushchev and Ulbricht thus mentioned it in their respective Party Congresses.

The commitment of the Soviets to MT is contemporary cybernetic's return to grace. It is from 1954, with Arnost Kolman's talk, and the first MT computer demonstration in New York, that the possibility of work on MT was considered.

In 1956, a resolution of the 20th Communist Party Congress explicitly promoted MT as a priority scientific project. In 1958, after the translation of Wiener's book, two journals were created where articles on MT were published, *Problemi kibernetiki* and *Mašinnyj Perevod i Prikladnaja Linguistika.*[8]

However, contrary to the USA, MT did not occupy a key position in the Soviet Cold War strategy. There was little funding, and computers were reserved to secret services and to strictly military aims. The researchers who were involved in MT belonged to speculative disciplines like mathematics or mathematical linguistics which were considered inoffensive ideologically. Hence, they benefited from some tranquillity, and their situation, other things being equal, could be compared with the British, who were also little subject to economic and strategic pressures.

The authorities required less to translate English into Russian than Russian into the other languages of the Soviet Union. MT was regarded as the first step of a more general program of information processing, of its retrieval and storage from written texts in various languages. Other tasks such as editing, summarising and providing bibliographic references were taken into account.

In their early works, Russian researchers attempted to keep pace with the Americans, who were pioneers in the domain and whose works were key references in those times of cold war and competition.[9] The Russians criticised the conception of translation inherited and promoted by Weaver, assuming that languages were codes and translation was decoding. On the contrary, translation, defined as the transfer of meaning from one language to another, cannot be handled as a mere code change, that is, of forms only. This view led them to develop a semantic approach to MT, at the expense of syntactic analysis, then dominant in the USA. It also led them to give more importance to the synthesis into the target language, rather than the analysis of the source language, hence the development of intermediary languages.

Models of Intermediary Languages[10]   Several models were used as intermediary languages, Russian, international languages and the idea of protolanguage, all of them anchored in the long-term history of the Russian cultural and linguistic tradition. D. Ju. Panov (1956) eliminated artificial languages, such as international languages which he thought were incapable of conveying the richness of natural languages. He also discarded the idea of building a specific language for translation and put forward Russian as an intermediary language. The arguments in favour of Russian were both economical and linguistic. Russian was presented as involving specific properties such as the morphological non-ambiguity of verbs allowing a verb form to be accurately identified even out of any context.

Nikolaj Dmitrivic Andreev (1920–1997) led the experimental MT laboratory at the University of Leningrad, which was part of the Institute of Mathematics and Mechanics. His model of intermediary language originates in the idea of

---

[8] In English: *Problems of Cybernetics, and Machine translation and Applied Linguistics*

[9] Respective works were well-known on both sides of the Iron Curtain. One of the MT pioneers, D. Ju. Panov, attended the first computer demonstration of MT in New York. Russian works on MT or information retrieval were systematically translated by an American service, the Joint Publication Research Service (JPRS) as soon as 1956.

[10] See Archaimbault and Léon (1997).

Fig. 7.5 Andreev's	*the*	*sun*	*is*		*a*	*yellow*	*star*
hieroglyphs	φ5τ4	+ δ1	+ φ1	φ8 τ5	+ φ6 τ4	+ δ2τ2	+ δ3 τ1

unequivocal information language promoted by Drezen (Andreev 1967). His method of construction rests on the statistical treatment of linguistic invariants and on the conception of languages as social facts. Thus, the structures which are sufficiently distributed in the natural languages under examination do not belong to the intermediary language. Presence or absence of these structures is weighted by the number of speakers of the language and the number of texts already translated. This method based on statistical data (number of common structures, number of speakers, number of translated texts) is reminiscent of the nineteenth-century method of a posteriori international languages as well as the trend, well-known in the USSR, towards statistical language planning. Besides using the term "hieroglyph" for naming the basic elements of his intermediary language, Andreev revived one of the old myths of the search for a perfect language based on non-alphabetical symbols, such as some nineteenth-century schemes of pasigraphy. Andreev suggested calculating, for each language, a congruence index from the number of corresponding hieroglyphs (when the hieroglyph of the source language is the same as the target language's one) and non-corresponding hieroglyphs comprised by each language, and the weighting it is given. Consider the following English sentence and its translation into hieroglyphs (Fig. 7.5).

Semantic hieroglyphs δ correspond to lexical units: for example, δ1 is the semantic hieroglyph of sun.

Formal hieroglyphs f correspond to grammatical information: f5 is the formal hieroglyph of the definite article.

Tectonic hieroglyphs express word order: t4 is the tectonic hieroglyph indicating that the article is followed by a noun.

I.A. Mel'čuk, (born in 1932), specialist in Spanish and French, worked at the Linguistic Institute of the Academy of Sciences of Moscow. In 1956, with the mathematician Olga Kulagina (1932–2005), he developed a MT system for French and Russian before working on a translation algorithm from Russian to Hungarian which led him to design an intermediary language (Kulagina and Mel'čuk 1967). Hungarian presents interesting characteristics concerning the translation process: while word order can be considered negligible for the translation of languages such as Russian, English, French and German, it plays a significant role in the translation from Hungarian to Russian. The solution consists either in designing a specific procedure to take into account the change of word order for each pair of languages, or in considering a method dissociating the processes of analysis and synthesis in such a way that the problem of word order transfer is neutralised. This method is based on an intermediary language.

Mel'čuk's works were inspired by Vyacheslav Ivanov (1929–2017), who was his PhD supervisor. Ivanov suggested to reinvest theoretical work on historical and comparative linguistics in the theoretical reflection on intermediary language. This work is in the direct line of Baudoin de Courtenay with the explicit references made by Ivanov to the theory of language mixity. This theory is based on the idea that the methods comparing language facts had been proven useful by experience, but that a metatheory able to describe the formal structure of comparison, a theory on linguistic systems relations, still remained to be elaborated. It should rest on an abstract language, named protolanguage, which would be representative of an earlier stage of a given language, but which would constitute its abstract system, in the sense that it would contain all the potentialities common to a group of languages, whether these potentialities are expressed or not (e.g. in some languages, like Russian, aspect is morphologically marked; but not in English and French. In English, there are three genders, while in French there are only two, etc.).[11] It is this protolanguage that Ivanov put forward as an intermediary language for MT.

Mel'čuk conceived translation as the transfer of meaning from one language to another with the help of linguistic invariants. The issue was to deal with variant features through the intermediary language. Mel'čuk attempted to solve the problem raised by variations by borrowing the notion of grammatical meanings (as opposed to lexical meanings) from Franz Boas about which he learnt through an article written in 1959 by Jakobson "Boas' View of Grammatical Meaning" (Jakobson 1971a [1959]).

However, Mel'čuk did not hold grammatical meanings as universals (in his *Cours de morphologie générale*, he uses the term "inflection") and exploited the fact that they are not identical in terms of translation. He used them to differentiate the treatments of source and target languages. A large proportion of grammatical meanings (morpho-syntactic information) which are unique for each language and useful for the analysis of the source language text are no longer necessary for the translation stage itself. Consequently, there is no need to know gender, number and case of a Russian adjective when it is translated into French or German. What is important is to find, through the analysis step, the substantive it is in agreement with. The case is different for grammatical indicators of lexical meanings used to identify lexical elements necessary to translation (number of nouns, tense and mode of verbs, etc.).

Consequently, intermediary language should necessarily involve only two sorts of linguistic variations, lexical and syntactic meanings: first because they exist in every language; second because they are needed by translation. This particularity has consequences for the structure of intermediary language which has no real grammar because it should not take into account the grammatical meanings of the languages. On the contrary, syntactic meanings are stored in the form of the syntactic relations of intermediary language, and lexical grammatical features are stored in the form of words (or concepts) in a dictionary. Mel'čuk (1960, p. 25) meets Ivanov's position: "concretely relation meanings should be reflected not in grammar, but in machine vocabulary". In other words, a large part of the natural language grammar should be translated in the form of a dictionary. This is due, he explains,

---

[11] In these examples, aspect and gender are grammatical features that can potentially be expressed in a language or a group of languages. They are called potentialities.

to the fact that natural language grammars hardly conform to the logical syntax of a scientific language. Words and syntactic relations of intermediary language correspond to the alphabet and formation rules of the formal languages of mathematical logic.

Finally, the processing of linguistic variations imposes two constraints for the translation of the source language into the intermediary language: (i) no grammatical information from that language should be lost because such information may be needed in the synthesis stage for the translation into one of the target languages. Thus the number of nouns will be expressed in the intermediary language when it exists in the target languages (Russian, English, Hungarian, etc.) but not in Chinese: this allows loss and redundancy of information to be avoided; (ii) information should not be developed specifically when it is not clearly expressed in the source language, as the information may turn out useless in the translation into the target language. For example, in the translation from Japanese into Chinese, the introduction in the intermediary language of the number of nouns, which is not expressed in Japanese, requires the implementation of lexico-semantic statistical and contextual rules, which would be useless and redundant in this particular case. When this information is required for the output language, it is more economical to generate it during the process of the text synthesis, by means of contextual analysis.

Such an approach makes it possible to translate new languages without major changes in the intermediary language: new grammatical meanings are transformed into words of the intermediary language where they are introduced cumulatively without changing its structure.

Such an intermediary language cannot be entirely artificial or entirely natural. It is based on the retrieval of the properties of languages. For MT, Mel'čuk is led to privilege synthesis. He argues that, as meaning is the key element of translation, it is too difficult to begin with semantic analysis, as it supposes that the understanding of texts be mastered. This task was hardly considered feasible in the 1970s, as artificial intelligence was in its early beginnings. Besides, inserting information belonging to the source language during the synthesis stage turns out more economical than providing the intermediary language with this type of information.

The primacy given to synthesis will be one of the characteristics of the meaning-text model Mel'čuk developed in the late 1960s with Žholkovskij (see Mel'čuk and Žholkovskij 1970) from his works on intermediary language. This is what is shown by the orientation "meaning → text" rather than "text→ meaning".

In his presentation, Polguère (1998, p. 4) defines the meaning-text model in the following way: "… a meaning-text model is a virtual machine which takes as input (representations of) utterance meaning and provides as output a set of texts which comprises all the paraphrases expressing the meaning given as output".[12]

The meaning-text model is largely inspired by the former intermediary language: syntactic relations constitute dependency syntax; grammatical features become

---

[12] "[…]un modèle Sens-Texte est une machine virtuelle qui prend en entrée des (représentations de) sens d'énoncés et retourne en sortie un ensemble de Textes, qui contient toutes les paraphrases permettant d'exprimer le Sens donné en entrée" Polguère (1998, p. 4).

lexical functions. Remaining faithful to the idea that he must account for the variations between languages and for every possible type of linguistic structures, the model uses various formalisms. In the meaning-text model, intermediary language, initially designed to be linked to the implementation of concrete algorithms, is replaced by basic English and basic Russian, that is, by a set of deep lexico-syntactic structures which are needed by synthesis. Indeed, the viewpoint of synthesis is crucial. Here is the argument given by Polguère, less MT-oriented than Mel'čuk's (1960):

"The Meaning-Text correspondence has always been viewed from the perspective of synthesis – from Meaning to Text — rather than from the viewpoint of analysis — from Text to Meaning. The reason is that only the modelling of linguistic synthesis makes it possible to implement purely linguistic knowledge (contained in the dictionaries and grammars of the language). With analysis one must face the problem of disambiguisation, a problem which cannot be solved (by the speaker or by formal modelling) without the recourse to heuristics based on extra-linguistic knowledge" (Polguère 1998, p. 4).[13]

Meaning-text model is thus the most visible part of the horizon of projection of early 1950s MT works in the Soviet Union. Besides, Mel'čuk considers himself a typologist, and his view of non-universal grammatical meanings has been expressed in his *Cours de morphologie générale* (Mel'čuk 1993).[14]

7.2 Automation of Translation and Multi-word Lexical Units

The automation of translation provided an opportunity for new linguistic objects to emerge. This was the case of multi-word lexical units in 1960s French linguistics. Reflection on lexis was at the core of the computationalisation of the language sciences in France (see Chap. 8). It was one of the major thematics of the Colloque international sur la mécanisation des recherches lexicologiques organised in Besançon in June 1961 by Bernard Quemada (1926–2018). Quemada pointed out that phraseology was one of the less investigated lexicological areas. Even if much research on statistical studies of vocabulary was conducted simultaneously, both types of approach cannot be confused. Actually, even if it can be shown that works on lexicology are an outcome of computationalisation, they do not put in place a real mathematisation of language of a mathematical-logic or statistical order. They

---

[13] "La correspondance Sens-Texte est toujours envisagée sous l'angle de la synthèse — du Sens au Texte — plutôt que sous celui de l'analyse — du Texte au Sens. La raison en est que seule la modélisation de la synthèse linguistique permet de mettre en jeu les connaissances purement linguistiques (contenues dans le dictionnaire et la grammaire de la langue). L'analyse, elle, ne peut se faire sans que l'on soit confronté au problème de la désambiguïsation, problème qui ne peut être résolu (par le locuteur ou par une modélisation formelle) sans le recours à des heuristiques basées sur des connaissances extra-linguistiques" (Polguère 1998, p. 4).

[14] Concerning this horizon of projection, Ju. D. Apresjan's work on componential semantics should be mentioned.

attest to a renewal of French linguistics at the intersection of several trends: statistical studies of vocabulary associated with the French sociolinguistic tradition, structural linguistics, Guillaumian linguistics and machine translation.

Vocabulary studies are rooted in the French sociolinguistic tradition linking language, culture and society.[15] At the beginning of the twentieth century, Gilliéron's linguistic atlas implements a conception of vocabulary where words make it possible to reconstitute both history of language and history of nation. In the 1940s–1950s, it was studies on dialectology and the history of words, as well as etymological and stylistic studies, which led to lexicography.

At the junction of the sociological tradition of vocabulary studies and lexicography, there is the pioneering work of Mario Roques (1875–1961) and his *Inventaire Général de la Langue Française*, started in 1936, whose 6 million records (words with contexts from literary and technical texts) were dedicated to works on lexicography, rather than to the making of dictionaries which was common at the time.

In the 1950s–1960s, the use of statistical methods made vocabulary studies evolve towards statistical works, such as Pierre Guiraud's, and later Charles Müller's, or towards works with a pedagogic intention like *Français élémentaire* directed by Gougenheim. Finally, in the 1960s, MT and, more specifically, the possibility of automating translation, aroused a revival of reflection on lexis and the appearance of new units, multi-word lexical units.

Word groups, traditionally processed by grammarians with the help of operations of derivation and composition, did not arouse structuralist linguists' interest. As to "words", they were highly suspicious, and word groups were not investigated specifically. For Saussure, they are phrases, that is, consecutive units: compounded words, derivatives, parts of sentences or complete sentences. What interested him was less to define the structures and the boundaries of phrases than to determine their belonging to the order of language or speech. What argued in favour of speech is that a sentence, as the ultimate speech unit, is a phrase; the opposite argument is that units of speech are free by definition and that free phrases can be encountered (e.g. "prendre la mouche"). The identification of such non-free phrases as units of language constitutes everything that structuralism has to say on compounded units.

7.2.1 Lexies, Synapsies *and* Synthèmes

With MT, structuralist linguists were led to rethink the status of "word" and groups of word. Only graphic words, that is, series of letters between two spaces or two separators, can be identified by machine. Besides, the objective consisting in making a machine translate a text compelled them to define units that may be simultaneously units for text segmentation, language units, meaning units and translation

---

[15] For a survey on the importance of statistical studies in French linguistics, see Léon and Loiseau (eds) (2017).

units. The aim is to make graphic forms, syntactic units and translation units coincide. The definition criteria should make it possible to recognise these units in a text and to store them in a dictionary. Some terms had been coined by linguists to account for these types of units:

- *Lexies* by Bernard Pottier (b. in 1924)
- *Synapsies* by Emile Benveniste (1902–1976)
- *Synthèmes* by André Martinet (1908–1999)

Pottier (1962a, b) holds that lexis is one of the most complex areas of MT, either on the formal level (especially compound words) or on the semantic level (polysemy). He put forward *lexie* as a lexical and syntactic unit for the processing of texts.[16] Simple *lexies* ("chaise"), compound *lexies* ("sous-chef", "cheval-vapeur") and complex *lexies* ("pomme de terre", "prendre la mouche") cannot be shorter than the graphic word. Those that may cause problems for MT are complex *lexies*, since the others, simple and compound ones, can be identified graphically by the machine. It is actually rather difficult to distinguish them from groups or free word associations, the grouping of which is, as Pottier says, fortuitous in discourse. In fact, criteria making it possible to define complex *lexies* are manifold and they leave many areas of uncertainty.

In addition to the semantic criteria referring to stable designation and to object uniqueness, secured by this type of lexical unit, the main criteria that Pottier identifies as functional are syntactical. They indicate that the unit is inaccessible to any kind of insertion. A further criterion linked to translation comes from interlingual comparison: a complex *lexie* can be translated into a simple *lexie* in another language. It is the case of "cheval de course" and its Spanish equivalent "corcel". Pottier deals with areas of uncertainty through statistical criteria which determine a degree of lexicalisation: "pomme de terre" is more lexicalised than "crise de croissance". Finally, it is interesting to see that Pottier mentions the internal structure of these complex *lexies* in terms of categories (N, adj ou V) where a syntactic treatment can be seen to emerge.

Pottier introduces a categorisation which is related to the notion of head in phrase grammar: "plaque tournante" is categorised as a substantive because it is the highest category in the phrase. Thus S + A = S.[17]

What is new with Pottier, partly thanks to MT, is a unifying conception of lexical units. Simple, compound or complex *lexies* are simultaneously syntactic units, meaning units and translation units. This explains why Pottier is less interested in the morphological aspect of *lexies* than in their mode of construction and of syntactical categorisation.

---

[16] Bernard Pottier, a semanticist and Hispanist, was the only linguist, with his colleague Guy Bourquin, who was directly involved in practical MT projects. Most notably he founded the MT Centre of Nancy in 1960.

[17] "Lexies are of different types. (A) grouping of nominal elements. The resultative functional value is that of the highest level element: 'plaque tournante': S + A = S″ (Pottier 1962a, p.64).

A few years later, Benveniste[18] (1966, 1967) identified *synapsies* defined as groups of lexemes forming a new unit with a unique and constant signified. Following Darmesteter (1875), Benveniste was more interested in the internal structure of *synapsies* he regarded as strictly syntactic units. A *synapsie* comes from the nominal conversion of a predicative unit: "gardien d'asile de nuit" derives from the predicative utterance "il garde un asile de nuit". The syntactic nature of *synapsies* warrants its expansion and its productivity, as ("(gardien d'asile) de nuit") or as ("(gardien) d'asile de nuit"), which is completely innovating in the process of formation by composition. By implementing regular mechanisms of syntax, *synapsies* constitute a very productive mode of creation of new compounds, thus constituting the basic composition forming in technical nomenclatures.

For both Pottier and Benveniste, it was technological developments, MT for the former, technical nomenclature for the latter, which contributed to the identification of those new units. In both cases, we are facing a non-morphological approach to the composition process.

As to Martinet, it has been shown that his concern for compound lexical units came from Pottier and more generally from MT (Léon 2004). Thus, it is only from 1967 that the *synthème* appeared (Martinet 1967). It is a syntactical unit which groups all the forms built by derivation, composition and "figement" (fixation) and which is defined by a set of heterogeneous criteria of a morphological, flexional and derivational nature. Martinet was not interested in the modes of unit construction. *Synthèmes* do not make it possible to identify a specific level of lexis distinct from the morphological level. His views remained close to that of the structuralists according to whom all language units (words, phrases, sentences) are organised homogeneously and uniformly, that is, they are monemes or combinations of monemes. On the contrary, like Pottier's units, *synthèmes* are syntactic units with signifiers remaining stable in the utterance.

It should be noted that that work, stimulated by technological developments like MT and scientific and technological terminology, led to innovative developments in the areas of syntax and lexis. The fact that these lexical units are often specialised terms and that recognising them requires extra-linguistic knowledge makes them more likely to be dealt with by a discursive approach within the specific tradition of vocabulary studies. One can assume that these studies led to a type of lexicology rooted in discourse.

Internal unit constructions are linked to their syntactic function in the utterance and to their referential function in discourse. These features are characteristic of enunciation theories (*théories de l'énonciation*) which constitute one of the specificities of French linguistics in the second part of the twentieth century.

---

[18] Emile Benveniste was a major French twentieth-century linguist, a specialist in Indo-European languages and comparative grammar and above all a pioneer in Enunciation theory. He was not directly involved in MT projects but took part in committees evaluating French MT projects.

7.2.2   NLP and Complex Lexical Unit Processing

Started in the 1960s, this type of inquiry on complex lexical units gave way to achievements in NLP. It constitutes what is now called the "structural" approach of complex lexical unit analysis. An extended approach was added to that view within the frame of the second stage of the automatisation-mathematisation of language. It was called the "statistical approach" (Habert et Jacquemin 1993). Those research endeavours, which were specifically French in the 1960s, have now become international with the rise of computerised large corpora (see Chap. 10).[19] The structural approach considers that the identification of complex lexical units is a prerequisite to any automatic processing, while the statistical approach regards the step of identification as secondary.

Every approach in the structural trend shares common points, such as the need to identify complex lexical units, as well as to classify and to store them in dictionaries before undertaking any language processing which could be done only in a second stage.

Their divergence depends on the importance given to the internal analysis of units and to the search for formation and construction rules; it also depends on the preference given to the treatment, morphological or syntactic, of these construction rules and on the mode of identification of word groups. Either they are regarded as language data and listed a priori, or they should be identified by automatic processing.

For MT and text generation, the issue is to find equivalents in the target language, which, in most cases, implies (re)constructing complex lexical units, referring to the crucial principle of non-compositionality of meaning which characterises idioms. This means that idioms are characterised by complex forms that have meaning that can often not be decomposed in simpler units that would translate easily into other languages. In the statistical approach, collocations and idioms are not determined a priori but are located during processing and are assigned a status only in a second stage. The aim of this approach is to study the lexical functioning of a text or a corpus by statistical methods. All the approaches in this trend share common options: (i) priority given to text within the frame of a stylistic or discursive analysis; (ii) "word" is the basic unit and it is the functioning of texts which determines whether they should be grouped with the help of co-occurrences and collocations searching; (iii) the internal analysis of word groups is considered insignificant.

---

[19] In the 1950s, Bar-Hillel (1955) was one of the few researchers outside France to raise the issue of the automatic translation of idioms. He addressed cases in which the number of units forming the compound varies across languages and in which meaning cannot be translated unequivocally. Regardless of any linguistic conception of lexis, his only suggestion was to build an idiom dictionary.

7.3   Formalisation, Mathematisation and Automatisation

The three sets of research presented in this chapter have developed semantic methods to account for meaning transfer in MT. It is worth noting that each project resulted in forms of representation of lexical meaning in opposition to the dominant computational model developed by Bar-Hillel and Chomsky in the USA.

Besides, not all these incorporated a reflection on mathematisation. This is the case of Pottier, for example. In his preparatory works on MT, the idea of automatisation in an algorithmic form already exists and he puts forward rules, namely, for disambiguation, with the help of "ordinograms" called "schemas" (Pottier 1962b, p. 205).

The issue of automatisation, with or without mathematisation, was an issue for the human sciences at that time. One can recall Gardin's views (Gardin and Jaulin 1968) in his introduction to the proceedings of the congress held in 1966 on formalisation in human sciences.[20] For him, formalisation does not involve computation.[21] And computation does not involve mathematics. Gardin defines computation as "every sequence of operations each linked to the next following rules prescribed in advance to form a reasoning, a 'computation' applicable to qualitative or more specifically non numerical data. The common feature in both cases is the making explicit of every stage of the process [...] the important thing is to recognize the major trend towards algorithmisation of search procedures, in disciplines which had the reputation of neglecting them in favour of intuitive shortcuts with an immediate benefit" (Gardin et Jaulin 1968, p. 8).

What is placed at the forefront by Gardin, is the making explicit of "algorithmicised procedures" by rules involving discrete data, without computation in the mathematical sense of the term (i.e. counting, logico-mathematical formalisms, Boole's algebra, free monoids, etc.). It is what Pottier had implemented.

---

[20] Linguistics is not represented at all in this congress, reflecting that it played a specific role in the human sciences in the middle of the 1960s. In addition, heated debates opposed structuralist linguists to the supporters of information retrieval and universal semantic categories such as Gardin (see Chap. 9).

[21] Auroux (2009) distinguishes formalisation from mathematisation. He puts forward two definitions of formalisation: (i) formalisation in the strict sense of the term, that is, "formatting", "application of a form that language does not possess", does not involve mathematisation; (ii) in the specific sense of the term, formalisation can be defined as "the action of representing objects by a literal system that is not necessarily unequivocal". He glosses "literal" in the following way: "It is not in fact necessary that it should be a "letter" : A could be replaced by "suitcase", B by "terror" and G by "emptiness", but in order for substitution to mean something, it would be necessary to delete any meaning or to use words functioning as variables (such as "truc", "machin", "chose"). The use of letters originates from the use of alphabetic writing. Formalisation does not exist in oral societies" (Auroux 2009, note 11 p.25). See also the notion of weak formalisation put forward by Auroux (1998) – note 12, Chap. 4 in this volume.

See also Nefdt (2019, p. 1672) for a reflection on the difference between formalisation and mathematisation.

As we saw in Chap. 4, procedures had already been implemented in linguistics by American distributionalist linguists since Bloomfield, well before automatisation. It can be said that they were "discovered" with MT by the French linguists.

Contrary to Pottier's works, Mel'čuk's and CLRU's involved a formal dimension based on mathematical models (graph theory for the thesaurus, transformational generative grammar with a strong lexical component for the meaning-text model developed by Mel'čuk and Zholkovskij 1970 [1967]). In both cases, formalisation and mathematisation are associated. For Mel'čuk, the aim was to adapt an existing model, transformational generative grammar, so that it admitted lexical transformations. For example, new operators should be defined.

The debate between Masterman and Bar-Hillel (Masterman et al. 1959), even if it is on logico-mathematical formalisation (especially on the notion of "normal" language), questions the relationship between formalisation and language. For Masterman, formalisation is not an internal characteristic of language so that it should not be a priori. It comes as a second step, as a mode of representation.

It cannot be said that the works of the CLRU resulted in new forms of mathematisation of the language sciences, "intrinsic" mathematisation (Auroux 2009) creating new concepts inseparable from their mathematical formulation. However, we do not encounter mere artificial applications of mathematical models to linguistic objects either. The use of lattice theory by the members of the CLRU constitutes an original importation of a mathematical model into the language sciences since it aims at representing lexical meaning by a network, and these semantic networks constituted new objects for linguistics.

Chapter 8
The French Linguistic Tradition and External Reception of the Computational Mathematisation of Language

France played a specific role in the process of the computational mathematisation of the language sciences. Although it was one of the "winners" of World War II and can be included among MT pioneers, it started experiments only in 1959, namely, 10 years after the USA. Several factors may account for this French specificity: the lack of a proper configuration of the war sciences, the lack of roots in mathematical logic and philosophy of language which characterised the first mathematisation, the need to catch up with the American development in computing and the lack of specific training in the universities. The convergence of these various factors had the effect that the computational mathematisation of the language sciences was integrated in a totally external way. I therefore suggest speaking of external reception rather than of integration for the French case. External reception can be defined as a process which does not rely on any anchorage in tradition or in the horizon of retrospection of the research field which receives it.

8.1 The French Tradition and the Horizon of Retrospection of the War Sciences

France remained outside the logico-formalist movement of the 1930s where the first twentieth-century mathematisation was anchored. This situation can be explained by the disaffection with the teaching of logic involved by the tragic fate of French logicians (among them Jean Cavaillès and Jacques Herbrand) killed during the 1914–1918 war, by the attraction of French philosophers by the German Nietzschian Heideggerian philosophical tradition and the radicalism of the structuralist movement (see Dosse 1991).

This chapter is a summary of Léon (2010c).

© The Author(s), under exclusive license to Springer Nature Switzerland AG 2021
J. Léon, *Automating Linguistics*, History of Computing,
https://doi.org/10.1007/978-3-030-70642-5_8

In the late 1950s, within the all-powerful Société de Linguistique de Paris (hereafter SLP), American structuralist works did not arouse much interest (Chevalier 1990). When they were reviewed in the *Bulletin de la Société de Linguistique* (BSL), which occurred only rarely, they were often severely criticised, as was Z.S. Harris's *Methods in Structural Linguistics* reviewed by Jean Cantineau in 1954. The situation improved a little once Georges Mounin joined the SLP in 1958. He was the reviewer of *Syntactic Structures* in 1961 (Mounin 1961).[1]

MT works were scarcely present. On the contrary, works coming from the countries of the Soviet block were systematically reviewed. As early as 1955, René Lhermitte wrote a regular review of the Russian journals *Oprosy Jazykoznanija* and *Izvestija Nauk SSSR*[2] where Soviet works and the main conferences on mathematical linguistics were published. As to Marc Vey, he reviewed Czech journals, among them *The Prague Bulletin of Mathematical Linguistics*. Thus, at the beginning of the 1960s, French linguists were better informed on Soviet works on mathematical linguistics than on American ones, either distributionalist or formalist. This situation partly explains, as we will see later, why in France new forms of mathematisation emerged, different from the conjunction syntax-formalism-computer programming present in the USA.

Finally, the war sciences configuration, in which the second mathematisation was anchored, was only partly represented in France.[3] Digital electronic computing, at the core of the computational mathematisation turn, was lagging behind in France, while in the USA the computer was one of the technological devices that best illustrated the success of the new alliance between sciences and war sciences engineering.

After World War II, digital electronic computing had proven its worth for scientific computing and for data processing. In France before the war, a tradition of analog computing for the sciences and punch-card processing in the commercial sector existed, but these traditions failed to produce a digital electronic computer after the war. Due to a number of factors, both economic and institutional, France was one of the last industrialised countries that built a digital electronic computer (see Ramunni 1989 and Mounier-Kuhn 2010 for details). French industry and the army showed only a slight interest in electronic computers. Universities manifested hostility towards general machines and information processing. As Mounier-Kuhn (2010) shows, pure mathematics dominated the French academic world leaving

---

[1] Marcel Cohen published a review of *Syntactic Structures* in *l'Année Sociologique* in 1962 (Cohen 1962). However, Chomsky's book published in 1957 was translated into French only in 1969 (by Michel Braudeau).

[2] *Issues in Linguistics* and *News about Sciences in USSR*

[3] The CNRS (Centre National de la Recherche Scientifique), when created in 1939, involved some features of the war sciences. Its vocation consisting in grouping human and social sciences and applied sciences under the control of specialised committees comprising scientists, industrialists and engineers seemed close to the vocation of MIT in the USA, that is, a research centre where sciences, engineer sciences and human sciences interacted. After being put on standby during World War II, the CNRS resumed its activities only in 1945 with a philosophy that differed from the initial project.

aside applied mathematics and computing which was not considered a topic for research. Very few mathematicians (Marcel-Paul Schützenberger was an exception) were concerned with areas related with computering and programming languages such as Boolean algebra, set theory, theory of formal languages, etc. Mounier-Kuhn underlines serious problems of reception since issues at stake at international level were not discussed by the French scientists. For example, Von Neumann's machine, which raised crucial issues on the status of computing as a science, was completely ignored in France.

In addition to the delay in the building of hardware, this disinterest implied an overall shortage of trained staff. This failure pushed the CNRS even to acquire a UK-built Elliott 402 computer in 1955. France's delay in building up a national computer industry or even research culture in the 1950s was only definitely reversed in 1966 when the government came up with its *Plan Calcul* to catch up with the digital age and its technologies.

8.2   The Context of the Appearance of the Second Mathematisation in France

While in the USA and in Great Britain the second mathematisation emerged from the teams experimenting with machine translation, in France theoretical research on MT played an important role too. But due to the 10 years delay and to the lack of anchorage in any tradition, it was not the only means and the only mode of reception of computational mathematisation in France.

As their first experiments on MT began 10 years after the USA and Great Britain, and about 5 years after the USSR, the French ignored the early methodological stages, namely, word by word translation.[4] They anchored their research directly in the syntactic parsers developed in the USA in the early 1960s while adopting some aspects of the models worked out in the Soviet Union. Finally, the French linguists' stance towards the new field was radically different from the American linguists. The fact that MT appeared in France in 1959 is linked to a special political context. MT centres were created in France in the wake of the advent of the Gaullist era which was characterised by the implementation of a genuinely scientific research policy. The CNRS (Centre National de la Recherche Scientifique), created in 1939, experienced unprecedented development and became a powerful war machine;

---

[4] In fact, the first French machine for automatic translation was invented and built by Georges Artsrouni (1893–1960), a contemporary of Trojanskij (see Chap. 7), between 1932 and 1935. Artsrouni constructed three machines, all of them purely mechanical and electrical, which were first used for intelligence and accounting services. Words were stored on a strip of cardboard with several columns: on the left input words in the source language, and on the right corresponding words in the target languages. The strip was activated by a set of perforations on each side of the cardboard, just like rolls of film. A keyboard was used as an input device (see Daumas 1965 for more details).

other institutes were created, comparable with the American model, such as the DRME (Direction des Recherches et Moyens d'Essais) where the army promoted the integration of research by both engineers and academics.

However – probably because of the weak interest for computers, as previously mentioned – it was neither an academic nor a scientist who promoted MT in France. It was Emile Delavenay (1905–2003), director of the UNESCO information and publishing service, who drew the attention of the CNRS and of linguists to MT works as early as 1957. In February and March 1958, he convened two meetings on "translation machine" at the Institut de Linguistique de la Sorbonne, in collaboration with André Martinet. Michel Lejeune, deputy director of the literary and human sciences sector of the CNRS, attended the meeting chaired by Benveniste, as well as the mathematicians Georges Guilbaud, Benoît Mandelbrot and Marcel-Paul Schützenberger. These mathematicians played a crucial role in the process of computational mathematisation.

Because of his functions at UNESCO, and his former position as the head of the translation and publishing service at the UN, Delavenay was very well aware of MT research around the world. He created a group for reflection and information exchange on the domain which became the ATALA (Association pour la Traduction Automatique et la Linguistique Appliquée) in April 1959. Since 1960, the association has published a journal *La Traduction automatique*, now called *TAL*. ATALA was established as a forum for discussions on machine translation, information retrieval and applied linguistics and was intended to be more than a research centre. The first MT centre was thus a learned society, and the spreading of the domain in France required someone to act as a conduit agent (Chiss and Puech 1999). Delavenay was neither an engineer nor a real academic, but a man of networks and a frontier runner.

Thanks to Michel Lejeune's help, the CNRS created the CETA (Centre d'Etude en Traduction Automatique/ Centre for Machine Translation Studies) in December 1959 within the Laboratory of Digital Computing at the Blaise Pascal Institute. The CETA had two sections, one in Paris led by Aimé Sestier and the second in Grenoble led by Bernard Vauquois. In the USA, many MT centres were created at universities, within language departments. In France they were created at the CNRS by mathematicians. Sestier was an army engineer from the Ecole Polytechnique, and Vauquois was a physicist, a specialist both in astrophysics and computers. The only exception was Bernard Pottier and Guy Bourquin who were both linguists. They created the Centre for MT at the University of Nancy in 1960. In the MT centres, the language specialists graduated in languages, especially in Russian, but they were not academics. MT was an electronic computing problem, that is, a problem of storage capacity and speed, which only engineers and mathematicians could deal with. Applied mathematics was the discipline where MT research was carried out. Contrary to what their weak concern for American linguistics might have suggested, linguists took a real interest in MT. They did not work directly on MT — except for, as we said, Bernard Pottier and Guy Bourquin — but they presided over its destiny at the CNRS and within the framework of the ATALA, where they bestowed disciplinary status on it. They decided on the funding of MT research and assessed the results of experiments and research. This stance of the linguists, more observers, evaluators and legislators than actors, gave a specific physiognomy to the reception of formal languages in France. As for MT, the reception of computational linguistics required the intervention of intermediaries, conduit agents, be it either institutions or scientists.

8.3   Conduit Agents (1): Marcel-Paul Schützenberger and Maurice Gross

The creation of the CETA at the Blaise Pascal Institute closely linked MT to the development of digital computing and electronic computers. We previously mentioned the crucial role played by the CNRS. It is within one of its institutes, the Blaise Pascal Institute, that the new field was established. Dealing with mathematics, computer sciences, automata theory and formal languages, it had many similarities to MIT. Two major personalities played the role of conduit agents between the USA and France. They were genuine conduit agents and not mere importers of theories and methods, since their works helped to improve research on both sides of the Atlantic and in both directions. Both of them enriched American as well as French works.

Marcel-Paul Schützenberger (1920–1996) can be considered a genuine frontier runner between mathematics, computer sciences and formal languages on the one hand, and between American and French works on the other hand. He received a double training, first in medicine, later in mathematics in which he held a PhD. His early works on theoretical computer science were carried out in France in 1955 and focused on coding and automata theory. In his first article published in *l'Evolution psychiatrique* in 1949 "A propos de la cybernétique (Mathématiques et psychologie)", Schützenberger was involved in the relationship between the notion of information as it was worked out by Fisher in the 1930s and by Shannon in the late 1940s. In the wake of his second PhD, in mathematics, "Contribution aux applications statistiques de la théorie de l'information" which he defended in 1953, he was invited in 1956 by Shannon at MIT, at the Research Laboratory of Electronics (RLE). With Shannon, he worked on the semantics of formal languages and with Kleene on finite-state automata. At MIT, he met Chomsky with whom, during a second invitation to the USA in 1963 at Harvard Medical School, he worked on context-free grammars, thus contributing to the foundations of a general theory of computer languages. In the middle of the 1960s, he worked at the Blaise Pascal Institute within a group consisting most notably of Maurice Gross and André Lentin, in charge of research on applied algebra, theory of languages and automata theory. Then he devoted himself mainly to theoretical computer sciences and founded Word combinatorics, an area in which he worked with André Lentin.

Maurice Gross (1934–2001) can be considered a second frontier runner between the French and the American research, between formal languages and linguistics.

Trained as an army engineer at the Ecole Polytechnique, he was recruited at the CETAP in 1960 to set up an automatic dictionary and syntactic analysis programs for MT. From October 1961 to May 1962, he completed a research internship in two MT centres: at Harvard under the supervision of Antony Oettinger who led the MT centre and later at the RLE (Research Laboratory of Electronics) at MIT led by Victor Yngve.

Gross attended Chomsky's lectures at RLE and presented his work on Tesnière's syntax at his seminar. He discussed with Bar-Hillel the problems raised by MT and the poor results obtained in the domain. After the CETAP was dissolved in 1962, he became a researcher at the CNRS Blaise Pascal Institute and worked with Schützenberger on automata theory and formal grammars. Benefiting from Schützenberger's contacts with Harris, he became a visiting lecturer at the University of Pennsylvania and started researching on French transformational grammar following the methods set up by Harris. When Gross came back to the Blaise Pascal Institute, he joined the group working on formalised grammar, which also included David Cohen who worked on a syntactic parser of Arabic. In 1966 he replaced Jean-Claude Gardin at the head of the SAD (Section d'Automatique Documentaire) which became the LADL (Laboratoire d'Automatique Documentaire et Linguistique) in 1970.

Until he encountered Harris, Gross was concerned more by problems raised by the new computer sciences, oriented towards compiler theory than to linguistics itself. After his second stay in the USA and after completing his works with Harris, he played an important role in disseminating information on formal grammars and largely contributed to spreading Harris's works and integrating them into French linguistics (see Chap. 9). Gross invited Harris to give lectures at the University Paris 8-Vincennes in 1973–1974. These lectures were published in 1976 by the Editions du Seuil in Paris under the title of *Notes du Cours de Syntaxe*.

8.4   Conduit Agents (2): ATALA and the Centre Favard

A second type of conduit agent can be identified: the learned societies. Blanckaert (2006) shows the crucial role played by the learned societies in the institutionalisation of disciplines in the nineteenth century, some of them being created entirely outside of universities. These societies anchored MT firmly in the French tradition. We have already mentioned the ATALA and its founder Emile Delavenay who played a crucial role of frontier runner for the establishment of MT in France. The ATALA included translators, documentalists, engineers, mathematicians and linguists. It essentially committed oneself to the information about and disseminating MT, of formal linguistics and the computational mathematisation of linguistics.

Training was provided by another association, the Centre Favard, created in March 1960, in particular with its Quantitative Linguistics Seminar, at the Henri Poincaré Institute where teaching on linguistics for mathematicians was provided by André Martinet and Jean Dubois; teaching on mathematical logic and information theory for non-specialists was provided by René Moreau and Daniel Hérault. In 1962–1963, an additional course on language theory was given by Jacques Pitrat and Maurice Gross. These courses led to the publication in 1967 of the book by Gross and Lentin *Notions sur les grammaires formelles*, a genuine introduction to the area, sufficiently explicit and clear to be understood by the linguists. These centres for information and training, although open to anybody, were mostly attended by young researchers. Unfortunately, this type of courses was not available for students in linguistics, who did not receive formal and computational training at that time. There was nothing of that kind in the universities, and the strict separation between the Sciences faculty and the Arts faculty did not foster the development of such courses where several disciplines interacted.

It was at EPHE (Ecole Pratique des Hautes Etudes) 6th section that such a training was implemented for a few years (1967–1970). EPRASS (Enseignement préparatoire à la recherche approfondie en Sciences sociales) [a preparatory program for advanced research on social sciences] added a section on linguistics and semantics in 1966 led by A-G. Greimas. Greimas attempted to organise a specific course for linguists including training in formal linguistics (logic, mathematical formalisation, programming, information retrieval). Scholars such as Marc Barbut, Oswald Ducrot, Algirdas-Julien Greimas, Christian Metz, Jean-Blaize Grize, Yves Gentilhomme, Frédéric François, Michel Pêcheux, etc. taught at EPRASS. This course, for the first time in France, aimed at training linguists in every field of linguistics, thus reversing the current trend of the time which privileged isolated courses and training over more general training.

By consulting EPRASS program contents, it can be appreciated how challenging it was to organise a course on formal linguistics in France. Both worlds, mathematics and logic on one side and linguistics on the other, hardly succeeded in talking to each other. Teachers were aware of the fact that a too hasty confrontation between linguistics and formalisation might have negative implications which would be contrary to the desired objectives. In the 1966–1967 program two difficulties were mentioned. It is "dangerous for the researchers interested in general linguistics to ignore the extension given by mathematics and logic to the notion of language, in the same way as the functions of language revealed by its psychological and sociological study". Conversely, students with previous mathematical training "regard as taken for granted the division of utterances into words and the classification of clauses into main and subordinate ones. As a result, logic and mathematics are applied to a conception of language that has been called into question a long time ago, that is, typically, the conception which underpins 20 years old school grammars"; those various stances being obstacles to "any further collaboration between linguistics and the formal disciplines" (EPRASS archives, EHESS).

8.5   Hazards of External Reception (1): MT as Computational Linguistics

French research on MT began only in 1959 and this had several consequences. While in the USA computational linguistics was established progressively starting from MT projects, in France MT and computational linguistics were integrated and developed simultaneously. The phase of MT as a war technology was hardly outlined by the CETAP (Paris) and was given up as soon as it was shut down. The CETAG (Grenoble) started to work directly on MT systems as formal systems without being forced to produce mass translations. After the ALPAC report, the CNRS, which was concerned only secondarily by the economic aspects of MT, continued to support the works of the CETA in Grenoble in order to confront questions and expectations raised by formal models and syntactic parsing within the community of linguists and applied mathematicians. Their approach consisted in equating natural languages with formal languages and programming languages, and, thanks to MT systems, in exploring the analogy between translation and compilation (the translation of a natural language into another and the translation of a programming language into machine language). In 1967, one year after the publication of the ALPAC report, the CETA was flourishing and gaining an international profile by organising the second international conference on natural language processing ("Deuxième conférence internationale sur le Traitement Automatique des Langues"). The first one took place in New York in 1965 under the title International Conference on Computational Linguistics.

However, the debate on the theoretical aspects of the automatisation of linguistics versus the practical aspects of linguistic engineering was not over. Vauquois was severely criticised by Gross in his CNRS report on the CETA in 1967. Gross, who was a member of the CETAP at the time of its dissolution and who had met Bar-Hillel shortly after the publication of his 1960 report, did not find it feasible to carry out research on computational linguistics and experiments on MT simultaneously: either one does MT with the unique aim of providing an industry-ready finished product, or one devotes oneself to the theoretical analysis of the structures of artificial languages and natural languages. MT, he said, is by no means a problem of application, that is, a problem concerning the adaptation of linguistics to computers or the adaptation of computers to linguistics. During the next decades, this tension between theoretical aspects and applied and industrial aspects would remain vivid within the developments of natural language processing.

8.6   Hazards of External Reception (2): American Models Versus Russian Models

In 1960, the Americans were not the only ones to develop models for MT. The British and the Soviets also outlined their own models, which, contrary to the Americans, were not exclusively based on syntactic analysis (see Chap. 7). Besides, among syntactic models, other models than those founded on phrase grammars were developed. Thus, the French experimenters could implement parsers by testing and comparing various existing models.

Soviet works on mathematical linguistics were well known in France. As we saw, the reviews published in the *Bulletin de la Société de Linguistique* reflected the French linguists' interest in Soviet works, especially on mathematical linguistics, even more than in American works. Many members of the ATALA association and of the Centre Favard were members of the Communist Party in France. Researchers of Romanian origin, like George Moisil and Solomon Marcus, ensured the dissemination of works coming from the countries of the Eastern bloc. ATALA received the French translations of Russian works, carried out by the research service of the French army (CASDEN, Comité d'action scientifique de défense du centre d'exploitation scientifique et technique du ministère de la Défense) and was a subscriber to the Joint Publications Research Service, an American service specialised in the translation of Russian works into English.

Contrary to American MT experimenters, who rarely mentioned Russian works even when they were translated, ATALA members published and discussed Russian works in several publications: *TA Informations*, the *Documents de linguistique quantitative* and the series published by Dunod, such as I.I. Revzin's, I.A. Mel'čuk's and S.K. Shaumyan's works, among others.

As to the Grenoble MT group, Bernard Vauquois and Jean Veyrunes visited the Soviet Union in 1962 and made contact with Igor Mel'čuk and Andreev's group who worked on MT methods based on intermediary languages. At the CETAG, Vauquois developed his own model of intermediary language called "pivot language". Close to Mel'čuk's model, it was a syntactic-semantic model ensuring the independence between analysis and synthesis phases in the translation process.

The French models were also involved with and compared to Chomskyan models. David Hays (1964) worked out his model of "dependency grammar" based on Tesnière's grammar. In his conflict model, Lecerf (1960) put forward the idea of a unique representation by automatically associating a Chomsky graph (phrase structure trees) and Tesnière graph (stemma) to a given sentence (see Chap.6 §6.3). The comparison between the two models led him to distinguish two main tendencies in linguistics: the tendency to work on word strings (most notably Bar-Hillel, Chomsky and Yngve) and the tendency to describe the languages in terms of words, of "dependency" or "hierarchy" of words (Tesnière, Hays). In the second model, intermediary categories between sentence and words, like phrases, for example, are not required.

In order to implement parsers for MT, the CETA members simultaneously relied on Russian models of intermediary languages, American models of syntactic parsers, such as David Hays's dependency grammar and Sydney Lamb's stratificational grammar, formalisms developed by the British such as the lattices worked out by the Cambridge Language Research Unit and finally tree structures coming from Chomskyan grammars. What constituted CETA's originality was the setting up of a writing language for syntactic rules as well as pivot language.

8.7   Hazards of External Reception (3): Statistics and Formal Languages

8.7.1   Information Theory and Statistical Studies of Vocabulary

The formal trend stemming from the logico-mathematical developments of the 1930s–1940s and from the automatisation of language of the 1950s is not the only form of mathematisation of language in the post-World War II period. A second approach originates from the statistical and probabilistic works of the early twentieth century, as modified and strengthened by the appearance of information theory. As we saw in Chap. 5, the application of information theory to the language sciences generated a heterogeneous set of concepts and methods which met various destinies. One can identify two sets of research in that field, just as there were two major conduit agents who contributed to the transfer of methods and concepts from information theory to French linguistics, in particular to statistical studies of vocabulary, traditionally anchored in the French stylistic studies of the 1940s–1950s.

Benoît Mandelbrot (1924–2010) was a frontier runner. He carried out the circulation of theories between France and the USA and therefore contributed to enriching them. Even more so than Schützenberger and Gross, he pursued a Franco-American scientific career in American laboratories at the core of the war sciences. After being trained at the Ecole Polytechnique in France, he spent 2 years (1947–1949) at Caltech (California Institute of Technology) where Weaver had taught in the 1930s; he worked for 1 year (1953–1954) with Von Neumann at the Institute for Advanced Study in Princeton. From 1953 to 1971, he regularly taught at MIT, in other American universities and at the Collège de France.

In 1954 Mandelbrot published an article in the journal *Word* entitled "Structure formelle des textes et communication". It was a mathematical work on the Estoup-Zipf law, reexamining the data within the frame of Shannon's theory. He was concerned by empty forms (lemmes) as opposed to Zipf who was interested in inflected forms (word-forms) whose frequencies would have intrinsic properties. As this view seemed quite questionable to Mandelbrot, he rethought Zipf's law as a theoretical law for organising texts.

Mandelbrot's works drew Chomsky's attention. In his early works, Chomsky rejected any real significance of Zipf's law for grammar, holding in particular that the notion of grammaticality could not be defined through statistical properties[5] (see Leon 2007d). While acknowledging the importance of Mandelbrot's work, he still doubted of the explanatory significance of statistical studies for linguistics. He concluded that the changes made by Mandelbrot, although they brought real theoretical

---

[5] "If we rank the sequences of a given length in order of statistical approximation to English, we will find both grammatical and ungrammatical sequences scattered throughout the list; there appears to be no particular relation between order of approximation and grammaticalness" (Chomsky 1957: 17).

importance to Zipf's works, were not relevant for grammar.[6] It is worth noting that he seemed more favourable to that kind of methods when working with George A. Miller on the distinction between competence and performance in 1963. Competence could be taken into account only through cognitive hypotheses and transformational grammar. On the other hand, performance could be dealt through stochastic and finite-state models (Léon and Riemer 2015).

In France, statistics and probabilities united the interests of both linguists and mathematicians who shared common objects that can be dealt with by statistical methods, such as letters, words and texts, relevant to the French linguistic tradition, dominated in the 1950s by historical linguistics and philology, and that can be dealt with by statistical methods (see Chap. 7). Consequently, statistical methods benefited from a wide interest among linguistic academic institutions where major issues on the relationship between statistics and linguistics were discussed. Among them: (i) Is frequency an intrinsic property of words? (ii) Are word frequencies a property of languages, a property of texts or a property of speech or discourse? (iii) Should statistics be regarded as mere tools or models for language?

Reviews on books and articles on lexical statistics multiplied and crossed each other in the BSL in the 1950s involving mathematicians and stylisticians like Pierre Guiraud – Guiraud reviewed Mandelbrot, and Mandelbrot Guiraud (Mandelbrot 1954b), and Mandelbrot reviewed Herdan – as well as presentations within the SLP. Thus this debate fully contributed to linguistics research in France.

Unlike Zipf and Mandelbrot, Guiraud did not see Zipf's law as a characteristic of the vocabulary of words in texts, but a characteristic of the lexicon of potential words in a language. In other words, frequency is a property of language: "language is essentially a statistical phenomenon; that is to say subjected to constant and digital laws and, as such, open to quantitative definitions and interpretations"[7] (Guiraud 1960, p.16). However, he was severely criticised by mathematicians, namely, Mandelbrot and René Moreau, for his incompetence in mathematics.[8]

The crucial role of Marcel Cohen should be mentioned. Especially within the SLP, he played a major role in spreading new theories concerning vocabulary statistics. He published several reviews of Zipf's works in the BSL as soon as they were published (Cohen 1932, 1950), as well as one of the first French articles on linguistic statistics (Cohen 1949).

The question remains to determine whether vocabulary statistics constituted a real mathematisation of linguistics and whether it produced results. Pêcheux (1969)

---

[6] "The real import of Mandelbrot's work for linguistics seems to be that it shows that rank-frequency distributions of the type that Zipf and others have found are consistent with a very wide class of plausible assumptions about linguistic structure, and consequently, that we learn practically nothing about words when we discover this rank-frequency relation. In other words, this way of looking at linguistic data is apparently not a very fruitful one" (Chomsky 1958: 102).

[7] "le langage est un phénomène essentiellement statistique; c'est-à-dire soumis à des constantes et à des lois numériques et susceptibles, à ce titre, de définitions et d'interprétations quantitatives" (Guiraud 1960, p.16).

[8] On early debates on the statistical studies of vocabulary, see Léon (2017).

considers that these methods conveyed a pre-Saussurian (i.e. pre-scientific) concept, that is, the bi-univocity of the relationship between signifier and signified.

Auroux (2009) qualifies as "superficial mathematisation" (*mathématisation courante*) the quantitative approaches tackling language "on top" by counting observable elements, such as words, and by giving them a property or a number; he contrasted it with "substitutive mathematisation" worked out by formal languages which substitute variables and constants for language.

This debate, which is still vigorous nowadays, would take a new turn in the 1990s with the availability of large computerised corpora which, in France, started with lexicometry, Charles Muller's works, and the setup of the Trésor de la Langue Française at the beginning of the 1960s. In these years, the automatisation of this approach competed with the formal approach in France.

8.7.2   The Naming War and the Boundaries of the Field

Although it was considered marginal by the Chomskyans and researchers on computational linguistics, the field of lexical statistics, deeply anchored in the French tradition and revived by information theory, played a crucial role through the rivalry it had introduced between both approaches, formal and quantitative. This is shown by the multitude of designations naming the field and subfields the Americans have referred to as "computational linguistics".[9]

The Centre Favard explicitly chose the name "séminaire de linguistique quantitative" (quantitative linguistics seminar) in order to avoid dissociating the formal aspects of linguistics from statistical methods. Desclés and Fuchs (1969) discuss the classification put forward by Solomon Marcus during the Séminaire International de Linguistique Formelle that took place in Aiguille in 1968.[10] Among his classes, Marcus distinguished between algebraic linguistics (for instance, Chomsky-Schützenberger's work on monoids), mathematical linguistics (using Markov chains) comprising probabilistic linguistics and quantitative linguistics, automatic, computational and cybernetic linguistics, finally applied linguistics. Marcus did not include within computational linguistics either works on formal grammars or vocabulary statistics. It is the term "formal linguistics" which subsumed the whole set.

Vauquois, who was still in 1969 the director of the CETA and the chairman of the ATALA, curiously grouped generative grammar and statistical studies of vocabulary on one side, and natural language processing and semantic formalisation on the other side. His reasons were probably more political than epistemological. Actually, what his classification reveals, as well as the appearance of the term "linguistique formelle" in France, is the emergence of the Culiolian trend of semantic

---

[9] See Cori and Léon (2002).

[10] This seminar was organised by Antoine Culioli and Daniel Hérault.

formalisation based on enunciation theory in the late 1960s.[11] By promoting natural language processing and semantic formalisation against formal grammar and statistics, Vauquois aimed to ensure that natural language processing would be recognised by the CNRS.

These various classifications do not reflect the distinctions made by computational linguistics as defined in 1962 by the Association for Machine Translation and Computational Linguistics (AMTCL) and the ALPAC report in 1966 (see Chap. 6). Computational linguistics claimed to involve, while distinguishing them explicitly, every theoretical aspect of the interaction between formal languages, linguistics and programming on the one hand, and the practical aspects of language engineering on the other hand. The whole set would be carried out by NLP in the 1970s.

That profusion of terms shows the diversity of the domains involved as well as the complexity of their integration within the field of the language sciences in France. As the first mathematisation was missing, the second computational mathematisation had to cope with particularly heterogeneous and disparate sources: automated devices and non-automated ones, American and Russian methods, formal grammar and statistical studies of vocabulary, theoretical studies and industry-oriented applications. Most of the time they were completely external to the French intellectual tradition and to the horizon of retrospection of French linguistics. That situation would have a significant impact on the second automatisation turn in the 1990s (see Chap. 10).

8.8   Hazards of External Reception (4): Reception, Reflexivity and Double Externality

Concerning historiography and reflexive studies on the mathematisation of language, the situation in France is, here again, very different from the USA. Until the middle of the 1960s, it was Chomsky himself who provided the synthesis of works on formal grammar (see Chomsky and Miller 1963). The task was taken over in the 1980s, once the formal limitations of the transformational model had been acknowledged, by books rehabilitating context-free models in preference to transformational grammars (see among others Savitch et al. 1987). More generally, it was in the journal *Computational Linguistics* that critical articles on the formalisation of linguistics could be found. Formal languages and models of the mathematisation of language were most of the time associated with algorithm studies, programming languages and more generally with computer sciences (Perrault 1984).

In France, for want of proper anchoring and interest in the field, early works on formalisation, at least part of them, turned out to be reflexive from the outset. As we saw, syntactic parsers had been developed from existing models. In parallel, for

---

[11] The examination of this trend, which largely exceeds our study of the reception of computational linguistics, should be undertaken thoroughly.

want of specific courses, a demand for courses and handbooks appeared instantaneously. It is thus not surprising that the textbook introducing formal languages *Notions sur les grammaires formelles* written by Gross and Lentin (1967) was published more than 10 years before its American counterpart *Fundamentals of Mathematics for Linguistics* published in 1978 by Barbara Hall Partee. The former stems from the seminars in quantitative linguistics dedicated to training or more simply informing linguists, while the latter was a course given by the author from 1962 onwards within the frame of a universitary course and evolving every year.

As soon as the late 1960s, as a complement to the ATALA journal, then entitled *TA Informations*, the journal *Mathématiques et Sciences humaines* regularly reviewed the domain (in 1971, 1982 and 1988) with special issues on the theme "Mathematics and Linguistics". In these issues, the authors compared grammatical formalisms and took a critical view towards generative grammar. In the 1980s, they noted certain developments such as the return of logic, the emergence of artificial intelligence and of other models of mathematisation, such as graph theory and topology.

Externality is then assumed by reflexivity. However, even if some forms of institutionalisation took over as, for example, specific courses on NLP, the question remains whether the computational mathematisation really succeeded in being integrated in the language sciences in France.

8.9   Conclusion

In conclusion and to complete the reception of computational linguistics in France, a few words should be said about the reception of formal grammars and, more generally, of American works by the new generation of French linguists.[12]

According to the testimonies collected by Chevalier (2006), the few young linguists who read American works at the beginning of the 1960s worked in isolation and for personal reasons. Within the frame of his PhD, which he defended in 1955, Bernard Pottier read all the American works which were available in *Word* and *Language*. However, he was not a "spreader"; he used his readings for his own work but did not teach them.[13]

Gross and Ruwet read *Syntactic Structures* in the very early years in the 1960s, the former in 1961 before his first stay in the USA, the latter in 1960 when he found it on Lacan's desk. Both acknowledged they understood the text only after becoming familiar with American works, in particular that of Harris. Ruwet read them systematically; Gross worked with Harris directly. In effect, it was Harris's texts

---

[12] For the previous generation, the crucial role played by Knud Togeby in the spreading of American linguistics should be emphasised (see Chap. 9).

[13] However, one can suggest that this thorough knowledge of American works played a significant role, which explains why Pottier was the only French linguist who undertook MT works in the early 1960s.

that allowed them to get into the American linguistic context, which their training and the French and Belgian context made inaccessible. It was only in 1965–1966 that American works, among them works on formal grammars, were spread among linguists systematically – and even to a more general public – well beyond the specialised circles of the ATALA and the Centre Favard. It was also in 1966 that Gross, according to his own testimony, who until then felt as a computer scientist isolated from the linguists he only met at the Centre Favard, began to integrate himself into the French linguistic community. The editorial policy setup in the journal *Langages* (created in 1966) by Jean Dubois, consisting in systematically translating and spreading American works, was an important vector of the integration of formal linguistics, as shown by some of the first issues of the journal edited by Tzvetan Todorov, Oswald Ducrot, Nicolas Ruwet, Maurice Gross and Jean Dubois.

It is worth emphasising that the penetration of American linguistic works in France coincides with the editorial explosion of 1966 qualified by Dosse (1991) as "structural year" ("l'année structurale"), when linguistics dominated as the pilot science and which led to the climax of structuralism in 1967.[14] A lot of conditions thus seemed to be satisfied for the "new linguistics" finally to find its place.

---

[14] 1966 was also the year when an international conference was organised at the University Johns Hopkins which gathered most of the structuralist theoreticians on the theme "Critical Languages and the Sciences of Man".

Chapter 9
Automatic Documentation and Automatic Discourse Analysis: Specificity of Harris's Reception in France

There are two domains of the automation of language in France which should be linked, automatic documentation and automatic discourse analysis (AAD – for Analyse Automatique du Discours – below). One reason for this linking is Harris's reception in France, and more broadly the prestige of structural linguistics in the 1960s. In contrast to machine translation, the French were pioneers in the area of automatic documentation, most notably with Jean-Claude Gardin's works (1925–2013) at the Section d'Automatique Documentaire (SAD) created in 1961 by the CNRS at the Blaise Pascal Institute. The SAD was later directed by Maurice Gross (1934–2001) who succeeded Gardin in 1966. It was there that work was undertaken based on Harris's transformational grammars. Still in the wake of automatic documentation and Harris's reception, Michel Pêcheux (1938–1984) developed Analyse Automatique du Discours.

Finally, it should be noted that a non-automated version of "French discourse analysis", inspired by Harris but without any link with automatic documentation, appeared in the 1960s with Jean Dubois's works (1920–2015).

In this chapter, I will examine the two sides of automation associated with Harris's works, that is, automatic documentation and automatic discourse analysis. More generally, I will study Harris's reception in France and his influence on French discourse analysis.

9.1 Automatic Documentation

9.1.1 History of Documentation Systems

The appearance of early documentation systems can be located at the end of the 1950s, that is, about 10 years after the beginnings of MT. As for MT, the development of automatic documentation needed to keep abreast of the increase of

© The Author(s), under exclusive license to Springer Nature
Switzerland AG 2021
J. Léon, *Automating Linguistics*, History of Computing,
https://doi.org/10.1007/978-3-030-70642-5_9

knowledge and documents during the post-war period. Automatic documentation, including the automatic analysis of documents and information retrieval, had recourse to the same tools as MT, and both domains were often associated with the same publications (see Kent 1961). The problems that needed to be solved were partly the same: homonymy and polysemy, anaphora resolution and analysis of syntactic facts.[1] In the USA, it developed in the wake of early syntactic parsers so that many automatic documentation pioneers were also MT pioneers. It was the case of Victor Yngve, whose programming language COMIT, devised for syntactic parsing and machine translation, was used to program the General Inquirer (Stone et al. 1966).[2] It was also the case of Ida Rhodes's predictive analysis (developed by Oettinger at Harvard) and of Harris's string analysis (Harris 1962a).[3] Harris (1970 [1959]) himself undertook a project of information retrieval. In the ALPAC report (1966) information retrieval is mentioned as a priority that should be developed together with machine-aided translation. Finally, one of the report authors, David G. Hays, worked on syntactic parsers and automatic content analysis simultaneously. In France Maurice Gross abandoned MT for automatic documentation by working on formal languages and Harrissian transformational linguistics. In USSR, tools like intermediary languages based on logic and semantics had been developed for automatic documentation as well as for MT.

On the technological level, the automation of documentation experienced progressive development, from mechanography to electronic computers, whereas MT, implying formal languages, algorithms and programming, needed to use computers from the outset and followed their appearance.[4] Automatic documentation, aiming at classifying documents and fields of knowledge has sources older than MT which emerged only in 1942 with cryptographers. The decimal system of library classification was created by the American Melvil Dewey in 1876 and was complemented by the universal decimal classification of the Belgians Henri La Fontaine and Paul Otlet. It aimed to establish a universal and exhaustive bibliography by classifying the whole set of human knowledge by using complex indexes which are still used nowadays in libraries and documentation centres.

---

[1] These are major linguistic difficulties for natural language processing of texts. Homonymy refers to words which sound alike or are spelled alike, but have different meanings. Polysemy refers to words which have multiple meanings. *Anaphoric pronoun* refers to a pronoun which refers back to another constituent in the sentence.

[2] The General Inquirer is one of the first computerised systems for content analysis.

[3] String analysis is a method of syntactic parsing, intermediary between immediate constituent analysis and transformational analysis. Whereas immediate constituent analysis depends on the order of word concatenation, and whereas transformational analysis breaks down sentences into kernel sentences and operations, string analysis decomposes sentences into kernel sentences (subject verb, subject verb object) and adjuncts (adjectives, etc.) (see Daladier 1990 for more details).

[4] Cros et al. (1964) repeatedly praise the punch cards device called "peek a boo", that is, punch cards "with visual selection" by which holes allow the light pass through thus helping with the selection of certain cards. These cards correspond to the books searched for.

This is not the place here to write the history of the domain.[5] However let us note that the beginnings of the automation of documentation systems were punctuated by conferences which marked the beginning of information processing (Coyaud 1966): the Dorking conference organised in 1957 by the London Classification Research Group; the International Conference on Scientific Information in Washington in 1958; the International Conference for Standards on a Common Language for Machine Searching and translation in Cleveland in 1959 the proceedings of which constitute the state of the art for automatic documentation and machine translation (Kent 1961); and the first congress of AFCALTI (Association Française de Calcul et de Traitement de l'Information) in Grenoble in 1960. For Europe, the EURATOM (Communauté Européenne de l'Energie Atomique), a strategic institution created in Bruxelles in 1957, included the development of the automation of documentation systems among its missions.[6] It organised preparatory training courses for automatic documentation techniques in 1960. It was thanks to a EURATOM contract that Gardin's team developed SYNTOL (Syntagmatic Organisation Language) in 1960–1962 within the frame of the SAD (Section d'Automatique Documentaire) and in collaboration with the 6th section of EPHE (Ecole Pratique des Hautes Etudes).

SYNTOL was one of the earliest and most significant systems developed at the beginning of the 1960s, together with SMART (System for the Mechanical Analysis and Retrieval of Text) designed by Gerard Salton (1927–1995) at Harvard and at Cornell, and the Harvard General Inquirer, which was more oriented towards content analysis (Stone et al. 1966).

9.1.2 SYNTOL

As early as 1955, in one article published in the journal *Diogène*, Jean-Claude Gardin, an archaeologist and logician, analysed the specific problems of documentation in the human sciences.[7] He outlined the methods starting from mechanography dedicated to the systematisation of documentation analysis and classification in archaeology. His aim was to develop rules for inventorying archaeological objects in order to encompass all the characteristics of every considered object, from whatever place and period it came from. These characteristics were translated into an artificial documentary language in order to "provide a way of expressing, by means of a relatively limited set of unambiguous elementary features, a large number of

---

[5] For a prehistory of automatic documentation, see Krajewski (2011). In his book, *Paper Machines, About Cards & Catalogs 1548–1929*, the author explores the history of the card catalog, a long-standing storage technology, that shifted between World War I and World War II from libraries to offices.

[6] It was at CEA (Centre de l'Energie Atomique) that Paul Braffort developed a documentation system in 1955–1956 (Braffort and Jung 1956).

[7] For Gardin's scientific development, see Plutniak (2017).

intricately linked features in the objects to be described and classified, which have vague names or which do not have names in ordinary usage" (Gardin 1959, p. 76).[8]

Gardin conceived of SYNTOL as "a set of rules and procedures pertaining to the recording and retrieval of scientific information" with a double objective: translating a text written in natural language into a standardised language with its own syntax and proceeding with the automatic search of the analysed documents. One of the characteristics of the system was that the expressions that made it possible to represent the content of scientific documents could be reduced to strings of elementary "syntagms", that is, to pairs of keywords Mi, Mj, explicitly linked by a relation Rn. Hence its name "Syntagmatic Organisation Language". However, Gardin denied using "syntagm" in the linguistic sense of the term:

> The use of the word "syntagm" is a liberty we took with regard to its traditional sense in linguistics; this concerns a syntactic unit which is defined not in a natural language, in fact, but in the conventional language that we chose to express and record scientific information, for the purpose of subsequent mechanical searches. (Cros et al. 1964, p. 20)

The omnipresence of linguistic terminology expressed the pervasiveness of structural linguistics in the mid-twentieth century, most notably within documentary languages. Mounin (1963) dedicated several pages to the terms Gardin borrowed from linguistics, while he attempted to show that SYNTOL inherited more from structural semantics than from phonology. It was also Greimas's position.

According to Coyaud (1966), in the courses he gave on structural linguistics in 1963–1964, Greimas emphasised the similarity between the construction of a documentary language and that of a semantic theory. Gardin's borrowings from linguistic terminology are numerous. In 1956, he used the term "distinctive features" which he replaced later by "elementary features" (see quotation above) in order to characterise his documentary language, borrowing the term from Martinet who had just published *Économie des changements phonétiques*. Martinet himself had borrowed the term from Jakobson (see Chap. 5).[9]

SYNTOL was an unequivocal artificial language with its own lexicon and syntax. However, Gardin pointed out (Cros et al. 1964, p. 20) that even if the fact that this syntax exists justifies speaking of a "language", it does not comprise double articulation. It should be noted that he also invoked Harris's transformations in order to justify some normalisations inside his documentary language (ibid, p. 54). As to "documentary lexicons" or codes, these are a set of dictionaries of keywords and thesaurus which Gardin referred to as linguistic tools in his preface to the second edition of SYNTOL in 1968:

> Linguistic tools, which are used in practice for automating information retrieval, remain the same (descriptor lexicon and thesaurus for the control of scientific vocabulary; role indica-

---

[8] "Fournir une manière d'exprimer, par le moyen d'un ensemble relativement limité de traits élémentaires non-ambigus, un très grand nombre de caractères intriqués les uns dans les autres dans les objets à décrire et classer, qui ont des noms très vagues ou qui n'ont pas de noms du tout dans l'usage ordinaire" quoted by Mounin 1964, p.114.

[9] Gardin 1956 p.13 [quoted by Mounin 1964, p.115].

tor and logical relations to express the potential syntactic relationships between descriptors, etc.). (Cros et al. 1968 [1964], p. i)

However, he adds that SYNTOL is not strictly speaking a language immediately defined by its proper lexicon and syntax, but rather a logico-linguistic frame into which most of documentary languages thus defined can fit, at any stage of development and for any field of application.

In fact, the documentary language SYNTOL was an artificial language whose units should be unequivocal and unambiguous – Mounin even relates it to universal languages, notably to Leibniz's *Caracteristica* – as were current documentary languages of the period. In fact, that search for an unequivocal artificial language for representing meaning would lead Gardin to turn to artificial intelligence and expert systems in the 1980s.

9.1.3   SYNTOL and the Unification of Human Sciences

Very early, SYNTOL was applied to several areas of the human sciences. The first experiments were conducted within the frame of the SAD (Section d'Automatique Documentaire). Started in 1963 and supervised by André Martinet, Maurice Coyaud's doctoral dissertation dealt with 3000 documents on psychophysiology, psychology and cultural anthropology (originating from the Bulletin signalétique of the Centre de Documentation du CNRS) and involved machine tests (on an IBM 7090). The second experimentation was conducted by the anthropologist Françoise Lhéritier (then named Françoise Izard) on 5000 abstracts provided by the Centre d'Analyse Documentaire de l'Afrique Noire.

Meanwhile, Gardin had been associated with several projects dealing with documentation lexicons (or codes) specialising in various areas of the social sciences (cartography, ethnography, history, archaeology): in 1959, a code developed by René Labat from the Collège de France which aimed at establishing a systematic inventory of the events related in Akkadian tablets; in 1960, a code on rural sociology was set up on the initiative of the Ecole Pratique des Hautes Etudes; in 1961, a code for the analysis of graphic documents was established for the Laboratoire de Cartographie de l'Ecole Pratique des Hautes Etudes, led by Jacques Bertin; again in 1961, a code for a general bibliography on prehistory for the Centre de Documentation Préhistorique du Musée de l'Homme led by André Leroi-Gourhan; in 1962, a code for ethnographic films was devised by Marie-Salomée Lagrange for the Comité International du Film Ethnographique led by Jean Rouch (Cros et al. 1964).

These codes came in addition to those developed by Paul Braffort at the CEA (Centre d'Energie Atomique), and those concerning the social sciences developed by Robert Pages for social psychology in 1959.

Gardin was then led to lay out the idea of a "basic lexicon" which would be common to all the human and social sciences and could be devised for any of them according to its specific needs while respecting the compatibility of results.

SYNTOL constituted the unificatory frame for those various documentation lexicons. A few years later, Gardin et al. (1981) pursued this aim by proposing "to clarify the concepts underpinning the human sciences, as they appear in practice, by the joint study of symbolic systems, which are the material, and of the series of operations which govern the architecture" (Gardin et al. 1981, p. 5).

9.1.4 Institutionalisation of Automatic Documentation and Formalisation of the Human Sciences

This project, which was of international dimensions, had to be firmly institutionalised. It could be performed only within the frame of a documentation centre. In 1958, Gardin became the director of the Centre d'analyse documentaire pour l'archéologie (CADA) and directed the Section d'Automatique Documentaire (SAD), created in 1960 at the Blaise Pascal Institute, which grouped together the major computer laboratories of the CNRS, including MT centres.

He envisaged that the Maison des Sciences de l'Homme would take part in the project of code harmonising and in linking the specialised centres with the creation of a central library, an office for specialised bibliographic studies and the opening of a computer centre. Even if the documentation centre, the Centre de Documentation pour les Sciences Humaines (CDSH), continued to be entrusted to the CNRS as well as the creation of the Service de Calcul pour les Sciences Humaines (SCSH), Gardin's collaborators obtained the direction of the latter. Thus Monique Renaud, a former collaborator of Gardin at the SAD, became the head of the SCSH in 1976. When it was transformed into the Laboratoire pour les Sciences de l'Homme (LISH) in 1981, Mario Borillo and Jacques Virbel, both former members of the SAD and the CADA, became the heads of the centre.

As to the Centre de mathématique et de calcul (CMAC) created in 1969 at the Maison des Sciences de l'Homme, it was founded and directed by the logician Bernard Jaulin (1934–2010), a friend of Jean-Claude Gardin and a contributor to the book *Archéologie et calculateurs* (Gardin 1970). Gardin and Jaulin (1968) also co-edited the proceedings of the Conference Calcul et formalisation dans les sciences de l'homme which took place in Rome in 1966.

9.2 Harris and Automatic Documentation in France

Harris's works on string grammar and information retrieval from 1959 to 1962 constituted inescapable references in automatic documentation. The General Inquirer (Stone et al. 1966) identified Harris's system as a system based upon linguistics. It shows that distributional analysis can be used in content analysis as a procedure permitting the identification of words and expressions which belong to identical categories. Automatic documentation is one of the main paths of Harris's reception in France. However, that reception took various forms: mere mentions by Gardin, critical analysis by Coyaud and use of Harrissian works in "automatique documentaire" by Maurice Gross.

9.2.1 Documentary Languages and Distributional Analysis

Cros et al. (1964) cite Harris several times. Besides the use of the term "transformation" to account for certain normalisations, Gardin mentions Harris's string analysis which makes possible the automatic recognition of sentence structure as a preliminary to information retrieval strictly speaking (Cros et al. 1964: note 1 p. 32).

In his doctoral dissertation on documentary languages, Coyaud (1966) classified them into several categories: documentary languages based on logico-mathematics such as some models developed for geometry and chemistry; languages including syntactic relations, such as those by Braffort, Pagès as well as Gardin's SYNTOL; some other languages can be regarded as purely linguistic-based, such as those by Yngve and Harris. Coyaud knew Harris's works well.[10] For his PhD, he worked with Naomi Sager, one of Harris's close collaborators, on the transformational grammatical analysis of two sentences extracted from a psychophysiology corpus which would be used as the input for a SYNTOL analysis. Coyaud (1966) devoted twelve pages to Z. S. Harris's project. The application of his theory of transformations should allow information retrieval since, according to Harris, a sentence carries the same information as its transformed form. For Coyaud, linguistic-based systems like Harris's one present several advantages: no need for abstracts, classifications and indexations; no loss of information; updating the system is easier (no need to reclassify); no limitation of the scope of questions in/within/inside the part dedicated to information retrieval.

However, he criticised Harris's system on several points. String analysis does not provide for the resolution of inter-sentence anaphora or for the treatment of compound words – for example, "thyroid gland" constitutes a single word for a documentation system. It is difficult to justify undertaking the operations of analysis and information retrieval exclusively in natural language and with the sole help of grammatical analysis (see the criticism of the application of string analysis to the analysis of documents in Climenson et al. 1961).

From the documentation point of view, string analysis and distributional criteria should make it possible to identify the "centre" of an utterance as a kernel sentence, which is a potential candidate for the indexation of documents. However, for Coyaud, it is difficult to prove that the content of an utterance can be assimilated to its "centre"; a systematic concordance does not exist between central sentences (i.e.

---

[10] After having worked on documentation languages, Coyaud entirely focused on the study of East Asian languages in which he became a specialist.

kernel sentences used to index documents on the formal level) and "central" sentences from the semantic point of view (that from its informational value). In fact, Harris himself would consider later that this way of characterising the informational value of utterances is too rough: transformational analysis does not produce any hierarchy between kernels on the informative level while, on the documentation level, it is necessary to distinguish between significant and insignificant kernels. In fact, it was on the analysis of information that Harris would focus more systematically from the 1980s onwards (Léon 2011a).

9.2.2   Maurice Gross: Harris's "Documentation" Inheritance

We have seen (see Chap. 8) that Maurice Gross played the role of a frontier runner for language automation. He was a pioneer both in MT and automatic documentation. Appointed to the CNRS from 1963 to 1967, at the mechanics section of the Laboratory of Digital Calculus at the Blaise Pascal Institute, he worked under Marcel-Paul Schützenberger's direction on automata theory, formal languages and the syntactic analysis of French. During that period, he spent a year and a half at the University of Pennsylvania in order to work with Harris. He was appointed director of the Section d'Automatique Documentaire in 1966 which he swapped in 1970 for the Laboratoire d'Automatique Documentaire et Linguistique.[11] What interested Gross was neither Gardin's artificial documentary languages nor Harris's information works developed at the end of his life. Gross implemented a specific approach to NLP based on morpho-syntax as early as his first works on MT and his research at the Blaise Pascal Institute. It should be said however that even if the ultimate aim was information retrieval from texts (Harris's information retrieval), it was not the priority. For the purpose of the automatic treatment of texts, an exhaustive description of languages, French in that case, had to be done by classifying the analyses and by storing them in electronic dictionaries. At the beginning, Gross devoted himself to the syntactic analysis of verbal structures by means of Harris's distributional and transformational analysis. This would be the subject of his PhD, which he defended in 1967 at the Faculté des Lettres of Paris, "L'Analyse formelle comparée des complétives en français et en anglais", which led to the publication of the book *La Grammaire transformationnelle du français. Syntaxe du verbe* in 1968. As Fuchs points out in her book on paraphrase:

Gross's aim "is not to seek to define paraphrase relation (the judgement of identity of meaning being considered the baseline given by intuition), but to extend it empirically to new areas at the boarders of syntax and lexis, by attempting to

---

[11] See Maurice Gross's career file CNRS 910024 DPC, archives CNRS.

conduct lexically exhaustive surveys of pairs of structures in paraphrastic relation" (Fuchs 1982 p. 132).[12]

Until his death in 2001, Maurice Gross and his LADL team would aim at continuing those descriptions, ensuring their computational storing through "lexiques-grammaires" (syntactic data bases) and electronic dictionaries, and the implementation of automata dedicated to providing a syntactic analysis prior to information retrieval (Courtois and Silberztein 1990).

9.3   Automatic Discourse Analysis

With automatic discourse analysis (Analyse automatique du discours – AAD) developed by Michel Pêcheux (1938–1983) and his team, we are in the presence of two successive stages of Harris's reception in France: the documentation stage, the main outlines of which have been traced in the previous section, and the implementation of paraphrase as the cornerstone of discursive construction.[13]

9.3.1   Social Psychology, Content Analysis and Documentation Systems

It can be assumed that AAD was developed by Michel Pêcheux as a documentation machine to compete with existing systems, especially SYNTOL which was well established in the formalisation of several human sciences at that time. Social psychology, chosen by Michel Pêcheux as a field of application for his researches on the history of science and the theory of ideology, was one of the human sciences where the automation of documentation and content analysis was the most advanced.[14] It was in social psychology that the General Inquirer developed one of its early thesauruses (the Harvard 3rd *Psychosociological Dictionary*). According to Cartwright (quoted by Pêcheux), it was the proper object of social psychology which required the use of that type of method:

---

[12] "L'objectif de Gross "n'est pas de chercher à définir la relation de paraphrase (le jugement d'identité de sens étant considéré comme une donnée de base livrée par l'intuition), mais de l'étendre empiriquement à de nouveaux domaines aux frontières de la syntaxe et du lexique, en cherchant à faire des relevés lexicalement exhaustifs des paires de structures en relation paraphrastique" (Fuchs 1982 p. 132).

[13] Voir Léon (2010a).

[14] Documentary analysis and content analysis should be distinguished. According to Gardin, documentary analysis, unlike content analysis, transforms the text. "However, documentary analysis always keeps a part of sentence structures at least – by expressing certain logical relations between significant units — while often content analysis is limited to a mere juxtaposition of 'key-words' without any syntactic link" (Gardin 1962, p.88). It should be noted that what Pêcheux criticised in both methods is a priori semantic categorisation.

The proper object of social psychology can be reduced, to a large extent, to verbal manifestations and other symbolic behaviors such as they appear in society [...] The systematic description of these phenomena by psychologists and sociologists involves that these symbolic acts had been observed and registered methodically by classifying and categorizing them, as by calculating their frequencies and determining their interrelations [...] The classification and categorization task is generally named 'content analysis' or 'coding'. (Cartwright 1963, p. 482–3)[15]

The Laboratory of Social Psychology of the Faculty of Arts and Social Sciences of the University of Paris, founded in 1952 by Daniel Lagache, can be counted among the pioneers in the area of documentation. It comprised a documentation centre and his researchers very early developed methods and a documentary language for human sciences (Pagès 1959, Bouillut 1967). These authors are quoted by Cros et al. (1964) several times for their major advances in the area of classification in social psychology. The Laboratory of Social Psychology also pioneered in the technological level and was one of the first to use "Peek-a-boo" punch cards. Consequently, Michel Pêcheux, together with his activities as a philosopher within Marxist and Althusserian reflection groups,[16] decided to develop epistemological reflection on social psychology, once he was appointed as a junior researcher at the CNRS in 1966.[17] It should be said that Pêcheux pointed out that he owed to Jean Bouillut the principle of the comparison between binary relations, strings formation and grouping into equivalence classes (Pêcheux 1968, p. 117).[18] Jean Bouillut had been recruited in the Laboratory of Social Psychology to develop a documentary language inspired by SYNTOL for social psychology. Thus, certain parts of AAD procedures were borrowed from SYNTOL: in particular, the representation of a sentence by a graph of binary relations was very close to SYNTOL strings of elementary syntagms, that is, (see Sect. 9.1.2 above) graphs of keyword pairs Mi, Mj, linked by a relation Rn. AAD automatic procedure involved two stages, once the

---

[15] L'objet même de la psychologie sociale se ramène, dans une large mesure, à des manifestations verbales et d'autres comportements symboliques tels qu'ils apparaissent dans la société [...] La description systématique de ces phénomènes par les psychologues et les sociologues suppose qu'on ait observé et consigné ces actes symboliques avec méthode en les classant et en les catégorisant, comme en calculant leurs fréquences et en déterminant leurs interrelations [...] Le travail de classement ou de catégorisation est, en général, désigné sous le nom d'"analyse du contenu" ou de "codage" (Cartwright 1963, p. 482–3).

[16] Althusser's followers, as philosophers, were encouraged to make an entry into human sciences in order to transform them according to their own view on the epistemology of sciences. In a totally different perspective, for Desanti's followers, the aim for philosophers was to be trained and to work in various human sciences (I am grateful to Sylvain Auroux for this information).

[17] It was in psychology journals that Michel Pêcheux published his early works: he was a member of the editorial board of *Psychologie Française*, the journal of the Société française de psychologie, where he published one of his first texts on AAD (Pêcheux 1968). He also published in the *Bulletin d'Etudes et Recherches Psychologiques* (below CERP) (Pêcheux 1967a). Finally, AAD would be published in 1969 by Dunod, in the series *Behavior Sciences* directed by two psychologists F. Bresson and M. de Montmollin (Pêcheux 1969).

[18] In the mimeo version of his doctoral dissertation (1967b), Pêcheux had reserved thirty pages (pages 58 à 88) for Jean Bouillut to explain the method used in AAD.

corpus had been constituted: (1) the coding of the sentences of the corpus into "elementary utterances" (a series of morpho-syntactic categories) linked by dependence operators (each pair of elementary utterances forms a "binary relation". Each surface sentence is represented by a graph of binary relations) and (2) the constitution of equivalence classes (semantic domains) from the comparison of lexicon within an identical environment (strings of elementary utterances and dependence operators).

Let us take the simplified examples extracted from Léon and Torres-Lima (1979, p. 30). The sentence: "Les pays occidentaux et ceux du Tiers-Monde risquent de manquer de matières premières" [occidental countries and those from Third World may run out of raw materials] is coded in elementary utterances and in binary relations in the following way:

List of elementary utterances (Fig. 9.1).

List of binary relations (which can also be represented by a graph) with the following connectors: 06 = infinitive; 91, 92 = N1 determination; 40 = coordination

01 06 02
01 92 03
01 91 04
02 91 03
02 91 04
03 40 04

Here is an example of equivalence classes (semantic domains) obtained by the comparison of the lexicon within an identical environment (extracted from Léon and Torres-Lima 1979, p.38). See Fig. 9.2.

Nr	D1	N1	V	ADV	PP	D2	N2
01	LS	pays	risquer	ø	ø	ø	ø
02	R	pays	manquer	ø	de	ø	matieresprem
03	R	pays	E	ø	ø	ø	occidental
04	R	pays	E	ø	de	le	Tiers Monde

Fig. 9.1 AAD elementary utterances (Léon and Torres-Lima 1979)

En1	N1	V	PP	ADV	N2	Co	En2	N1	V	PP	ADV	N2
172	programme	E	à	ø	intellectuel	40	173	programme	E	à	ø	culturel
481	épanouissement	E	à	ø	intellectuel	40	482	épanouissement	E	à	ø	culturel
519	développement	E	à	ø	intellectuel	40	520	développement	E	à	ø	culturel
818	développement	E	à	ø	intellectuel	40	819	développement	E	à	ø	culturel
689	épanouissement	E	à	ø	culturel	40	690	épanouissement	E	à	ø	intellectuel
549	développement	E	à	ø	intellectuel	91	550	développement	E	à	ø	meilleur
519	développement	E	à	ø	intellectuel	91	521	développement	E	de	ø	l'homme
589	potentiel	E	à	ø	intellectuel	91	590	potentiel	E	de	ø	l'homme
588	potentiel	E	à	ø	culturel	40	589	ordre	E	à	ø	intellectuel
936	ordre	E	à	ø	culturel	40	937	ordre	E	à	ø	intellectuel
383	niveau	E	à	ø	culturel	40	384	niveau	E	à	ø	intellectuel

Fig. 9.2 AAD semantic domains (From Léon and Torres-Lima 1979)

9.3.2   *The Criticism of SYNTOL*

Gardin's projects particularly interested Michel Pêcheux and Paul Henry, a mathematician close to Pêcheux and Althusser, and a researcher at the Laboratoire Européen de Psychologie Sociale led by Serge Moscovici (1925–2014). They most particularly criticised the reduction of natural language synonymy and polysemy when translated into documentary languages. In those languages, terms have an equivocal and consensual meaning for a given disciplinary field. SYNTOL comprises a system of cross-referencing between words, a sort of semantic network which structures information unequivocally.

In a special issue of the 1967 Bulletin du CERP, entirely devoted to content analysis and documentary systems, Paul Henry criticises SYNTOL while admitting the need for a necessary limited language of science involving invariants and logical links. Moreover, he acknowledges the interest of SYNTOL for making explicit the requirements needed by formalisation which compelled researchers to do more rigorous and systematic analysis. However, Henry criticises the analyst's subjective interventions at several key stages of the procedure in the absence of any control and any rule. He also shows that the analysis made by SYNTOL fragments the texts and destroys the logic of the classification proposed by the subject, however legitimate and natural, by keeping no trace of shifts of meaning.

Pêcheux devoted the beginning of his article (Pêcheux 1967a) to an epistemological issue, the constitution of codes institutionally determined for sciences. He questions "the technological analysis aimed at establishing the identifying of all the distinctive features needed to describe objects […] It is because an institutionally-guaranteed discourse on the object already exists that the analyst can rationalize the system of semantic features which characterizes that object […] the analysis system will then have the theoretical age (the level of development) of the institution which norms it […]" (Pêcheux 1967a, p. 216).[19] To that norm guaranteed a priori by the institution, Pêcheux contrasts taking into account the processes of production of texts which are the only ones likely to determine meaning. These are the processes which should be theorised:

> Any semiological system [represented by an empirically-given discourse] should be referred to the places from where the corresponding discourses can be respectively uttered and heard, which involves a psycho- sociological understanding of the conditions of communication, bringing to light the system of the potential places. (Pêcheux 1967a, p. 219–220)[20]

---

[19] "L'analyse technologique destinée à établir le recensement de tous les traits distinctifs nécessaires à la description des objets […] C'est donc parce qu'il existe déjà un discours institutionnellement garanti sur l'objet que l'analyste peut rationaliser le système de traits sémantiques qui caractérisent cet objet […] le système d'analyse aura donc l'âge théorique (le niveau de développement) de l'institution qui le norme […]" (Pêcheux 1967a, p. 216).

[20] "Tout système sémiologique [représenté par un discours empiriquement donné] doit être référé aux places d'où les discours correspondants peuvent être respectivement prononcés et entendus, ce

Starting from Saussurean concepts he developed extensively, Pêcheux adopted, in opposition to the practice of content analysis in the human sciences, a non-reductionist conception of language and a constructivist and structuralist stand on meaning. He would systematise his criticism in an article in 1968 (Pêcheux 1968) showing the implicit hypotheses at work in the various practices of content analysis, among them automatic documentation systems such as SYNTOL, which postulate a priori equivalence classes. To these hypotheses, he opposed counter hypotheses in order to found "discourse analysis technics" where equivalence classes had not been given a priori but were produced as results: after assessing the semantic comparability of two configurations, strings of semantic resemblance were formed which were likely to be grouped into equivalence classes, that is, semantic domains. It can be said that, in 1968, AAD procedures were developed as a system of discourse analysis and as an alternative to systems of documentary analysis. From its publication in 1969 (Pêcheux 1969), it became a system of discourse analysis only and was called AAD69.[21]

9.4 Harris's *Discourse Analysis* and French Discourse Analysis

9.4.1 Paraphrase: The Second Stage of Analyse Automatique du Discours

As it was developed as a documentation system outside of linguistics, the initial version of the AAD system may explain the little importance given to Harris. Harris is only mentioned once concerning a minor transformation (the addition of a copula in the case of epithet adjectives) although the representation of elementary utterances as kernel sentences and the equivalence classes method and even the name of "analyse du discours" were owed to him. Such a method made it possible to provide the conditions of interpretation of discourse without using meaning a priori as did documentary systems. In fact, even if Pêcheux adopts the idea of equivalence classes to "generate" discourses, defined as semiological systems, he criticised "taxonomy" as thought out by Harris for whom equivalence classes are stable throughout the discourse, which did not make it possible to account for the "forms of discourse progress". Moreover, Pêcheux proposes an outline of discourse typology where "the presentative form (report, narrative, story, legend)" would be opposed to "the

---

qui suppose une saisie psychosociologique des conditions de communication, mettant en évidence le système des places possibles" (Pêcheux 1967a, p. 219–220).

[21] One should mention the irreducible hostility opposing Gardin and Pêcheux's teams. Among the most vehement criticisms of AAD69 can be found those by Gardin's followers, Mario Borillo and Jacques Virbel. Gardin does not mention either Pêcheux or AAD69 (or Dubois's work either) in his book *Les analyses de discours* published in 1974 (Gardin 1974).

demonstrative form (evidence, justification, argumentation)" (1967a, p. 221). His criticism of Harris for whom a discourse was formed by only one text was not yet on the agenda.[22]

Later, Pêcheux made amends several times by acknowledging the debt he owed to Harris. In particular, within the frame of the major changes in AAD presented in *Langages* 37 (1975), he discussed key aspects of Harris's theory which were missing in AAD69 because they did not represent any issue at that time: the notion of paraphrase and the related questions of identity and synonymy, and the opposition to Harris's view of a corpus reduced to a single text. When AAD69 was developed, linguistics did not belong to Pêcheux's horizon of retrospection. It became part of it in 1975.

9.4.2   The Third Pathway of Harris's Reception in France: From Togeby to Jean Dubois

Even if Jean Dubois's works on discourse analysis had not been thought out as computerised procedures, at least at the beginning, they constitute the third pathway of Harris's reception in France. It should be said that the different trends of discourse analysis were not completely distinct. Jean Dubois worked with the LADL led by Maurice Gross (see the issue of the journal *Linx* 34–35 1996); some of his followers, namely, Denise Maldidier and Jacques Guilhaumou, had been part of the team "Analyse du Discours et Lectures d'Archive", created by Pêcheux in 1982. Finally, both trends, Pêcheux's and Dubois's, had been identified as forming "French discourse analysis", although they originate from distinct and sometimes opposite sources, such as the link between discourse analysis and sociolinguistics advocated by Marcellesi and Guespin (Dubois's followers).

The term "French discourse analysis" was forged by Guespin (1971, p. 15) in his presentation of the issue of the journal *Langages* devoted to political discourse. For him, this term encompasses the works of Pêcheux and that of Dubois and his followers (Maldidier, Marcellesi and Guespin) under the triple mentoring of the "American School" (Harris), the "European School" (Jakobson, Benveniste) and content analysis (including Gardin's documentary analysis), which the notions of "condition of production" and "condition of production process" come from.[23]

---

[22] Moreover, the examples put forward by Pêcheux in AAD69, that is, excerpts from *Alice in Wonderland* and from Joan of Arc's life, looked strangely similar to the type of examples used by Harris, such as the fable The Very Proper Gander, which he submitted to his own discourse analysis method.

[23] In the issue 140 of *Langage et Société*, published in June 2012 and entitled "Analyse du discours à la française", a strange title, the editors underline the heterogeneity of references and trends by stressing the predominance of sociolinguistics in both trends (Dufour & Rosier 2012). This is quite strange because this aspect was strongly criticised by Pêcheux.

La structure immanente de la langue française **(1951) by Knud Togeby: the introduction of American structural linguistics in France.** The crucial role of Knud Togeby's book *Structure immanente de la langue française* should be emphasised. It was published in French in 1951 in *Les cahiers de linguistique de Copenhague*.[24] Togeby was one of Hjelmslev's followers, and his starting point, the Saussurean immanence principle, implied the rejection of meaning in linguistics. His book, establishing a typology of the different structuralist methods, European and American, experienced a real success in France when it was published. It was reviewed in many journals, mainly French journals,[25] and was republished by Claude and Jean Dubois with Larousse in 1965.

Togeby was the author of one of the first reviews of Harris's *Methods in Structural Linguistics* published in 1951,[26] and he knew Harris's works well. In *Structure immanente*, he devoted several pages to Harris and underlined his crucial role in distributional analysis. Before Togeby's review, there were only a few references to Harris and a few scattered reviews in French linguistic works which, clearly, had not grasped the issues of his work (see Chap. 8). One can say that Togeby is really the one who introduced American structural linguistics in France. Works by American linguists were translated into French only at the end of the 1960s. It was Maurice Gross who translated the first article by Harris "From Morpheme to Utterance", published in a French journal – the special issue of *Langages* dedicated to models in linguistics, published in 1968. It was followed by the article "Discourse Analysis" (1952) translated by Françoise Dubois-Charlier in a 1969 issue of *Langue Française*; Harris's 1968 book, *Mathematical Structures of Language*, was translated in 1971 by Catherine Fuchs; finally, "The Two Systems of Grammar: Report and Paraphrase" was translated in an issue of *Langages* edited by Danielle Leeman in 1973.

Jean Dubois and the lexicological trend of French discourse analysis. Dubois cited Togeby[27] and Harris's *Methods in Structural Linguistics* in his thesis dissertation *Histoire du mouvement ouvrier et vocabulaire politique* published in 1962, and he was probably the first linguist to use Harris's distributional method. In his dissertation, Dubois distinguished himself from the works on lexicology and stylistics of the period by starting work on structural linguistics for which the unequivocity between signifier and signified was not taken for granted.[28] He addressed complex nominal groups as semantic units having specific discursive functions for a given

---

[24] I would like to thank Jean-Claude Chevalier who drew my attention to the importance of Togeby in Harris's reception in France and his influence on Dubois's works.

[25] For the 1951 edition, nine reviews were published in the following journals: *Journal de Psychologie normale et pathologique*, *BSL*, *Language*, *Word*, etc. Martinet, Pottier, Wagner, etc. were among the authors. For the 1965 edition, Bonnard, Prebensen and Arrivé, respectively, wrote reviews in the *Journal de Psychologie normale et pathologique*, *Langue française* and *Langage*.

[26] See *Modern Language Notes* 68.19–194 (1954).

[27] We saw that Larousse republished *Structure immanente* in 1965.

[28] See also Jean Dubois 1960, "Les notions d'unité sémantique complexe et de neutralisation dans le lexique", *Cahiers de lexicologie*, vol. 2, p.62–66.

Affranchissement	Du prolétaire Du prolétariat Des travailleurs	Avènement politique	De la classe ouvrière Des travailleurs
Emancipation	Des masses Du prolétariat De la classe ouvrière Des travailleurs	Aspirations	Des classes ouvrières Du prolétariat Du peuple Ouvrières
Avènement	De la classe ouvrière Du prolétariat Des travailleurs	Amélioration du sort	Des travailleurs Des conditions des classes ouvrières
		Cause	Des travailleurs Des masses Du peuple

Fig. 9.3 Dubois' equivalence classes (1962)

discourse. With the help of equivalence classes, he established semantic units, which enabled him to study the social vocabulary of the given period discursively:
Especially see the table (Fig. 9.3) in his thesis (p.186).

As Chauveau (1971) and Guespin (1971) pointed out, the sources of Dubois's discourse analysis are multiple, namely, Harris's distributional method as well as Jakobson's and Benveniste's enunciation theories. Chauveau justified the recourse to enunciation theories by Europeans because of the differences of status and treatment between sentence and discourse. In the European tradition, the limits imposed on the sentence are of a theoretical order because the difference between the sentence and discourse beyond the sentence is qualitative: in sentences "langue" (a system of signs) is at work; beyond sentences, "parole" and discourse are at work and analysis procedures are not identical. These procedures pertain to Enunciation Theory.

There was no such distinction in the American tradition where utterance, defined in Behaviourist terms, was considered to obviously pertain to linguistics, whatever its length. It was describable by procedures which were similar at any level (Chauveau 1971, p. 12).[29]

In his article published in the *Cahiers de Lexicologie*, Dubois (1969b) claimed that the lexicologist's ambition is above all to develop a science of utterance. His aim was lexicological, and the starting point was the analysis of vocabulary which should be included as a part of discourse analysis. Consequently, for Dubois, discourse analysis needed a typology of discourses determining the relations between enunciation and "enunciated" (utterance); especially, he made a distinction between polemical discourses and didactic discourses. On the methodological level, Dubois adopted Harris's method, that is, distributional analysis, accompanied by transformational manipulations leading to the constitution of equivalence classes. Transformational manipulations aimed at classifying passives and actives as well as noun complements and adjectives in the same equivalence classes. In the same way,

---

[29] "Rien de tel dans la tradition américaine où l'énoncé, présenté dans les termes du behaviorisme, est considéré, quelle que soit sa longueur, comme relevant en droit de la linguistique, et descriptible selon des procédures similaires à tous les niveaux" (Chauveau 1971, p. 12).

complex sentences were transformed into two-argument clauses. The analysis consisted in studying the distribution of cooccurrent words in the same types of clauses, as, for example, the term "student" in May 68 texts. These linguistic operations once performed, linguistic models (models of the analysis of utterances on the basis of lexical clauses and discourse models) and sociological models, defined as ideological structures, can be matched:

> When, with lexical analysis, one chooses a certain number of terms in a corpus, one claims at the same time that the clauses gathered around these terms are representative of the corpus and make it possible to establish a relation with the ideological model of the author. (Dubois 1969b, p. 117)[30]

9.4.3 Discourse Analysis *as a Founding Text*

To conclude this section dedicated to Harris's reception in French discourse analysis, it is worth noting that both trends of discourse analysis claim as a founding text Harris's *Discourse analysis* (1952) is. As Marandin stated, citing Harris:

> French discourse analysis refers to discourse analysis as a foundational text. Indeed, it defines a research area: 'The continuation of descriptive linguistics beyond the limits of a single sentence at a time', 'the correlation between culture and language (i.e. non-linguistic and linguistic behavior)' [Harris 1970 [1952]: 314]. (Marandin 1979 p. 19)[31]

Beyond Guespin's attempt to gather under the same term the different French trends, which may seem hazardous, the idea of the homogeneity of discourse analysis in general is far from unanimous. For Chauveau (1971), European views and American views were incompatible, which is shown by the recourse to the specific treatment of discourse by enunciation theory in France. Moreover, it can be shown that the text which inspired Pêcheux's AAD on the one hand, and Dubois lexicodiscursive studies (1960 et 1962) on the other hand, was *Methods in Structural Linguistics* and not *Discourse Analysis*.

In his early articles, Pêcheux does not refer to *Discourse Analysis* but to *Discourse Analysis Reprints* published in 1963 (Harris 1963) which were described by Harris as reprints of 1957 working papers not claiming to represent the latest development of the discourse analysis method.

In his 1969 text (Dubois 1969b), although he quotes *Discourse Analysis* – which he had just helped to disseminate in French – Dubois uses the method and not the

---

[30] "Lorsque, par analyse lexicale, on choisit dans ce corpus un certain nombre de vocables, on émet du même coup l'hypothèse que les propositions réunies autour de ces termes sont représentatives du corpus et permettent d'établir une relation avec le modèle idéologique de l'auteur" (Dubois 1969b, p. 117).

[31] "L'analyse du discours française se réfère à *Discourse Analysis* comme à un texte fondateur. Il définit, en effet, un champ de recherche: "le prolongement de la linguistique "descriptive au-delà des limites d'une seule phrase à la fois", "les rapports entre la "culture" "et la langue" et la relation entre ces deux séries de faits [Harris 1969 [1952], p. 9]" (Marandin 1979 p. 19).

theoretical frame. In fact, his paper does not include any presentation of Harris's approach or theoretical aims. His position involves integrating Harris's method into his own views. In the 1971 issues of *Langages* and *Langue Française*, his followers mention Harris only sporadically. Harris's method is often promoted through Dubois's structural grammar (1965, 1967, 1969a). However, this method was not used on its own: it was associated with Dubois's lexicological method and with an enunciative frame inspired by Jakobson and Benveniste. As to transformations, they were referred to Chomsky, more cited than Harris in Dubois's bibliography.

In other words, within Pêcheux's trend, the attempt to found French discourse analysis on Harris's discourse analysis seems to have been created in retrospect. It is worth noting that Pêcheux himself erected *Discourse analysis* as a founding text, in a reflexive movement at the very time he abandoned AAD69 officially:[32]

The reworking of AAD69 is an attempt to [...] take 'modern linguistics' seriously, in particular the work of an American linguist, author of a text providentially entitled *Discourse analysis* and used as a scientific reference for linguists working in the area of discourse analysis in the wake of Jean Dubois. [...] From this point of view, the specificity of AAD version 69, was to drive Harrissian linguistics to its ultimate consequences [...]. (Pêcheux et al. 1982, p.97)[33]

In this excerpt, Pêcheux, by endorsing *Discourse analysis* as a founding text, made two moves: (1) he placed his own work in the wake of Jean Dubois's ones, thus acquiring a linguistic legitimacy which he lacked until then; (2) he conferred a scientific status on Harris's work, whose hypotheses and consequences should be tested. This double move allowed him to abandon AAD69, to legitimise it in retrospect, and establish discourse analysis in the field of linguistics.[34]

---

[32] The official abandonment of AAD69 in 1982 (Pêcheux et al. 1982) brought syntax back to the centre of Discourse Analysis. The main hypothesis was that no manipulation of linguistic expressions was possible without taking into account their syntactic structure. However, it was considered that questioning the autonomy of syntax in discursive structures implies that other dimensions such as enunciation, lexis and sequence are taken into account. Thus, sequence and intra-discourse phenomena and their apprehension through "syntagmatic algorithms" had been legitimised in the same way as the dimension of utterance, a traditional one for AAD, was apprehended by "paradigmatic algorithms".

[33] "La mise au point de l'AAD69 constitue une tentative, parmi d'autres, de réaliser ce programme, en s'efforçant de prendre au sérieux 'la linguistique moderne', et en particulier les travaux d'un linguiste américain, auteur d'un texte providentiellement intitulé *Discourse Analysis* qui servit pendant toute une période de référence scientifique concrète aux linguistes travaillant dans le champ de l'analyse de discours, sur la lancée des travaux de Jean Dubois. [...] De ce point de vue, la spécificité de l'AAD version 69, dans l'espace des travaux d'analyse du discours, ce fut d'abord me semble-t-il, de pousser la linguistique harrissienne jusqu'au bout de ses conséquences [...]" (Pêcheux et al. 1982, p.97).

[34] Although it raises much more complex issues, Puech's analysis of Saussure's *Cours de linguistique générale* as a founding text can be used as a comparison (see Puech 2008). This construction made in retrospect, at the very moment when an entire part of the theory was abandoned, was used to legitimise what had been in the name of what would be.

9.5 Conclusion

Coming back to Harrissian legacy, it should be noted that from 1965, Harris had no longer published articles in *Language* (Matthews 1999) and hardly anything in the USA.[35] As other Neo-Bloomfieldian works, his works had been overshadowed by the rise of the Chomskyan trend in the 1960s. If, nevertheless, the Harrissian trend has survived, that was thanks to Harris's reception outside the USA, mainly in the area of NLP.

In France, as we saw, works on discourse analysis, documentation analysis, computerised dictionaries and string analysis all referred to Harris. In Canada, works on sublanguages, namely, the machine translation project TAUM-Météo developed in 1975 by John Chandioux (Chandioux and Guéraud 1981), and continued in the 1980s (Kittredge and Lehrberger 1982), were directly derived from Harris's works. However, the debate on Harris's legacy is not yet closed and positions are contradictory. In his biography of Harris, Barsky (2011) doubts the significance of Harris's works nowadays, his legacy and his importance in the history of linguistics.[36] Nevin's book (2002), on the contrary, gives arguments for a legacy of NLP approaches originating from Harris's computable theory of language. This position, as well as the whole book, was severely criticised by Anne Daladier (2003) in her review in the BSL. So many considerations showing that Harris's legacy and his impact on the language sciences still remains a largely open debate.

---

[35] In his biography of Harris, Barsky (2011) notes that when Harris passed away in 1992, some American linguists had even forgotten he was alive and thought he had already been dead for a long time.

[36] It should be noted that Barsky is Chomsky's biographer and was encouraged by him to undertake a biography of Harris. There is no doubt that his aim was to present him more as a Zionist activist, admired by Chomsky, than as an outstanding linguist (see Léon 2013b).

Chapter 10
The Empiricist Turn of Automation-Mathematisation: Large Corpora, Restricted Languages and Sublanguages

With large corpora, one can identify a second turn in the automation-mathematisation of linguistics in the early 1990s. This turn can be characterised by the following points:

1. Contrary to the emergence of MT and of computational linguistics in the 1960s, there is no discontinuity in a break in the horizon of retrospection.
2. The turn refers more to automation than to mathematisation. Methods, of statistical and probabilistic nature, are in the continuation of the methods from information theory outlined in the 1950s–1960s. The only innovation, definitely a crucial one, is that they become applicable to large amounts of data. At the present time, the development of mixed methods for Natural Language Processing, both probabilistic and computational, shows that there is no discontinuity on the level of mathematisation. Besides, some probabilistic corpus studies were developed within the framework of connectionism, reconnecting with first cybernetics (see Chap. 6, §6.5). This is the case of dynamic models for the study of polysemy (Fuchs and Victorri 1996).
3. What constitutes the main development for linguistics is the automation of data introducing drastic changes in linguists' practices. That is why, what is presently called "corpus linguistics" – called "Linguistiques de corpus" (in the plural) in French – refers to very diverse fields in linguistics (Habert et al. 1997). Objectives, methods and even definitions of "corpus" are diverse. It is very rare that linguists, whatever their theoretical obedience, dispense with the possibilities offered by large corpora.

It is worth noting that the emergence of large corpora was brought about through drastic technological changes, the appearance of micro-computers and generalised use of the Internet, which have modified the linguists's practical approaches towards data. Here again, it is a real renewal of empiricism in linguistics. However, this upheaval, which impacts many other domains of knowledge and society in general,

© The Author(s), under exclusive license to Springer Nature Switzerland AG 2021
J. Léon, *Automating Linguistics*, History of Computing,
https://doi.org/10.1007/978-3-030-70642-5_10

does not justify that some linguists, such as Leech (1992), calling it a new discipline, "a new linguistics" and this for legitimisation purposes.

In this chapter, three points will be examined: the British sources of corpus linguistics; the debates between the Chomskyans and the British empiricists on the use of corpora; and the new linguistic objects which appeared at the crossroads of the empiricist approach and automation.

10.1   The British Sources of Corpus Linguistics

10.1.1   The "First" Computerised Corpus: Various Claims

The debate determining the "first" computerised corpus is relevant because it shows that the methods based on the use of corpora belong to several traditions and that their automation does not provoke a break.

In the received history, shared by most Natural Language Processing specialists, the first computerised corpus is the Brown Corpus, developed at Brown University by Twadell, Kucera and Francis in 1963. The first results were published in 1967 (Kucera and Francis 1967). It can easily be shown that the Brown Corpus had a predecessor, the Survey of English usage, created in 1960 by the Englishman Randolph Quirk (1920–2017). The Brown Corpus is entirely organised along the Survey of English Usage's guidelines. The initial project was to compile 200 texts (spoken and written) of various genres comprising each 5000 words for a total of 1 million words. Quirk, the author of the Survey of English usage (Quirk 1960), was a member of the Brown team when the corpus specifications were settled.

A second candidate for the role of precursor is the Trésor de la Langue Française whose creation was decided on in 1957 during a conference organised by the CNRS (Centre National de la Recherche Scientifique) in Strasbourg, under the lead of Paul Imbs, one of Mario Roques's pupils (see Chap. 7, Sect. 7.2). This corpus of modern French literature (from 1789) comprised 80 million occurrences. Its computerisation was decided on as soon as 1957 and was carried out by Bernard Quemada, Imbs's assistant.[1]

The received history assigning a pioneering role to the Brown Corpus shows several things. First, corpora have been part of the methodology of American anthropological and descriptive linguistics for a long time. Second, the Americans are pioneers in the computerisation process of linguistics. It is thus not surprising that they were the first to provide a whole computerised corpus. It is not surprising either that the French, who were lagging behind in every area of computer sciences in general, and especially in the domain of the automation of language – Machine translation, Computational Linguistics and Natural Language Processing – were unable to stabilise the methods anchored in their own tradition, such as the

---

[1] For the history of TLF, see Cerquiglini (1998) and Chevalier (2006).

statistical studies of vocabulary which the TLF comes from, and to make them bear fruit. At the time of the institutionalisation of corpus studies, they struggled to be well-positioned on the international stage and in the end lagged behind British works.

As to the British, their descriptive-oriented conception of corpora was designed for automation. Notwithstanding with the fact that the Brown Corpus, whose example was followed by all the corpora for the study of English variation, had been thought out on the model of the British SEU, there is no doubt that the theoretical background of corpus linguistics analysis comes from that tradition.

10.1.2 Meaning in Context, Usage, Lexicogrammar, Text, Corpus: The Empiricist British Tradition

The term "Corpus Linguistics" appeared in 1984 in the British tradition, in the title of the collective book edited by Aarts and Meijs *Corpus Linguistics: Recent Developments in the Use of Computer Corpora in English Language Research*. This book grouped British, Scandinavian and Dutch works on computerised corpora dealing with the English language. Ever since, corpus linguistics has strengthened its institutionalisation with the creation of specialised journals and conferences. However, despite its homogenous appearance, two trends, corpus-based and corpus-driven, can be distinguished, corresponding to two different options on corpus constitution and analysis, both originating from the works of John Rupert Firth (1890–1960). As the corpus-driven option promotes the use of authentic and integral texts, the corpus-based one rests on sampled corpora, each trend involving specific assumptions on the relation between language and corpus (Léon 2008b).

Both trends of corpus linguistics share some common features pertaining to the British tradition and inherited from Henry Sweet[2] on the one hand, and from the late nineteenth-century Oxford English Dictionary on the other hand: the crucial role of phonetics and of spoken language; the importance of text; linguists' training in non-European languages related to the British Empire and decolonisation; the strong tradition focused on usage and descriptive linguistics in which theoretical linguistics and applied linguistics were tightly associated; finally, the refusal to accept any discontinuity between the different levels of language, in particular between syntax and lexis. It is interesting to see that the British linguistic tradition can be considered relatively homogenous and continuous. Differences appear between generations, often for external reasons (war, decolonisation), more than within one generation (Brown and Law 2002). What is called the London School gathers more or less most of the British linguists of the post-war period, more or less, around the ideas of

---

[2] Henry Sweet (1845–1912) was a phonetician, one of the pioneering leaders of the International Phonetic Association and of the Reform Movement. This movement, created at the end of the nineteenth century by the major phoneticians of the period, aimed at reforming language teaching from three main principles: primacy of speech; centrality of text; language teaching by spoken language (see Howatt 2004, Chapter 14 and here Chap. 3, Sect. 3.1).

J.R. Firth. This homogeneity not only characterises linguistics but the whole British linguistic tradition of that period. Some features, such as the determination of word meaning in context and by usage, belong to the philosophical tradition (Wittgenstein 1961 [1953]) or the anthropological one (Malinowski 1923, 1935) and strongly influenced linguistics and its computerisation, as we saw (Chap. 7, Sect. 7.1.2) with the CLRU led by Margaret Masterman, a philosopher and one of Wittgenstein's pupils.[3] Malinowski introduced the concept of situation in 1923, and Firth who had been his assistant in the 1930s, referred to it as soon as 1930 in Speech. In 1935, each of them published a paper developing in a distinct way the notion of context of situation, central in the British empirical tradition. The notion of context of situation, developed by Malinowski in *Coral Gardens and their Magic*, is ethnographic and includes, besides linguistic context, gestures, glances, mimics and context of perception. In his article "The technique of semantics", Firth puts forward the idea that context of situation can be defined as a set of linguistic and pragmatic categories. Those would be developed as categories of restricted languages from 1945 onwards (see Sect. 10.2.1 below).

Although many British linguists stayed in the USA several times, few of them became "Chomskyans"; those who are the closest to Chomskyan theory are very critical, such as John Lyons and Peter Matthews. Actually, the formalisation of language, from the debate between Bar-Hillel and Masterman at the end of the 1950s (see Chap. 7), as well as Chomsky's propositions, aroused strong debates as soon as they appeared. Rather than integrating the computational linguistics based in logico-mathematics that had been originated at MIT, the British linguists confronted it straight up and discussed it, which led to reinforcing their own empiricist position. Their strong attachment to lexis, that is, to word meaning in context and to the continuity between syntax and lexis (see Halliday's, Sinclair's and Quirk's works, Sects. 10.1.3 and 10.1.4 below) led to the interest in the role of probabilities in language, in the wake of information theory more than mathematical logics. That is why automation really developed with the apparition of large corpora, when the implementation of probabilistic hypotheses on big data became possible.

10.1.3   Halliday, Sinclair and the Corpus-Driven *Trend*

The notions of lexical meaning and text, which are crucial in Firth's approach (1957), are central in the corpus-driven trend which had been led, until recently, by John Sinclair (1933–2007). In Firth's polysystemic approach, opposed to European and American structuralisms, meaning by collocation refers to lexical meaning and corresponds to one of the five interrelated levels of language description, the four other levels being phonetics, morphology, syntax and semantics. At a given level,

---

[3] Besides, some linguists belonged to both groups, such as MAK Halliday, one of Firth's pupils and a pioneering member of the CLRU.

the meaning of a unit depends on the role played by that unit on the higher level (Léon 2007c). Meaning of collocation evolved over time in Firth's work into an automatisable object. While in earlier texts collocation referred to the co-occurrence of any linguistic elements within any stretch of text, it was later limited to words in relationships of mutual expectation. For example, in "dark night", the meaning of "night" is that it can be in collocation with "dark" and conversely (see Firth [1951] 1957e, p.196). Several methodological constraints appeared when Firth suggested ways to study and use collocations for practical aims: language teaching, translation and dictionary-making. Besides limiting collocation to words, he suggested study-ing collocations in restricted languages rather than in language in general (see Sect. 10.2.1 below). A third constraint concerns text: to tackle the issue of meaning, word collocations should be studied within authentic texts. Following Wittgenstein, Firth considers that word meaning should be defined by usage, that is, from its occurrence in contextually situated texts.

When Sinclair undertook automatic searching of collocation patterns in spoken and written English (OSTI project – UK Government Office for Scientific and Technical Information) in 1963, he stepped into the Firthian tradition (Sinclair et al. 2004). MAK Halliday (1925–2018), one of Firth's followers as well as supervisor of the project, had already laid the groundwork for his probabilistic theory of lan-guage resting on lexicogrammar, a continuum between lexis and grammar. Lexicogrammar can be analysed from collocation patterning, defined as a kernel item within a stretch of text comprising a given number of words on the right and on the left (Halliday 1966). In accordance with the Firthian approach, collocations should be searched in complete and authentic texts, and not in sampled corpora. Meaning is conceived of as a potential, depending on choices made in the integral text, thus likely to be analysed by probabilistic methods. Any text (e.g. a poem) can be considered a sample of a given language and makes sense only with respect to that language as a whole:

> A literary text has meaning only by comparison with a particular language at a particular time. Any stretch of language has meaning only as a sample of an enormously large body of text; it represents the results of a complicated selection process, and each selection has meaning by virtue of all the other selections which might have been made, but have been rejected... So a poem is a sample of a language; perhaps not a representative sample, but only carrying meaning because it can be referred to a description of a whole language. (Sinclair 1965, p. 76–77)

That probabilistic approach to meaning is possible only through the study of large corpora of texts. That is why Sinclair opposed methods based on sampled corpora and on a priori genres. That is also why this study remained at the draft stage till the late 1980s, as the 1960s technology was unable to deal with large amounts of textual data. In 1980, Sinclair resumed this work with the project COBUILD (Collins Birmingham University international language Database), a large lexical data base aimed at making dictionaries from a set of authentic and complete texts, the Birmingham Collection of English texts (BCE). The theoretical orientation of Sinclair's project was not modified by the twenty years' interruption. When Corpus Linguistics was in full rise, Sinclair put forward a corpus typology which still privileged corpora constituted by collections of complete texts (large text corpora).

10.1.4   *Quirk, Leech and the* **Corpus-Based** *Trend*

The corpus-based trend, at the time led by Geoffrey Leech, comes directly from Quirk's SEU with which it shares its main objectives. Although his interest for grammar keeps him away from Neo-Firthians' main concerns for meaning, in particular for their concern for lexical meaning in context, Quirk is related to the British empiricist lineage. This is evident in the importance he gives to Henry Sweet's lexicographical syntax (Sweet 1884, p. 585) that searched for grammatical patterns, and to the tradition of late nineteenth-century English dictionaries based on usage, such as the Oxford English Dictionary edited by James Murray, whose original title A New English Dictionary on Historical Principles, founded mainly on the materials collected by the Philological Society, shows that corpus-based methodology was already used. Contrary to Halliday and Sinclair, Quirk is in line with the Neo-Bloomfieldian tradition.[4] He owes to Charles Fries the idea of using recorded conversations, an idea which turned out to be totally coherent with the British tradition of the study of spoken language. He worked with Freeman Twaddell on the design of the Brown Corpus. He borrowed from Harris and American anthropological linguists, substituability tests and the use of informants, and from Hockett his idea of a grammar for the hearer. Quirk's objective (see Léon 2013a) is to make grammars confront the demand for English teaching as a foreign language in post-war years. He advocates a grammar designed from a corpus based on usage, that is, great amounts of attested, recorded or transcribed data, that he calls "a corpus of natural usage", "a body of full and objective data" and "a copious body of actually recorded usage".

The grammar should be both descriptive and prescriptive. New and objectively based prescriptions can be worked out from grammatical usage making it possible to obtain as systematic descriptive patterns as possible. For Quirk, usage is not a simple and obvious notion, and he attempted to draw a distinction between usage as observed in corpora, norm as prescribed by grammars and dictionaries, and speakers' beliefs. At that time, there were already animated debates on the Chomskyan notions of grammaticality, acceptability and native speaker intuition, so that Quirk paid much attention to the discrepancy between native speakers' and linguists' intuition and usage, that is, between the forms they accept as well-formed and those they actually produce. This frequent divergence between speakers' beliefs and real usage led Quirk to develop tests to evaluate that discrepancy and to consider acceptability as a multifaceted and continuous phenomenon that cannot be reduced to a

---

[4]After his PhD on syntax at University College of London, Quirk spent two years in the USA (1951–1952) where he met several Neo-Bloomfieldians.

strict yes or no statement. In some cases, he would speak of preference for usage of such and such form rather than of rules (Quirk and Svartvik 1966). Tests are only one part of the procedure making it possible to study usage. Studying variations is a key element. There are variations of the norm, and there is no variation without a linguistic cause; any variation, even apparently minor, should appear in the grammar and be explained. This strong interest in variation is another point relating Quirk to the Firthian trend. For his part, Sinclair did not pay any attention to variation, and regarded sampled corpora, which were a way to account for them, as "special" corpora, deviating from normal language, which remains, for him, the central core of description.

Quirk shared Halliday's hypothesis of a continuum between lexicon and grammar. However, while Halliday opposes a probabilistic model of lexicon (with open choices) to a model of deterministic grammar (with closed choices), Quirk and Mulholland (1964, p. 149) proposes a gradient even for grammatical classes. Between "in spite of", which is a quasi-preposition and "on the table near the door", which is completely free, there are different realisations, such as "in spite of the hotel", "at the sight of the hotel" and "in the lounge of the hotel", which can be identified on a continuum. This may lead to classify, from a dozen of distinctive features, the grammatical class of preposition to be classified, from a dozen of distinctive features, among open classes in English.

SEU should be a corpus built by the linguist, that is, it should be systematic, sampled and representative. Its objective is to account synchronically for the spoken and written language of adult educated British speakers, and to work out selective experiences likely to set up the rules accounting for infrequent variations and usages, for prescriptive purposes. Variations are tackled through some genres: literature, technical, scientific, legal, political, religious texts, newspapers, etc. However, Quirk is particularly interested in free variations that cannot be examined only by the corpus method (i.e. by the SEU). Elicitation tests should be used as well. Quirk started to implement them in collaboration with Jan Svartvik as early as 1966 (Quirk and Svartvik 1966).

To sum up, the data used by Quirk in order to make a grammar have various origins: some artificial data were produced experimentally while other data, written and spoken, were attested. Although Quirk and his collaborators set up automatised procedures in order to explore SEU data as early as the 1960s, the database itself was only computerised in the late 1980s, most notably with the creation of the ICE (International Corpus of English) in 1990, a corpus of texts organised according to genres for all the varieties of English in the world.

As noted above, the Brown Corpus, which is, rightly or wrongly, often regarded as the first computerised corpus, in fact constitutes one of the forms of the computerisation of the SEU. In the 1970s, it is on the model of the SEU and of the Brown Corpus that the compilation of the variations of English continued, especially with the development of large corpora in Scandinavia by Quirk's followers. Geoffrey Leech from Lancaster University, Jon Svartvik from Lund University and Norwegians from Oslo and Bergen undertook the London-Lund Corpus of Spoken English

(LLC) in 1975 and the Lancaster-Oslo-Bergen Corpus of British English (LOB) in 1978.

In the 1990s, when the very large computerised corpora became available, they were integrated in Natural Language Processing and regarded as large data sets making it possible to make all sorts of explorations, either based on statistical methods or based on searches of structures and specific linguistic hypotheses. The corpus-based trend has no definite scientific goal: rather it is a general frame for the multifarious use of corpora in Natural Language Processing projects.

10.2   Empiricism in Linguistics and in NLP: New Objects, New Challenges

For applied purposes, that is, teaching, translation and the dissemination of science, empiricist traditions have produced intermediary objects between data and theory, such as J.R. Firth's restricted languages and Harris's sublanguages. Under various names (registers, restricted languages, specialised languages) those objects became NLP objects, between probabilistic and computational methods.[5]

10.2.1   Restricted Languages and Registers (Firth, Halliday)

In Firth's theory restricted languages belong to situational categories, that is, to linguistic categories making it possible to analyse the concept of context of situation. Restricted languages also refer to the "technical" function of language, in the wake of Wittgenstein's views.[6] In fact, the notion of restricted languages mixes two distinct aspects that will lead to two notions. One of them, restricted languages, was developed by Firth himself; the second one was developed by his followers, among them Halliday, who put forward registers.

When he started developing this notion in 1950, Firth gave two examples, making it possible to identify both aspects. The first example is the analysis of an utterance in Cockney "Ahng gunna gi' wun fer Ber" (I'm going to get one for Bert) (Firth 1957d [1950a], p.182). When one utters such a sentence, one should ask some questions in order to provide a situation context typical of verbal action (also named "historical event"): How many participants? Where does the action take place? What are the relevant objects? What is the sentence's effect on the other speakers?

---

[5] See Léon 2007b, 2008c.

[6] In *Philosophical Investigations*, Wittgenstein (1961 [1953] I, 2, p.116) refers to language functions as tools. He gives the example of a primitive language constituted only by a few words, "blocks", "pillars", "slabs" and "beams", which could be sufficient to serve for communication for two builders. Firth was directly inspired by this idea when he promoted a restricted language allowing pilots to communicate with each other in Japanese (see his example 2 below).

For example, the participants are in a pub, the speaker stands up and gets a pint for Bert, etc. The second example refers to Firth's experience as a Japanese teacher during World War II. His objective is less to teach British pilots informal conversation aimed at social relations, than the language used by Japanese pilots, that is, a technical and restricted language. Firth only worked thoroughly on restricted languages derived from technical languages. Later situational categories would have various destinies among the Firthians –such as registers – and within the ethnography of communication.[7]

At first, the notion of restricted languages refers to three types of languages at the core of descriptive linguistics: the language of description, the language under description and the language of translation. In spite of the apparent confusion created by those multifarious functions of restricted languages, the notion is consistent with Firth's empiricist views. It was when he contrasted post-Saussurian structuralism and Neo-Bloomfieldians, that Firth put forward "restricted languages of linguistics", and more generally "restricted languages of sciences" to be used as a metalanguage. As to languages under description, they are restricted languages defined as subsets of a given contextually situated language: technical languages, for sport, engineering, aviation, business, administration, etc. Text is the empirical space materialising restricted languages. It can be limited to only one text or one author's work. Firth gives the examples of Swinburne's poetic work, and single texts such as the Magna Carta of medieval Latin and American Declaration of Independence. This characteristic would determine some basic features of the corpus-driven trend of corpus linguistics, such as Sinclair's claim that one single text (one poem) can be considered representative of the language as a whole.

Restricted languages are crucial for descriptive linguistics, which determines micro-grammars and micro-glossaries for each of them. Finally, they are the best for collocation searches. One can see here how Firthian descriptive linguistics is directly computerisable through corpora and probabilistic methods. One central characteristic of restricted languages, related to the fact that they are contextually situated, is that they are very suitable for the study of variation. Major languages, such as French and English, given the fact that they are used in different geographical and cultural contexts, are subject to linguistic variations. These languages, spoken in Africa, Asia, America as well as Europe, are not unified and cannot be taught and translated as homogeneous sets. Different spatial and time references determine different restricted languages that are not shared by all the French or English native speakers. This is why it could be said that restricted languages are closer to the notion of French, English, Portuguese hyperlanguage (see Auroux 1997).[8]

---

[7] See Léon (2019).

[8] "Human language is not autonomous; it is not an activity sphere per se. To function as a mean of communication, it should be situated within a given world and among social habits. There is no possible human language without hyperlanguage'… A Québécois (or a Brazilian) indeed uses the same expression as a Frenchman (or a Portuguese) when he speaks of a 'big tree'. Yet, from many textual indices, one notices that the expressions have different meanings: grammatical language

Moreover, restricted languages cannot be assimilated to artificial languages such as Basic English or le Français élémentaire, both dedicated to language teaching and grounded in a lexicon limited by definition. On the contrary, restricted languages involve wide-ranging micro-glossaries showing the richness of lexis in variation. In addition, Ogden's definition of lexis is based, in his Basic English, on a priori semantic categories, which is the opposite of Firth's view on meaning.

Restricted languages, at the core of British descriptive linguistics, have a dual status. They are, at the same time, at the centre of the study of variation and constitute areas of stability for teaching and translation, since they make it possible to reduce problems of understanding. Finally, they became crucial tools for NLP because they help define micro-grammars and micro-glossaries. As they are suited to the identification of collocations, they are very well adapted to corpus searching. As to registers, they can easily be grasped by probabilistic methods. Halliday defines them as continuous phenomena which cannot be differentiated from one speaker to another and which cannot be handled by categories or discrete methods. They can be handled through patterns of usage, obtained from large corpora by generalisation, rather than through rules.

10.2.2   Sublanguages (Harris)

Harris's sublanguages are objects which make it possible to implement empirical descriptive linguistics and to define partial grammars. Like restricted languages they are privileged objects adapted to NLP. It is worth noting that, in spite of significant differences largely due to their often incompatible theoretical backgrounds, sublanguages, restricted languages and registers had been mixed up in the NLP project.

Harris thought out sublanguages in 1968 as mathematical systems, defined by operations – transformations – and without empirical basis. Later, they became concrete discourse structures, which could be applied to real scientific texts, contextually situated and suitable for being processed automatically. They were at the basis of Naomi Sager's string analysis, of the Taum-Meteo[9] machine translation project, and of the project of sublanguages of sciences worked out by Harris and his team, in the domain of immunology (Harris 1988, 1991).

One source of Harris's project is his involvement in international languages. Following Sapir's project of scientific auxiliary language[10] (see Harris 1951b) and Carnap's logical syntax, Harris worked out a project of an international language of sciences in 1962. Contrary to Carnap's language, it should not be based on mathe-

---

has not changed, it is the world that has changed, producing a change in the hyperlanguage" (Auroux, 1997, p.114–115).

[9] TAUM means "Traduction Automatique à l'Université de Montréal".

[10] In the edition of Sapir's complete works, Swiggers (2008) points out Sapir's involvement in international auxiliary languages. Sapir dedicated four articles to that topic between 1925 and 1933.

matical logic, but should be a sublanguage of natural language (Harris 1962b). Contrary to Firth who had never been attracted by universal languages and whose restricted languages were irreducible sites for variation, Harris considers that the sublanguage of sciences is universal and identical for all languages. The case of weather reports is exemplary of the difference between their views. While Firth takes the view that, as any other "text", they are subject to variation from one language to another and even inside the same language spoken in distinct spaces (of English hyperlanguage), Harris thinks that they have a structure which is the same for every language. The first experiments of machine translation using sublanguages are the translation of Canadian weather reports (regarded as sublanguages) within the frame of the TAUM-meteo project.

The authors have very different views on the status of metalanguage. Firth (1968a [1955] p.46–47) promotes the setting of a metalanguage (a restricted language) aiming at handling natural language indeterminacy which may collocate technical terms and ordinary language terms. On the contrary, Harris thinks that, as each language contains its own metalanguage, there is no need for artificial metalanguages. In spite of the coincidence of the terms "lexicogrammar" (developed by MAK Halliday, one of Firth's followers) and "lexique-grammaire" (developed by Maurice Gross, one of Harris's followers), their views on lexicon are very different. For Harris, restrictions of selection on lexicon should be done in syntactical terms with operators and arguments; for Firth, meaning by collocation can be attained only by usage so that Halliday put forward the idea of a continuum between lexicon and grammar, only analysable by probabilistic methods.

For Firth, each restricted language has its own micro-grammar. Harris has a more elaborate approach: grammars of sublanguages are not subsets of the grammar of a given language as a whole. They are intersections. Sublanguages are the site where meaning is produced, as, for example, synonyms and homonyms which are not identical in sublanguages and in the language as a whole. For example, "cells have multiplied" and "cells have divided" are synonyms in the sublanguage of biology while they are not in general language. Likewise, nonsense does not exist in sublanguages: nonsense is simply out of the sublanguage.

Substantial theoretical differences remain and are irreducible, most notably concerning text, context, meaning and variation. Besides, Firth had always expressed a very critical view on distributional methods, and especially Harris's methods (Firth 1968a [1955], 1968b [1956], 1968c [1957]). He criticised distributional methods by quoting *Methods in Structural Linguistics* (Harris 1951a), which, Firth says, never produced any result:

> The main criticism to be offered of American structuralist linguistics based on phonemic procedures is that, having attempted just that, it has not furnished any valid grammatical analysis of any language by means of which renewal of connection in experience can be made with systematic certainty. (Firth 1968c [1957], p. 191)

However, one can claim that restricted languages and sublanguages share some features which relate them to the use of empiricism in linguistics: inductive methods and intermediary levels between data and linguistic descriptions suitable for abstraction. In addition, the use of those languages in practical applications reduces discrepancies. In NLP, some authors use registers and sublanguages in the same project, since sublanguages are limited to technical languages, and registers and genres to more general or literary forms, such as tales for children and literary criticism. Terms like "specialised languages" and "languages of speciality" which are increasingly used, tend to neutralise differences. Nowadays, there are descendants of sublanguages and restricted languages – the difference is not relevant any more – in various domains. From the 1980s, specialised operational languages were developed in air traffic communications (Airspeak), sea communications (Seaspeak) and police communications (Policespeak) within the Schengen area. These projects involve specialised languages, communications technologies, computerised procedures and multilingual interfaces. In general, one can wonder whether these practical objectives, of which NLP is unquestionably a part, do not tend to minimise theoretical differences, and even consider them negligible.

10.3 Corpora, Data and Debates Between Empiricists and Chomskyans

British linguists, instead of rejecting or integrating Chomskyan theory "en bloc", continually kept having thorough and long-term discussions with it, on points which concerned them directly. That stand, open but uncompromising, is characteristic of the automation-mathematisation within British empiricism. Three distinct moments can be observed in debates between British empiricists and Chomskyans. The first moment corresponds to the emergence of generative grammar and of the new issues it raised, including among empiricists who discussed the notions of grammaticality/ acceptability, gradience, competence/performance, etc. The second moment corresponds to the appearance of large corpora that led empiricists, like Sampson (2001), to contest generativists' views. The corpus-driven trend, most notably, raises questions for the Chomskyan notion of linguistic creativity, whose innate character is put into question by large corpora. As to the partisans of the corpus-based trend, they revisited Chomsky's arguments on the relevance of corpora and probabilistic methods for linguistic analysis. At the third stage, with the appearance of large corpora, Chomskyans and post-Chomskyans reconsidered their position on data, obtained either by intuition, by evidence from observation or by experimentation within a recent movement of Philosophy of linguistics.[11]

---

[11] "Philosophy of linguistics is the philosophy of science as applied to linguistics. This differentiates it sharply from the philosophy of language, traditionally concerned with matters of meaning and reference." (Scholz, Barbara C., Pelletier, Francis Jeffry and Pullum, Geoffrey K., 'Philosophy of Linguistics', The Stanford Encyclopedia of Philosophy (Winter 2011 Edition), Edward N. Zalta ed., http://plato.stanford.edu/archives/win2011/entries/linguistics/.

10.3.1   In the 1960s: Acceptability, Lexicality and the Probabilistic Nature of Language[12]

In the 1960s, the British linguists took up the new horizon of retrospection introduced by MT and computational linguistics in a very original way. As already seen, early experiments on MT were led in Great Britain, at Birkbeck College in London, without regard to any theoretical framework (see Chap. 7). These experiments, which seemed to come out of the blue, brought into play the same intuitions as those of the Russian engineer Trojanskij, i.e. an intermediary language based on Esperanto. However, the CLRU, which benefited from a background strongly anchored in mathematical logic and philosophy of language, conducted experiments based on the British tradition of meaning in usage and in context while discussing on formalisation and developing an original type of mathematisation.

The Chomskyan theory was received in the same state of mind. Far from the external and delayed reception of the French, the British linguists were ready to debate on equal terms about advantages and defects of the new theory, and to accept suggestions or to challenge others that had been judged better performing. About this type of reception, one could speak of "integration by confrontation". The objective of Randolph Quirk and his colleagues, without directly rejecting the idea of competence, was to test performance and acceptability experimentally, starting from the observation of the discrepancy between the speakers' judgement and their own productions. They advocated a gradient view of acceptability, from an empiricist approach to performance based on usage, that is, usage cognitively elicited by tests and usage studied from inductive corpora-based methods. It is to be noted that only that aspect remained in Quirk's further works and in the corpus-based trend based on them.

Halliday's approach was more clearly empiricist. He discussed the very notion of competence during the debate which followed Chomsky's presentation at the 9th Congress of linguists in 1962 (Chomsky 1964). Complementary to the Chomskyan notion of grammaticality, by nature discrete and non-gradient, he put forward lexicalness, a non-discrete notion only interpretable in terms of degrees. In addition, he contested the opposition between "possible" and "impossible" in language: what is possible is possible in a predictive way, in terms of probable or less probable and not in an absolute way. Halliday is determined not to concede anything in his conception of language as a social object in action. Following Firth and ethnographers of communication, he developed a socio-semiotics constituting one of the most active trends of functionalism.

---

[12] See Léon 2010b.

10.3.2 In the 1990s: Generative and Transformational Grammar Revisited

The debate on the use of corpora and probabilistic methods was revived when large corpora appeared in the 1990s.The arguments which were put forward could seem anachronistic since they revitalised a debate that had taken place thirty years before. In fact, they were discussed for the purpose of legitimation by the proponents of the corpus-based trend (Leech 1992). This trend, NLP-oriented and dedicated to objectives more practical than theoretical, claimed the idea of creating a new linguistics breaking with the Chomskyan theory. One cannot help but thinking that these arguments attempted to start everything again from the beginning. We are back to the middle of the 1960s when ALPAC erected computational linguistics as a "new linguistics" by relying on brand-new generative and transformational grammar to oppose distributionalists and their corpus methods. By reversing the arguments, they aimed at showing that corpus-based empirical linguistics, formerly wiped out by the Chomskyans, turned out to be much more efficient theoretically.

The debate revived by the supporters of the corpus-based trend is the same as the one which opposed, in the 1960s, Chomsky and the distributionalists concerning the conception of language and grammar. Language, which is infinite for Chomsky, is finite for the Neo-Bloomfieldians as a corpus of a set of utterances. Neo-Bloomfieldians's approach to corpora cannot be attributed to the Neo-Firthans for whom a corpus can extend infinitely, in particular in Sinclair's version. Besides, the first corpora of the corpus-based trend, such as the Brown Corpus, were used for statistical studies of vocabulary. But Chomsky was not interested in statistical models of vocabulary which, as they did not address or question his theory, he even occasionally approved (Chomsky and Miller 1963).

Chomsky particularly criticised Markov chains for syntax, because they cannot use the recursivity necessary to generate every grammatical sentence and only them; according to him, grammaticality is necessarily non-probabilistic (Chomsky 1957). Consequently, the debate, revived by the proponents of the corpus-based trend, seemed orchestrated for purposes more political than scientifical. One can put forward the following suggestion: as they were conscious of the major issues of corpus studies, they wished to erect them as the "new linguistics". However, as they had progressively given up theoretical aspects in favour of more practical objectives pertaining to NLP, the corpus-based trend needed to be re-legitimised. For this purpose, they chose a precursor, Chomsky, which in fact turned out to be an anti-precursor, and a pioneer which was an NLP object, the Brown Corpus.

It should be said that certain Chomskyan arguments remain relevant concerning NLP applications. Is it possible to establish the primacy of the "attested" as a dogma, at a time when some regard the whole of the web as "the" corpus. Is any form encountered in such a corpus well-formed? Can a corpus, how large it may be, comprise all the grammatical forms? Chomsky (1962, p.180) argues that the sentence "John ate a sandwich" is most unlikely to be encountered in a corpus, including the

Congress Library, although it is perfectly well-formed. In general, newly attested data do not necessarily constitute new linguistic facts.[13]

The debate which was oriented from empiricists towards Chomskyans in the 1990s as in the 1960s broadened and reached the domain of NLP in the 2000s. However, its practical application in NLP neutralised and weakened the issues at stake. Some opted for reconciliation and complementarity between computer-based NLP and probability-based NLP (Pereira 2002). Many started to use mixed methods. As to the funders, they favoured both types of method alternatively, according to results and current fashion.

10.3.3 Linguistic Creativity and Lexicon: An Ongoing Debate

One further aspect of the Chomskyan theory is questioned by the use of large corpora. It is linguistic creativity, which is related to the infinite and innate character of language. The debate, opened by Sinclair, addresses the creativity of the lexicon and the implication of memory in language learning and usage. Sinclair (1991) puts forward two complementary principles for interpreting the meaning of a text: the open choice principle according to which the speaker has a large choice of lexical possibilities, only restricted by grammatical constraints, and the idiom principle, according to which the speaker has only a limited choice of ready-made phrase structures. The idiom principle, and the existence of ready-made elements in language, makes it possible to rehabilitate the role of memory in language learning and production. Besides, the use of partially lexicalised elements does not necessarily call into question the innovative character of language. According to Joseph (2003), Chomsky rejects any "collocational" model of language on the grounds of infinite linguistic creativity, while for Sinclair and his followers, collocations, analysable within corpora, does not imply a lack of creativity. In addition, the existence of ready-made segments helps refute a strict separation between lexicon and grammar.

10.3.4 The Debate on Data Evidence in Post-Chomskyan Linguistics

New issues arose for Chomskyans when large amounts of data became available. In the late 1990s, the debate became widespread inside one trend of philosophy of linguistics aiming at discussing the notions of grammaticality and intuition, and more generally data evidence, in order to assess the issues for theoretical linguistics and deepen reflection on empiricism in post-Chomskyan linguistics (see Schütze 1996; Pullum 2007; Riemer 2009; Kertész and Rákosi 2012).

---

[13] For a critical study of corpus linguistics, see Cori and David (2008).

Kertész and Rákosi (2012) establish a state-of-the-art survey of existing debates. Adopting an exclusively post-Chomskyan perspective, they ignore distributionalist works using elicitation and Quirk's studies using experimental data in addition to attested data based on corpora. They describe a new generativist era, according to which introspection data are not sufficient any more. Results obtained by investigations based on corpora and experiments are also needed. Generativists, whose task is to identify the principles of universal grammar, use the results of typology and neuro- and psycholinguistics.

Errors and slips of the tongue, considered ungrammatical since Chomsky (1955), can now be used as weak evidence for studying grammaticality. Some data have a mixed status (i.e. intuition-based and corpus-attested): according to Schütze (1996), the web, because of its huge size, is the best corpus, on condition that it is controlled by the linguist's intuition. Questionaries, eye-tracking, neuro-anatomic measures, etc., are experiments based on responses to stimuli which are neither corpus nor introspection-based data. Thus, linguistic competence is no longer the only relevant factor to validate acceptability judgements.

The status of counter-examples has changed. Generativists think they adopt a pioneering strategy by ignoring counter-examples temporarily, assuming that at a further stage of development of the theory, tools would become available to solve discrepancies (Chomsky 2002). Intuition-based data do not meet empiricist criteria any longer. Corpus-based data, less prone to manipulation, are considered more objective than intuition-based data. Finally, the mode of argumentation becomes more cyclical than linear. In order to find a suitable solution, one has to go back and try another way. At each cycle, perspective changes, and linguistic theorisation obeys a heuristic process by applying problem-solving strategies.

10.4   Conclusion

It is interesting to see that British descriptive linguistics contained every potential development which had become feasible thanks to automation. Since Henry Sweet, it had involved theoretical as well as practical aspects such as language teaching, translation, machine translation, automatic search for collocations, etc. Automation had not constituted a break; on the contrary, it was in the direct continuation of applied methods in linguistics. What really led to a turning point was the large amount of data becoming available. Corpora as linguistic tools had existed since the 1960s, they could be implemented with the technological progress of computers in the 1990s, increasing their potentialities in an unprecedented way.

This aspect is emphasised by Halliday (2002). Until the 1990s, he says, linguistics had very little data at its disposal and was in the same situation as physics in the late fifteenth century before experimentation was made possible by technological progress. For Halliday, and some empiricist linguists, linguistics is an experimental science which achieved two major developments in the twentieth century thanks to technological advances: (1) the appearance of recorders and of computers in the

1950s allowing linguistics to catch up with phonetics, which had already been constituted as a laboratory science since the 1920s; (2) the evolution of computers in the 1990s making large amounts of data available to linguists: "From all this it should be possible in the next decade or two to crack the semiotic code, in the sense of coming fully to understand the relationship between observed instances of language behaviour and the underlying system of language" (Halliday 2002: 8).

Sampson (2001) argues in the same way in order to criticise the opposition between "possible" and "impossible" which pertains to the Chomskyan notion of grammaticality. This opposition, he says, involves negative evidence which is not observable and cannot relate to intuition. In the 1950s–1960s, empirical evidence was replaced by intuition, because of the lack of sufficient data. Now, thanks to large corpora, nothing prevents linguistics from being an empirical science in the same way as the other sciences. Even if one does not adopt an empirico-positivist view, it cannot be denied that corpora have become an auxiliary source of data for every linguist. Most of them use corpora to establish linguistic facts. Moreover, some domains, such as prosody and morphology, require their use even when a formalist or realistic approach has been adopted.

Internal debates within Post-Chomskyan linguistics (Sect. 10.3.4 above) show this evolution and urge generativist linguists to use corpora and experiments. In general, it is important to know whether corpora are new tools (within equipped linguistics, "linguistique instrumentée", Habert 2005), constitute a new observatory for linguistics (see Auroux 1998; Cori and David 2008; Girault and Victorri 2009, among others), or whether their use is only a new way for linguistics to experience its empiricism.

Chapter 11
General Conclusion

In conclusion, it is worthwhile to take up some theoretical issues that result from reading the history of Natural Language Processing, as the history of recent past. The appearance of machine translation as an event in the context of war has hastened the process of automation without that process being a continuation of a specific linguistic or intellectual tradition. The point of view I have adopted, that is, to study the modes of integration of machine translation, computational linguistics, information theory and information retrieval into linguistics, raises the issue of the relationship between horizon of retrospection and tradition; between institutional history and history of linguistic ideas; and the stakes of a unique periodisation for such a short history; finally, it would be worth determining whether we should speak of a revolution or of a new mode of historicity.

Besides, the automation turn anchored in the sciences of war took on more peripheral forms, such as the technologisation of language teaching and the institutionalisation of applied linguistics. It led to the emergence of new domains such as automatic discourse analysis. Finally, the second turn, the corpus turn, having its own characteristics involves different epistemological issues.

In the case of machine translation, I spoke of integration of a new horizon of retrospection rather than transfer of concepts and methods from one discipline to another – in our case from computer sciences and mathematics towards linguistics. Integration may involve transfer but is not similar to it. In the idea of integration, there is the idea of contextualisation and anchoring in a tradition. Integration means the contextualised transfer of concepts and methods.

Although it was drastically and suddenly imposed by machine translation and computational linguistics, the new horizon of retrospection was not completely foreign to the horizons of linguistics in certain traditions. According to its familiarity or its strangeness, several modes of integration were distinguished. I spoke of "adaptation" when the logico-mathematical and linguistic anchorage was sufficiently strong. This was the case for the Neo-Bloomfieldians who had some familiarity with the first mathematisation and with some of its principles such as

J. Léon, *Automating Linguistics*, History of Computing, https://doi.org/10.1007/978-3-030-70642-5_11

axiomatisation. Besides, "New [computational] Linguistics", based on phrase grammars, shared many options with American structural linguistics.

At the other end of the spectrum, I spoke of "external reception" as far as French linguists are concerned, for whom both movements, mathematisation of language and automation, established themselves from outside with no anchoring in their tradition at all. Conduits had to be imagined, such as learned societies, traditionally at the core of the constitution of disciplines; or such as scientific frontier runners had to be defined, likely to pass on methods and concepts from the USA to Europe in both directions, and from the language sciences to other disciplines.

The case of British linguists is particular. Their familiarity with the first mathematisation and with philosophy of language made them as capable as the Americans to integrate into linguistics the automation-mathematisation implemented in the area of computational linguistics. However, their empirical tradition led them to adopt a critical stand in discussions with the proponents of the "new linguistics" and to innovate in their own field rather than to adopt that new linguistics. Thus, one can speak of integration through confrontation.

The choice of treating separately the integration of computational linguistics and of information theory can be justified first because the forms of mathematisation are very different: logico-mathematical and based on the computation of discrete units for the first case and probabilistic and based on continuous methods for the second one. One cannot decide whether one is intrinsic and the other extrinsic (Auroux 2009) in so far as to the extent that some empiricists, like Halliday and Sinclair, claim that language has a probabilistic nature from arguments which have not yet been refuted. The point here is that integration of information theory differed considerably from that of computational linguistics. None of the linguistic traditions ignored statistical methods. This situation is probably due to the fact that Zipf's works on phonetics and lexicon had had an early reception by both British and French phoneticians in the International Phonetic Association.

The Neo-Bloomfieldians used Markov chains very early on to delimit units inside an utterance. Certain approaches in linguistics, such as most notably Jakobson's Distinctive Feature Theory, comprised aspects converging significantly with some notions of information theory; this is the case for the redundancy and binary principle, as we saw in Chap. 5. That is why I spoke of transfer and convergence of concepts and methods between information theory and linguistics. It is likely that the general interest for cybernetics, which had the ambition of unifying sciences and of which information theory was considered the quantitative part, had much facilitated its integration into linguistics, as it did for the other sciences. The historical moment of that integration is crucial. The 1960s were the period of the rise of structuralism that also had a universalist ambition. The complementarity or concurrence between both movements, information theory and structuralism, with equal universalist claims, remains to be studied.[1]

---

[1] See Ronan Le Roux's work on the convergence between cybernetics and structuralisms, most notably in Lévi-Strauss's and Lacan's works (Le Roux 2009, 2013).

Another question concerns periodisation. We saw that it could vary according to the perspective adopted. Choosing contextually situated modes of integration as a main thread leads to the adoption of different modes of periodisation and various focuses of historicisation, i.e. institutional history and/or history of ideas, alternatively or simultaneously. Institutional history has priority for analysing the "founding" event, which may be delimited by three institutional reports within a short period of 15 years.[2] Such a periodisation, focused on events, refers to the role played by key personalities at the beginning of the automation of linguistics. For some of these personalities I displayed biographical elements each time it was necessary without being committed to a narrative model of history of sciences.[3] This was the case for Yehoshua Bar-Hillel, Warren Weaver, Benoît Mandelbrot, Pierre-Marcel Schützenberger and Maurice Gross.

In this study, Zellig S. Harris was given a central role, and his works are cited in several chapters. As a Neo-Bloomfieldian linguist, one of the most committed to formalisation, he led a machine translation group, and his works directly benefited from the automation of translation. The distributional method, which he applied himself to information retrieval, became the best-known linguistic method in automatic documentation. His works, relayed by Maurice Gross and the proponents of French discourse analysis, had an original career in France, whereas they were forgotten in the USA; finally, one can assume that a large part of his inheritance is in the area of Natural Language Processing.

Concerning the sources of corpus linguistics, the analysis of lexical semantics and the making of intermediary objects for empirical descriptive linguistics, other types of periodisation are needed. Such kinds of investigations can only be long-term studies, following the history of ideas. The duration of that long term is variable and not necessarily linear. For example, the study of the origin and genesis of semantic networks establishes a periodisation going from the seventeenth century to the middle of the twentieth century. However, that periodisation is not linear, and we need to distinguish three discontinuous moments: Wilkins' Essay in the seventeenth century, Roget's thesaurus in the nineteenth century and intermediary languages for machine translation established by the Cambridge (GB) group in the 1950s. Firth's restricted languages developed in the 1950s are a continuation of Henry Sweet's descriptive linguistics but are rooted in previous British empiricism.

In this study, the notions of tradition and horizon of retrospection have been used in an equivalent manner. This position can be justified when one encounters national cultures which were still dominant in the middle of the twentieth century, at the threshold of the internationalisation of linguistics. For Auroux (1987, p.34), horizon of retrospection is transmitted by tradition; conversely, one may consider that tradition is one of the conditions necessary for changing horizons of retrospection. Thus, it is from a given tradition that automation gave rise to new issues and new objects

---

[2] In this case, institutional history puts forward the interaction of the sociological component with the practical component (the development of machine translation systems) which should be analysed first before the theoretical component (see the model of sciences proposed by Auroux 1987).

[3] For a criticism of such a model, see Auroux (1987).

for linguistics. Experiments during the first 15 years, that is, the event constituted by machine translation, are a finite and easily definable period. I tried to avoid a "presentist" stand (Fischer 1970) that would mean selecting only methods currently used today.[4] The experiments I chose to study were those which shifted lines, raised new questions or renewed them for linguistics. Such a stand is far from being without risk and sometimes arouses misunderstanding among linguists for whom those experiments are only "dusty old things".

As to the second automation phase, the issue is completely different; we are at the core of what is happening now in linguistics. When one aims at an epistemological study of the linguistic results achieved by corpus studies, one has to take into account procedures of assessment implemented by stakeholders themselves. It would be necessary, first, to think through and devise the theoretical framework making such research possible.

Another issue remains unsolved, that is, to know whether automation of language can be assimilated to a new technological revolution, which could be said to be equivalent to writing and to the grammatisation of vernaculars from the sixteenth century (Auroux 1994). One can draw parallels between the respective historical contexts of the grammatisation revolution on the one hand and of automation on the other hand. In both cases it was necessary to internationalise communication, in the first case in the wake of the great European discoveries of the world, in the second case after World War II,[5] using the latest technological innovations and creating new tools for linguistics. Automation, through data bases, large corpora, annotation, electronic dictionaries, etc., undoubtedly constitutes unprecedented tools for languages extending human competence and with an impact exceeding linguistics but reaching the society as a whole. Finally, the history of Natural Language Processing is not only the history of recent past but also ongoing history. Today, one can see an acceleration of the changes of methods, completely in parallel with technological developments, even dominated by them. The pressure of social demand in addition to the intrinsic ambiguities of NLP leads to accelerating cycles of abandonment-revival/forgetting-(re)discovery of methods.[6] Sometimes the alternation of models is so fast that some overlapping may happen.[7] Disturbance caused by the rapid pace

---

[4] "Sometimes called the fallacy of *nunc pro tunc*, it (the fallacy of presentism) is the mistaken idea that the proper way to do history is to prune away the dead branches of the past, and to preserve the green buds and twigs which have grown into the dark forest of our contemporary world" (Fischer 1970, p.136).

[5] Such parallels have been drawn between universal languages schemes of the seventeenth century in Great Britain (Cram 1985) and the revival of interest they aroused as machine translation methods.

[6] Alternation of short cycles, the ephemeral nature of research and its damaging effects on knowledge accumulation had been pointed out by some researchers as early as the 1990s (see Victorri 1995).

[7] On the 23rd of June 2009, during the ceremony celebrating the 50th anniversary of ATALA, a German NLP representative claimed that the current dominant trend in MT was based on statistical methods, while at the same time and at the same place, the American representative claimed that it was rule-based methods which were on the rise, without any of them referring to the other.

of alternations may be worsened by new alliances between proponents of computational methods and supporters of probabilistic methods, making theoretical divergences disappear for the benefit of practical applications. However, it is difficult to know whether that acceleration, impacting the society as a whole, really determines a new mode of historicity (Hartog 2003), and whether the mode of historicisation required by the need for sciences progress existing since the nineteenth century (Auroux 2007) is about to give way to a new mode based on the cult of present time. By abolishing the past and annihilating any possible projection, the new mode of historicisation which characterises NLP and also the entirety of the language sciences would be better suited to technological development and consumable industrial products than to sciences.

Finally, it is likely that new technological developments lead to new developments. For example, massive use of the Internet and of large amounts of data may be considered a new peak in language automation. That new turn, or "data turn", which appeared in computer science and in artificial intelligence in the 1990s extended to NLP through corpus linguistics. Contrary to Corpus Linguistics based on linguistic hypotheses, objects and structures, the linguistic status of data for the "data turn" is not a relevant issue. Its methods treat any data in the same way, whether the data are tables, numbers, "bag" of words or parts of syntactic trees. The only common characteristics they share is being organised as attribute-value pairs. Methods themselves are not differentiated: even if statistical and probabilistic methods are dominant, symbolic methods are also used. Hybrid methods become more and more frequent. In such a configuration, one wonders whether linguistics still plays a role, and which one. Linguistics as a tool and a mere source of resources? In that case, would linguistics be simply instrumentalised for the benefit of practical tasks? Can new issues for investigating languages emerge from that type of processing? In the long term, it might be possible that this new "turn" seems anecdotal and that its impact on the language sciences proves to be insignificant. It is difficult to entirely characterise the third technological revolution of the language sciences and to draw all the consequences from it. We are facing one of the limits of the history of the present and recent past.

Bibliography

Aarts, J., and W. Meijs, eds. 1984. *Corpus linguistics: Recent developments in the use of computer Corpora in English language research*. Amsterdam: Rodopi.

Abella, A. 2008. *Soldiers of reason: The Rand Corporation and the rise of the American Empire*. Orlando: Harcourt Inc.

Ajdukiewicz, K. 1935. Die syntaktische Konnexität. *Studia philosophica* 1: 1–27.

Akhmanova, O.S., I.A. Mel'čuk, R.M. Frumkina, and E.V. Paducheva. 1963. *Exact methods in linguistic research*. Berkeley: University California Press.

ALPAC. 1966. Language and Machines. Computers in translation and linguistics. A report by the Automatic Language Processing Advisory Committee (ALPAC), National Academy of Sciences, National Research Council.

Anderson, S.R. 1985. *Phonology in the twentieth century*. Chicago: The Chicago Press.

Andreev, N.D. 1967. The intermediary language as the focal point of machine translation. In *Machine translation*, ed. A.D. Booth, 3–27. Amsterdam: North Holland Publishing Company.

Archaimbault, S. 2001. Les approches normatives en Russie. In *History of the language sciences – An international handbook on the evolution of the study of language from the beginnings to the present*, vol 18(1), ed. E.F.K. Koerner, S. Auroux, H.J. Niederehe, K. Versteegh, 901–907. Berlin: Walter de Gruyter.

Archaimbault, S., and J. Léon. 1997. La langue intermédiaire dans la Traduction Automatique en URSS (1954–1960). Filiations et modèles. *Histoire Épistémologie Langage* 19 (2): 105–132.

Auroux, S. 1987. Histoire des sciences et entropie des systèmes scientifiques. Les horizons de retrospection. In *Zur Theorie und Methode der Geschichtsschreibung der Linguistik*, ed. P. Schmitter, 20–42. Tübingen: Narr.

———. 1994. *La révolution technologique de la grammatisation*. Liège: Mardaga.

———. 1996. *La philosophie du langage (avec la collaboration de J.Deschamps et D.Kouloughli)*. Paris: PUF.

———. 1997. La réalité de l'hyperlangue. *Langages* 127: 110–121.

———. 1998. *La raison le langage et les normes*. Paris: PUF.

———. 2007. *La question de l'origine des langues (suivi de L'historicité des sciences)*. Paris: PUF.

———. 2009. Mathématisation de la linguistique et nature du langage. *Histoire Épistémologie Langage* 31 (1): 5–45.

Bar-Hillel, Y. 1953a. The present state of research on mechanical translation. *American Documentation* 2: 229–236.

———. 1953b. A quasi-arithmetic notation for syntactic description. *Language* 29: 47–58.

———. 1955. Idioms. In *Machine translation of languages, 14 essays*, ed. W.N. Locke and A.D. Booth, 183–193. Cambridge, MA/New York: Wiley/MIT.

© The Editor(s) (if applicable) and The Author(s), under exclusive license to
Springer Nature Switzerland AG 2021
J. Léon, *Automating Linguistics*, History of Computing,
https://doi.org/10.1007/978-3-030-70642-5

———. 1960. The present status of automatic translation of languages. In *Advances in computers 1*, ed. F.C. Alt, 91–141. London: Academic.

Barsky, R. 2011. *Zellig Harris. From American linguistics to Socialist Zionism*. Cambridge, MA: MIT Press.

Benveniste, E. 1966. Formes nouvelles de la composition nominale. *Bulletin de la Société de Linguistique* 61: 82–95.

———. 1967. Fondements syntaxiques de la composition nominale. *Bulletin de la Société de Linguistique* 62: 15–31.

Biggs, B. 1957. Testing intelligibility among Yuman languages. *IJAL* 23 (2): 57–62.

Blanckaert, C. 2006. La discipline en perspective. Le système des sciences à l'heure du spécialisme (XIXe-XXe siècles). In *Qu'est qu'une discipline ?* ed. J. Boutier, J.-C. Passeron, and J. Revel, 117–148. Paris: Éditions de l'EHESS.

Bloch, B., and G. Trager. 1942. *Outline of linguistic analysis*. Baltimore: Linguistic Society of America.

Bloomfield, L. 1914. *An introduction to the study of language*. London: G.Bel and Sons Ltd.

———. 1926. A set of postulates for the science of language. *Language* 2: 153–164.

———. 1933. *Language*. New York: H. Holt and Company.

———. 1942. *Outline guide for the practical study of foreign languages*. Baltimore: Linguistic Society of America.

Booth, A.D. 1958. The history and recent progress of machine translation. In *Aspects of translation*, ed. A.D. Booth et al., 88–104. London: Secker and Warburg.

Booth, A.D., and R.H. Richens. 1955. Some methods of mechanised translation. In *Machine translation of languages, 14 essays*, ed. W.N. Locke and A.D. Booth, 24–46. Cambridge MA/New York: MIT/Wiley.

Bouillut, J. 1967. Problèmes et méthodes dans le traitement de l'information documentaire: application à la psychologie sociale. *Bulletin de Psychologie* 20: 1191–1206.

Braffort, P., and J. Jung. 1956. *Classification alphanumérique pour le fichier matières du service de documentation du CEA*. Rapport CEA 568, Saclay.

Brown, K., and V. Law, eds. 2002. *Linguistics in Britain: Personal histories*. Oxford: Publications of the Philological Society.

Cantineau, J. 1954. Compte-rendu de Zellig S. Harris methods in structural linguistics 1951. *Bulletin de la Société de Linguistique* 46 (2): 4–9.

Carnap, R., and Y. Bar-Hillel. 1952. *An outline of a theory of semantic information Massachusetts Institute of Technology, Research Laboratory of Electronics*, Technical Report 247, Oct. 27, 1952. Reprinted in Bar-Hillel, Y. 1964. *Language and Information*, 221–274. Reading: Addison-Wesley.

Cartwright, D.P. 1963. L'analyse du matériel qualitatif. In *Les Méthodes de recherche dans les sciences sociales 2*, ed. L. Festinger and D. Katz, 481–537. Paris: PUF.

Cerquiglini, B. 1998. Le Trésor de la langue française. *Modèles Linguistiques* 19 (2): 31–36.

Chandioux, J., and M.-F. Guéraud. 1981. METEO: un système à l'épreuve du temps. *Méta* 26 (1): 18–22.

Chauveau, G. 1971. Problèmes théoriques et méthodologiques en analyse du discours. *Langue française* 9: 6–21.

Cherrry, C. 1957. *On human communication*. Cambridge: The MIT Press.

Cherry, C., M. Halle, and R. Jakobson. 1953. Toward the logical description of languages in their phonemic aspect. *Language* 29: 34–46.

Chevalier, J.-C. 1990. La linguistique au CNRS 1939–1949. *Cahiers pour l'histoire du CNRS* 9: 39–80.

———. 2006. *Combats pour la linguistique, de Martinet à Kristeva*. Lyon: ENS Éditions.

Chiss, J.-L., and C. Puech. 1999. *Le langage et ses disciplines, XIXe–XXe siècles*. Paris et Bruxelles: Éditions Duculot.

Chomsky, N. 1955. The logical structure of linguistic theory. *MIT*.

———. 1956. Three models for the description of language. *IRE (Institute of Radio Engineers) Transactions on Information Theory* IT-3: 113–124.

———. 1957. *Syntactic structures*. London: Mouton.

———. 1958. Review of Vitold Belevitch *Langage des machines et langage humain* 1956. *Language* 34 (1): 99–105.

———. 1962. Explanatory models in linguistic. In *Logic, methodology and philosophy of science*, ed. E. Nagel, P. Suppes, and A. Tarski, 528–550. Stanford: Stanford University Press.

———. 1964. The logical basis of linguistic theory. In *Proceedings of the 9th International Congress of Linguists 1962*, ed. H. Lunt, 914–978. The Hague: Mouton.

———. 2002. *On nature and language*. Cambridge: Cambridge University Press.

Chomsky, N., and G.A. Miller. 1963. Introduction to the formal analysis of natural languages. In *Handbook of mathematical psychology 2*, ed. D. Luce, R. Bush, and E. Galanter, 269–321. New York: Addison-Wiley.

Chomsky, N., and M-P. Schützenberger. 1963. The algebraic theory of context-free languages. In *Computer programming and formal systems*, Studies in logic and the foundations of mathematics, ed. P. Braffort and D. Hirschberg, vol. 14, 118–161. Amsterdam: North-Holland Publ. Co.

Church, K.W., and L.M. Robert. 1993. Introduction to the special issue on computational linguistics using large corpora. *Computational Linguistics* 19 (1): 1–25.

Climenson, W.D., N.H. Hardwick, and S.N. Jacobson. 1961. Automatic syntax analysis in machine indexing and abstracting. *American Documentation* 12 (3): 178–183.

Cohen, M. 1932. Compte-rendu de George Kingsley Zipf Selected Studies of the principle of relative frequency in language, Cambridge, Mass., Harvard University Press, 1932. *Bulletin de la Société de Linguistique* 33: 10–11.

———. 1949. Sur la statistique linguistique. Conférences de l'institut de linguistique de l'université de Paris. Klincksieck, Paris, pp. 7–16.

———. 1950. Compte-rendu de George Kingsley Zipf Human Behavior and the principle of least effort. An introduction to human ecology, Cambridge, Mass., Harvard University Press, 1949. *Bulletin de la Société de Linguistique* 46: 12–13.

———. 1962. Compte-rendu de Chomsky Syntactic Structures 1957. *L'Année sociologique*: 528–530.

Conway, F., and J. Siegelman. 2005. *Dark hero of the information age. In search of Norbert Wiener the father of cybernetics*. New York: Basic Books.

Cori, M., and S. David. 2008. Les corpus fondent-ils une nouvelle linguistique ? *Langages* 171: 111–129.

Cori, M., and J. Léon. 2002. La constitution du TAL. Etude historique des dénominations et des concepts. *Traitement Automatique des Langues* 43 (3): 21–55.

Cori, M., and J.-M. Marandin. 2001. La linguistique au contact de l'informatique: de la construction de grammaire aux grammaires de construction. *Histoire Épistémologie Langage* 23 (1): 49–79.

Coste, D. 2012. A propos d'un manuel français de linguistique appliquée. In *Les dossiers de HEL*, La disciplinarisation des savoirs linguistiques 5 SHESL, ed. Chiss et al. Paris. http://htl.linguist.univ-paris-diderot.fr/hel/dossiers/numero5

Courtois, B., and M. Silberztein, eds. 1990. Dictionnaires électroniques du français. *Langue française* 87: 3–4.

Cowan, J.M. 1991. American linguistics in peace and at war. In *First Person Singular II. Benjamins (SiHoLS 61)*, ed. E.F.K. Koerner, 69–82. Amsterdam: Benjamins.

Cowan, J.M., and M. Graves. 1986 [1976]. Report of the first year's operation of the Intensive Language Program of the American Council of Learned Societies 1941–1942. In Notes on the development of the Linguistic Society of America 1924–1950. ed. M. Joos, 97–113. Ithaca: Linguistic Society of America

Coyaud, M. 1966. *Introduction à l'étude des langages documentaires*. Paris: Klincksieck.

Cram, D. 1985. Universal language scheme in 17th century Britain. *Histoire Épistémologie Langage* 7 (2): 35–44.

Cros, R-C., J-C. Gardin, and F. Lévy. 1964. L'automatisation des recherches documentaires. Un modèle général. Le SYNTOL. Gauthier-Villars Paris; 2nde edition revue et augmentée 1968.

Dahan, A., and D. Pestre, eds. 2004. *Les sciences pour la guerre (1940–1960)*. Paris: Éditions de l'EHESS.

Daladier, A. 1990. Aspects constructifs des grammaires de Harris. *Langages* 99: 57–84.

———. 2003. Compte rendu de Nevin Bruce E. & Johnson eds, 2002, The Legacy of Zellig Harris, Amsterdam, Benjamins. *Bulletin de la Société de Linguistique* 98 (2): 50–61.

Darmesteter, A. 1875, (2e ed, 1893) [1967]. *Traité de la formation des mots composés dans la langue française comparée aux autres langues romanes et au latin*. Paris: Honoré Champion.

Daumas, M. 1965. Les machines à traduire de Georges Artsrouni. *Revue d'histoire des sciences et de leurs applications* 18 (3): 283–302.

Davies, A.L. 1990. Obituary of Stephen Pit Corder *BAAL Newsletter*, 36, Summer 1990.

Davis, B.H., and R.K. O'Cain. 1980. *First Person Singular*. Amsterdam: Benjamins (SiHoLS 21).

Delavenay, E. 1959. *La machine à traduire*. Paris: PUF. English translation: An introduction to Machine translation. Thames & Hudson, London 1960.

Desclés, J.-P., and C. Fuchs. 1969. Le séminaire international de linguistique formelle. *TA Informations* 1969 (1): 1–5.

Dosse, F. 1991. *Histoire du Structuralisme. I. Le champ du signe 1945–1966*. Paris: Éditions La Découverte.

Dostert, L. 1954. Pedagogical concepts for the use of certain audio aids in language teaching. *Monograph series on languages and linguistics* 6: 1–6.

———. 1955. The Georgetown-IBM experiment. In *Machine translation of languages, 14 essays*, ed. W.N. Locke and A.D. Booth, 124–135. Cambridge, MA/New York: MIT/Wiley.

———. 1957. Brief review of the history of Machine translation research. *Monograph Series on Languages and Linguistics* 10: 3–10.

Dubois, J. 1960. Les notions d'unité sémantique complexe et de neutralisation dans le lexique. *Cahiers de lexicologie* 2: 62–66.

———. 1962. *Le vocabulaire politique et social en France de 1869 à 1872. A travers les œuvres des écrivains, les revues et les journaux*. Paris: Larousse.

———. 1964a. La traduction de l'aspect et du temps dans le code français (structure du verbe). *Le Français moderne* 32 (1): 1–26.

———. 1964b. Compte-rendu de Roman Jakobson Essais de linguistique générale Les Éditions de Minuit. *Le Français moderne* 32 (4): 303–307.

———. 1965. *Grammaire structurale du français, nom et pronom*. Paris: Larousse.

———. 1967. *Grammaire structurale du français, le verbe*. Paris: Larousse.

———. 1969a. *Grammaire structurale du français, la phrase et les transformations*. Paris: Larousse.

———. 1969b. Lexicologie et analyse d'énoncé. *Cahiers de Lexicologie* 15: 115–126.

Dufour, F., and L. Rosier eds. 2012. Analyses du discours à la française: continuités et reconfigurations. *Langage et Société*, 140

Dupuy, J.-P. 1994. *Aux origines des sciences cognitives*. Paris: La Découverte.

Fehr, J. 2000. Visible speech and linguistic insight. In *Shifting boundaries of the real, making the invisible visible*, ed. H. Nowotny and M. Weiss, 31–47. Zürich: Hochschulverlag AG an der ETH.

———. 2003. Interceptions et interférences: la notion de 'code' entre cryptologie, télécommunications et les sciences du langage. In *History of linguistics 1999*, ed. S. Auroux, 363–372. Amsterdam: Benjamins (SiHoLS 99).

Ferguson, C. 1959. Selected readings in applied linguistics. *The Linguistic Reporter Supplement* 2: 1–4.

Firth, J.R. 1930. *Speech*. London: Benn's Sixpenny Library.

———. 1957a. *Papers in linguistics (1934–1951)*. Oxford: Oxford University Press.

———. 1957b [1935]. *The technique of semantics*. Papers in linguistics (1934–1951), 7–33. Oxford: Oxford University Press

———. 1957c [1936]. *Alphabets and phonology in India and Burma.* Papers in linguistics (1934–1951), 54–75. Oxford: Oxford University Press.

———. 1957d [1950a]. *Personality and language in society.* Papers in linguistics (1934–1951), 177–189. Oxford: Oxford University Press.

———. 1957e [1951]. *Modes of meaning.* Papers in linguistics (1934–1951), 190–215. Oxford: Oxford University Press.

———. 1968a [1955]. Structural linguistics. In *Selected papers of J.R. Firth (1952–59),* ed. F.R. Palmer, 35–52. London/Harlow: Longmans, Green and Co Ltd.

———. 1968b [1956]. Descriptive linguistics and the study of English. In: *Selected papers of J.R. Firth (1952–59),* ed. F.R. Palmer, 96–113. London/Harlow: Longmans, Green and Co Ltd.

———. 1968c [1957]. A synopsis of linguistic theory 1930–55. In *Selected papers of J.R. Firth (1952–59),* ed. F.R. Palmer, 168–205. London/Harlow: Longmans, Green and Co Ltd.

Fischer, D.H. 1970. *Historians' Fallacies. Towards a logic of historical thought.* New York: Harper & Row Publishers.

Fortun, M., and S.S. Schweber. 1993. Scientists and the legacy of World War II: The case of operations research (OR). *Social Studies of Science* 23: 595–642.

Fries, C.C. 1927. *The teaching of the English language.* New York: Thos Nelson & Sons.

———. 1940. *American English Grammar, the grammatical structure of present-day American English with especial reference to social differences or class dialects.* New York/London: Appleton-century Company.

———. 1945. *Teaching and learning English as a foreign language.* Ann Arbor: University of Michigan Press.

———. 1949. The Chicago Investigation. *Language Learning* 23: 89–99.

———. 1961. The Bloomfield 'school'. In *Trends in European and American linguistics 1930–1960,* ed. C. Mohrmann, A. Sommerfelt, and J. Whatmough, 196–224. Utrecht: Spectrum.

Fuchs, C. 1982. *La paraphrase.* Paris: PUF.

Fuchs, C., and B. Victorri. 1996. *La polysémie, construction dynamique du sens.* Paris: Hermès.

Gardin, J.-C. 1955. Problèmes de la documentation. *Diogène* 11: 107–124.

———. 1956. *Le fichier mécanographique de l'outillage: outils en métal de l'âge du bronze, des Balkans à l'Indus.* Beyrouth: Institut français d'archéologie.

———.. 1959. On the coding of geometrical shapes and other representations, with reference to archaelogical documents. In *Proceedings of the International Conference of Scientific Information,* Washington, DC, 16–21 November, 1958, National Academy of Sciences-National Research Council, pp 75–87.

———. 1962. Documentation sur cartes perforées et travaux sur ordinateurs dans les sciences humaines Revue Internationale de. *Documentation* 29 (3): 84–92.

———., ed. 1970. *Archéologie et Calculateurs.* Paris: Éditions du CNRS.

———. 1974. *Les analyses de discours.* Neuchâtel: Delachaux et Niestlé.

Gardin, J.-C., and B. Jaulin, eds. 1968. *Calcul et formalisation dans les sciences de l'homme, Actes des Journées internationales d'études sur les méthodes de calcul dans les Sciences de l'Homme, Rome 4–8 juillet 1966, Unesco et MSH.* Paris: Éditions du CNRS.

Gardin, J.-C., M.-S. Lagrange, J.-M. Martin, J. Molino, and J. Natali. 1981. *La logique du plausible, Essais d'épistémologie pratique.* Paris: Éditions de la Maison des Sciences de l'Homme.

Garvin, P. 1967. American Indian languages: A laboratory for linguistic methodology. *Foundations of Language* 3 (3): 257–260.

———. 1968. Machine translation today: The Fulcrum approach and Heuristics. *Lingua* 21: 162–182.

Girault, S., and B. Victorri. 2009. Linguistiques de corpus et mathématiques du continu. *Histoire Épistémologie Langage* 31 (1): 147–170.

Giroux, H.A. 2007. *The University in chains: Confronting the Military-industrial-academic Complex.* Boulder: Paradigm Publishers.

Gleason, H.A. 1969. *An introduction to descriptive linguistics.* Revised Edition. London/New York/Sydney/Toronto: Holt Rinehart Winston.

Graves, M. 1951. Report on the annual round table meeting on linguistics and language teaching. In *Monograph series on languages and linguistics*, ed. John De Francis, 1: 1–45.

Gross, M. 1964. The equivalences of models of language used in the fields of mechanical translation and information retrieval. *Information Storage and Retrieval* 2 (1): 43–57.

———. 1968. *Grammaire transformationnelle du français. Syntaxe du verbe*. Paris: Larousse.

Gross, M., and A. Lentin. 1967. *Notions sur les grammaires formelles*. Paris: Gauthier-Villars.

Guespin, L. 1971. Problématique des travaux sur le discours politique. *Langages* 23: 3–24.

Guiraud, P. 1954. *Les Caractères statistiques du vocabulaire*. Paris: PUF.

———. 1960. *Problèmes et méthodes de la statistique linguistique*. Paris: PUF.

Gumperz, J., and D. Hymes. 1972. *Directions in sociolinguistics: The ethnography of communication*. Rinehart and Winston/Holt: New York.

Habert, B. 2005. *Instruments et ressources électroniques pour le français*. Paris: Ophrys.

Habert, B., and C. Jacquemin. 1993. Noms composés, termes, dénominations complexes: problématiques linguistiques et traitements automatiques. *TAL* 34 (2): 5–43.

Habert, B., A. Nazarenko, and A. Salem. 1997. *Les linguistiques de corpus*. Armand Colin. Paris: Masson.

Hall, R.A. 1991. 165 Broadway – A crucial node in American structural linguistics. *Historiographia Linguistica* 18 (1): 153–166.

Halliday, M.A.K. 1966. Lexis as a linguistic level. In *In memory of J.R. Firth*, ed. C.E. Bazell, J.C. Catford, M.A.K. Halliday, and R.H. Robins, 148–162. London: Longmans.

———. 2002. *The collected works of MAK Halliday 1*, ed. Jonathan Webster. London/New York: Continuum.

Halliday, M.A.K., A. McIntosh, and P. Strevens. 1964. *The linguistic sciences and language teaching*. London: Longmans.

Harper, K.E. 1961. Soviet research in machine translation. In *Proceedings of the national symposium on machine translation*, ed. H.P. Edmundson, 2–12. Los Angeles: University of California.

Harris, Z.S. 1946. From Morpheme to Utterance. *Language* 22 (3): 161–183.

———. 1951a. *Methods in structural linguistics*. Chicago: The University of Chicago Press.

———. 1951b. Review of Mandelbaum ed. 1949 Selected writings of Edward Sapir in language, culture and personality. *Language* 27: 288–333.

———. 1952. Discourse analysis. *Language* 28: 18–23.

———. 1954. Transfer grammar. *International Journal of American Linguistics* 20 (4): 259–270.

———. 1955. From phoneme to morpheme. *Language* 31: 190–222.

———. 1957. Co-occurrence and transformation in linguistic structure. *Language* 33: 283–340.

———. 1959. Linguistic transformations for information retrieval. In *Proceedings of the International Conference on Scientific Information*, Washington, DC, 16–21 November 1958, 937–950. Washington, DC: National Academy of Sciences, National Research Council.

———. 1962a. *String analysis of sentence structure*. The Hague: Mouton.

———. 1962b. A language for international cooperation. In *Preventing World War III: Some proposals*, ed. Q. Wright et al., 299–309. New York: Simon & Schuster.

———. 1963. *Discourse analysis reprints*, Papers on formal linguistics. The Hague: 2 Mouton.

———. 1968. *Mathematical structures of language*. New York: Wiley.

———. 1969. *The two systems of grammar: Report and paraphrase*, Transformations and discourse analysis Papers 79. Philadelphia: University of Pennsylvania.

———. 1970 [1959]. *Linguistic transformations for information retrieval*. Papers in structural and transformational linguistics, 458–471. Dordrecht: D. Reidel.

———. 1976. *Notes du cours de syntaxe*. Paris: Le Seuil.

———. 1988. *Language and information*. New York: Columbia University Press.

———. 1991. *A theory of language and information: A mathematical approach*. Oxford/New York: Clarendon Press.

Harris, Z.S., and C.F. Voegelin. 1975 [1939]. *Lowie Robert H. Hidatsa texts; with grammatical notes and phonograph transcriptions*. New York: AMS Press.

Hartley, R.V.L. 1928. Transmission of information. *Bell System Technical Journal* 7: 535–563.

Hartog, F. 2003. *Régimes d'historicité. Présentisme et expériences du temps*. Paris: Éditions du Seuil.

Harwood, F.W. 1955. Axiomatic syntax. The construction and evaluation of a syntactic calculus. *Language* 31 (3): 409–413.

Hays, D.G. 1964. Dependency theory: A formalism and some observations. *Language* 40 (4): 511–525.

Heims, S.J. 1993. *Constructing a social science for Postwar America: The cybernetics Group, 1946–1953*. Cambridge, MA: The MIT Press.

Henry, P. 1967. Analyse de contenu, connaissances scientifiques et langage documentaire ; questions méthodologiques. *Bulletin du CERP* 16 (3): 245–263.

Hickerson, H., G.D. Turner, and N.P. Hickerson. 1952. Testing procedures for estimating transfer of information among Iroquois dialects and languages. *IJAL* 18 (1): 1–8.

Hill, A.A. 1964. History of the Linguistic Institute. *Bulletin of the Indiana University Linguistic Institute* 16–32.

———. 1979. Martin Joos. *Language* 55 (3): 665–669.

Hockett, C.F. 1952. Report on the 3rd annual round table meeting on linguistics and language teaching, Castiglione Salvatore J (ed). *Monograph Series on Languages and Linguistics* 2: 3–10.

———. 1953. Review: The mathematical theory of communication by Claude L. Shannon and Warren Weaver. *Language* 29 (1): 69–93.

———. 1954. Translation via immediate constituents. *International Journal of American Linguistics* 20 (4): 313–315.

———. 1958. *A course in modern linguistics*. New York: The Macmillan Company.

———. 1968. *The state of the art*. The Hague: Mouton.

Hockett, C.F., and R. Ascher. 1964. The human revolution. *Current Anthropology* 5: 135.

Howatt, A.P.R. 2004 [1984]. *History of English language teaching*. Oxford: Oxford University Press.

Hutchins, W.J. 1986a. *Machine translation, past, present, future*. Chichester ltd: Ellis Horwood.

———. 1986b. Direct translation systems since 1965. In *Machine translation, past, present, future*, ed. W.J. Hutchins, 209–223. Chichester ltd: Ellis Horwood.

———. 1995. 'The whisky was invisible', or persistent myths of MT. *MT News International* 11: 17–18.

———. 1996. ALPAC: The (In)famous report. *MT News International* 14: 9–12.

———. 1997. From first conception to first demonstration: The nascent years of machine translation, 1947–1954. A chronology. *Machine Translation* 12 (3): 192–252.

———., ed. 2000a. *Early years in machine translation*. Amsterdam: Benjamins (SiHoLS 97).

———. 2000b. Gilbert W. King and the IBM-USAF translator. In *Early years in machine translation*, ed. W.J. Hutchins, 171–176. Amsterdam: Benjamins (SiHoLS 97).

Hymes, D. 1962. The ethnography of speaking. In *Anthropology and human behaviour*, ed. T. Gladwin and W.C. Sturtevant. Washington, DC: Anthropology Society of Washington.

Hymes, D., and J. Fought. 1981. *American structuralism*. The Hague/Paris/New York: Mouton Publishers.

Jakobson, R. 1953. Patterns in linguistics. In *Results of the conference of anthropologists and linguists*, ed. C. Levi-Strauss, R. Jakobson, C.F. Voegelin, T. Sebeok. Memoir 8 of the International Journal of American Linguistics. Indiana University Publications in Anthropology and Linguistics: 11–21.

———. 1958. Typological studies and their contribution to historical comparative linguistics. In *Actes du 8e Congrès international des linguistes*, ed. E. Sivertsen, 17–35. Oslo: Presses Universitaires d'Oslo.

———. 1971a [1959]. *Boas' view of grammatical meaning*. Selected writings II, 489–496. s-Gravenhage: Mouton.

———. 1971b [1961]. *Linguistics and communication theory*. Selected writings II, 570–579. s-Gravenhage: Mouton.

Jakobson, R., and M. Halle. 1956. *Fundamentals of language*. The Hague: Mouton.

Jakobson, R., C.G. Fant, and M. Halle 1952. *Preliminaries to speech analysis. The distinctive features and their correlates*, Technical report 13. Cambridge: MIT Acoustic Laboratory.

Joos, M. 1942. Statistical patterns in gothic phonology. *Language* 18 (1): 33–38.

———. 1948. Acoustic phonetics, Supplement to Language, *Language Monograph* n° 23.

———. 1951. Report on the 2nd annual round table meeting on linguistics and language teaching. John De Francis ed. Georgetown: The Institute of Language and Linguistics School of Foreign Service, Georgetown University 13–14.

———. 1956. Review of "Machine translation of languages: Fourteen essays, ed. by William N. Locke and A. Donald Booth 1955". *Language* 32 (2): 293–298.

———. 1957. Readings in linguistics. The development of descriptive linguistics in America 1925–1956. Chicago: The University of Chicago Press.

———. 1986 [1976]. *Notes on the development of the Linguistic Society of America, 1924–1950*. Ithaca: Linguistica.

Joseph, J.E. 2002. *From Whitney to Chomsky. Essays in the history of American linguistics*. Amsterdam: Benjamins (SiHoLS 103).

———. 2003. Rethinking linguistic creativity. In *Rethinking linguistics*, ed. H.G. Davis and T. Taylor, 121–150. London/New York: Routledge Curzon.

Josselson, H.H. 1971. Automatic translation of languages since 1960: A Linguist's view. *Advances in Computers* 11: 1–58.

Kaplan, R.B., ed. 2002. *Oxford handbook of applied linguistics*. Oxford: Oxford University Press.

Kent, A., ed. 1961. *Information retrieval and machine translation*. New York/London: Interscience Publishers.

Kertész, A., and C. Rákosi. 2012. *Data and evidence in linguistics. A plausible argumentation model*. Cambridge: CUP.

Kittredge, R., and J. Lehrberger, eds. 1982. *Studies of language in restricted semantic domains*. Berlin/New York: Walter de Gruyter.

Koerner, K. ed. 1991. *First Person Singular II*. Amsterdam: Benjamins (SiHoLS 61).

Koutsoudas, A. 1956. Report from the international conference on mechanical translation (MIT, 20 octobre 1956). *Machine Translation* 3 (2): 34.

Krajewski, M. 2011. *Paper machines, About cards & catalogs 1548–1929*. Cambridge, MA: The MIT Press.

Kucera, H., and W.N. Francis. 1967. *Computational analysis of present day American English*. Providence: Brown University Press.

Kulagina, O.S., and I.A. Mel'čuk. 1967. Automatic translation: Some theoretical aspects and the design of a translation system. In *Machine translation*, ed. A.D. Booth, 137–173. Amsterdam: North Holland Publishing Company.

Lahaussois, A., and J. Léon. 2015. Transcription and translation of unwritten languages in American linguistics (1950s to 2000s). In *La traduction dans l'histoire des idées linguistiques*, ed. E. Aussant, 235–257. Paris: Geuthner.

Lamb, S.M. 1962. On the mechanisation of syntactic analysis. In *Proceedings of the International Conference on Machine translation and Applied Language Analysis, Teddington 1961*, 673–686. London: HMSO.

Le Roux, R. 2009. Lévi-Strauss, une réception paradoxale de la cybernétique (avec une réponse de Cl. Lévi-Strauss). *L'Homme, Éditions EHESS* 189: 65–190

———. 2013. Structuralisme(s) et cybernétique(s). Lévi-Strauss, Lacan et les mathématiciens. In Les dossiers de HEL (Histoire Épistémologie Langage) 3 Les structuralismes linguistiques, ed. C. Puech. Problèmes d'historiographie comparée. http://htl.linguist.univ-paris-diderot.fr/hel/dossiers/numero3

Lecerf, Y. 1960. Programme des conflits, modèle des conflits. *La Traduction automatique* 4–5: 17–36.

Leech, G. 1992. Corpora and theories of linguistic performance. In *Directions in Corpus Linguistics*, ed. J. Svartvik. Proceedings of Nobel Symposium, 4–8 August 1991. Berlin/New York: Mouton de Gruyter, pp 105–122.

Léon, J. 1992. De la traduction automatique à la linguistique computationnelle. Contribution à une chronologie des années 1959–1965. *Traitement Automatique des Langues* 33 (1/2): 25–44.

———. 2001. Conceptions du mot et débuts de la traduction automatique. *Histoire Épistémologie Langage* 23 (1): 81–106.

———. 2004. Lexies, synapsies, synthèmes: le renouveau des études lexicales en France au début des années 1960. In *History of linguistics in texts and concepts. Geschichte der Sprachwissenschaft in Texten und Konzeptionen*, ed. G. Hassler, 405–418. Nodus Publikationen: Münster.

———. 2006a. La traduction automatique In: les premières tentatives jusqu'au rapport ALPAC. In *Handbücher zur Sprach- und Kommunikationswissenschaft*, ed. S. Auroux, E.F.K. Koerner, H.J. Niederehe, and K. Versteegh, vol. 3, 2767–2774. Berlin: Walter de Gruyter and Co.

———. 2006b. La traduction automatique II: développements récents. In *Handbücher zur Sprach- und Kommunikationswissenschaft*, ed. S. Auroux, E.F.K. Koerner, H.J. Niederehe, and K. Versteegh, vol. 3, 2774–2780. Berlin: Walter de Gruyter and co.

———. 2007a. From universal languages to intermediary languages in Machine translation: The work of the Cambridge Language Research Unit (1955–1970). In *History of linguistics 2002*, ed. E. Guimarães, D. Luz Pessoa de Barros, 123–132. Amsterdam: Benjamins (SiHoLS 110).

———. 2007b. From Linguistic events and restricted languages to registers. Firthian legacy and Corpus Linguistics. *The Bulletin of the Henry Sweet Society for the History of Linguistic Ideas* 49: 5–26.

———. 2007c. Meaning by collocation. The Firthian filiation of corpus linguistics. In *History of linguistics 2005*, ed. D. Kibbee, 404–415. Amsterdam: Benjamins (SiHoLS 112).

———. 2007d. Claimed and unclaimed sources of Corpus Linguistics. In *Corpus linguistics: Critical concepts in linguistics 1*, ed. R. Krishnamurthy and W. Teubert, 326–341. London/New York: Routledge.

———. 2008a. Théorie de l'information, information et linguistes français dans les années 1960. Un exemple de transfert entre mathématiques et sciences du langage. In *Actes du Congrès Mondial de Linguistique Française*, ed. J. Durand, B. Habert, B. Laks. Paris, 9–12 juillet 2008. pp 923–938. https://doi.org/10.1051/cmlf08142

———. 2008b. Aux sources de la 'corpus linguistics': Firth et la London School. In *Construction des faits en linguistique: la place des corpus*, ed. M. Cori, S. David, and J. Léon. Langages 171: 12–33.

———. 2008c. Empirical traditions of computer-based methods. Firth's restricted languages and Harris' sublanguages. Beiträge zur Geschichte der. *Sprachwissenschaft* 18 (2): 259–274.

———. 2010a. AAD69. Archéologie d'une étrange machine. *Semen* 29: 79–98.

———. 2010b. British empiricism and transformational grammar: A current debate. In *Chomskyan (R)evolutions*, ed. D. Kibbee, 421–442. Amsterdam: Benjamins.

———. 2010c. Automatisation-mathématisation de la linguistique en France dans les années 1960. Un cas de réception externe. In *Actes du 2e Congrès Mondial de Linguistique Française*, ed. F. Neveu, V. Muni-Toke, J. Durand, T. Kingler, L. Mondada, and S. Prévost, 825–838. www.linguistiquefrancaise.org. Paris: EDP Sciences. https://doi.org/10.1051/cmlf2010158.

———. 2011a. S.Z. Harris and the semantic turn of mathematical information theory. In: Hassler G (ed) *History of Linguistics 2008*. Selected Papers from the Eleventh International Conference on the History of Language Sciences, 28 August–2 September 2008 Postdam, 449–458. Amsterdam: Benjamins (SiHoLS 115).

———. 2011b. De la linguistique descriptive à la linguistique appliquée dans la tradition britannique. Sweet, Firth et Halliday. *Histoire Épistémologie Langage* 33 (1): 69–81.

———. 2013a. Quand usage et prescription sont fondés sur la description systématique de l'usage: Randolph Quirk et le "Survey of English usage". In *Bon usage et variation sociolinguistique: Perspectives diachroniques et traditions nationales*, ed. W. Ayres-Bennett and M. Seijido, 161–170. Lyon: ENS Éditions.

———. 2013b. Review of "Barsky, Robert, 2011, Zellig Harris. From American Linguistics to Socialist Zionism Cambridge Mass, MIT". *Language and History* 56 (2): 119–122.

———. 2014. Early machine translation. Integration and transfers between computing and the language sciences. In *Computability in Europe 2014*, Lecture notes in computer science, ed. A. Beckmann, E. Csuhaj-Varjú, and K. Meer, vol. 8493, 275–282. Cham: Springer.

———. 2017. The statistical studies of vocabulary in the 1950–60s in France. Theoretical and institutional issues. In *Quantitative linguistics in France*, ed. S. Loiseau and J. Léon, 9–28. Lüdenscheid: RAMVerlag.

———. 2019. Les sources britanniques de l'ethnographie de la communication et de l'analyse de conversation. Bronislaw Malinowski et John Rupert Firth. *Linha d'Agua* 32 (1): 23–38.

———. 2020. Traduction, procédures, formalisation : le tournant de l'automatisation de la linguistique structurale américaine. In *Travaux linguistiques du CerLiCO 31: Transcrire, Ecrire, Formaliser 2*, ed. F. Toupin and C. Collin, 137–154. Rennes: Presses Universitaires de Rennes.

———. 2021. On the history of models in American linguistics. In *The philosophy and science of language*, ed. R.M. Nefdt, C. Klippi, and B. Karstens, 349–373. London: Palgrave Macmillan.

Léon, J., and S. Loiseau, eds. 2017. *Quantitative linguistics in France*. Lüdenscheid: *RAMVerlag*.

Léon, J., and N. Riemer. 2015. Genèse et développement du concept de grammaticalité dans la pensée de Chomsky (1951–1965). *Histoire Epistémologie Langage* 37 (2): 115–152.

Léon, J., and M.E. Torres-Lima. 1979. Etudes de certains aspects du fonctionnement d'AAD69: traitement des syntagmes nominaux en expressions figées et segmentation d'un corpus en séquences discursives autonomes. *T.A Informations* 20 (1): 25–46.

Leslie, S.W. 1993. *The Cold War and American Science: The military-industrial-academic complex at MIT & Standford*. New York: Columbia University Press.

Linn, A. 2008. The Birth of applied linguistics: The Anglo-Scandinavian school as 'discourse community'. *Historiographia Linguistica* 35 (3): 342–384.

Linn, A., D. Candel, and J. Léon eds. 2011. Disciplinarisation de la linguistique appliquée. *Histoire Épistémologie Langage, 33*(1).

Linx 34-35. 1996. Lexique, syntaxe et analyse automatique des textes. Hommage à Jean Dubois, Centre de Recherches Linguistiques de l'Université Paris X-Nanterre

Locke, W.N., and A.D. Booth, eds. 1955. *Machine translation of languages, 14 essays*. Cambridge MA, New York: MIT/Wiley.

Loffler-Laurian, A.-M. 1996. *La traduction automatique*. Lille: Septentrion.

Malinowski, B. 1923. The problem of meaning in primitive languages. In *The meaning of meaning*, ed. C.K. Ogden and I.A. Richards. London: Kegan Paul Supplement 1.

———. 1935. *Coral gardens and their magic*, The language of magic and gardening 2. London: Allen & Unwin.

Mandelbrot, B. 1954a. Structure formelle des textes et communication. *Word* 10 (3): 1–27.

———. 1954b. Compte-rendu de l'ouvrage Pierre Guiraud 1954 Les caractères statistiques du vocabulaire. Essai de méthodologie, Paris, PUF. *Bulletin de la Société de Linguistique* 50: 16–21.

Marandin, J.-M. 1979. Problèmes d'analyse du discours. Essai de description du discours français sur la Chine. *Langages* 55: 17–88.

Marcus, S. 1988. Mathématiques et linguistique. *Mathématiques et sciences humaines* 103: 7–21.

Markov, A.A. 1913. Exemple d'une étude statistique d'un texte extrait de 'Eugène Oniguine' illustrant les probabilités liées. *Bulletin de l'Académie Impériale des Sciences de St Pétersbourg*: 153–162.

Martinet, A. 1955. *Économie des changements phonétiques*. Berne: Francke.

———. 1957a. Compte-rendu de George A. Miller Langage et communication PUF 1956. *Bulletin de la Société de Linguistique* 53: 25–26.

———. 1957b. Compte-rendu de Vitold Belevitch Langage des machines et langage humain Paris, Hermann 1956. *Bulletin de la Société de Linguistique* 53: 27–29.

———. 1957c. Substance phonique et traits distinctifs. *Bulletin de la Société de Linguistique* 53: 72–85.

———. 1967. Syntagme et synthème. *La Linguistique* 2: 1–14.

———. 1970 [1960]. *Eléments de linguistique générale*. Paris: Armand Colin.

———. 1993. *Mémoires d'un linguiste*. Paris: Quai Voltaire.

Martin-Nielsen, J. 2010. 'This war for men's minds': The birth of a human science in Cold War America. *History of the Human Sciences* 23: 131–155.

Masterman, M., A.F. Parker-Rhodes, K. Sparck Jones, M. Kay, E.B. May, R.M. Needham, E.W. Bastin, C. Wordley, F.H. Ellis, and R. McKinnon Wood. 1959. Essays on and in Machine translation by the Cambridge Language Research Unit, dedicated to Yehoshua Bar-Hillel [Archives HTAL].

Matthews, P.H. 1999. Obituary of Zellig Sabbettai Harris. *Language* 75 (1): 112–119.

Mazziotta, N. 2016. Drawing syntax before syntactic trees: Stephen Watkins Clark's Sentence Diagrams (1847). *Historiographia Linguistica* 43 (3): 301–341.

McIntosh, A., and M.A.K. Halliday. 1966. *Patterns of language, papers in general, descriptive and applied linguistics*. London: Longmans.

Mel'čuk, I.A. 1960. K voprosu o grammatičeskom v jazyke- posrednike. *Mašinnyj Perevod i Prikladnaja Linguistika* 4: 25–451. English translation The problem concerning the 'grammatical' in an intermediate language. JPRS/8026 [archives HTAL].

———. 1961. *Some problems of MT abroad, USSR*. Reports at the conference on Information Processing, 1–44. Moscow: MT and Automatic Text Reading, Academy of Science, Institute of Scientific Information 6. English translation JPRS/13135, pp 1–75 [archives HTAL].

———. 1993. *Cours de Morphologie Générale 1. Introduction et première partie: le mot*. Paris: Montréal. Presses de l'Université de Montréal, CNRS Éditions.

Mel'čuk, I.A., A.K. Žholkovskij. 1970. Sur la synthèse sémantique. T.A. Informations 2: 1–85 [Problemy Kibernetiki 19 1967: 177–238].

Melby, A. 1992. The translator workstation. In *Computers in translation, A practical appraisal*, ed. J. Newton, 147–165. London: Routledge.

Micklesen, L.R. 1956. Form classes: Structural linguistics and mechanical translation. In *For Roman Jakobson, Essays on the occasion of his sixtieth Birthday 11 Oct 1956*, ed. M. Halle, H.G. Lunt, H. McLean, and C.H. van Schooneveld, 344–352. The Hague: Mouton.

Mildenberger, K.W. 1962. The National Defense Education Act and linguistics. *Monograph Series on Languages and Linguistics* 13: 157–165.

Miller, G.A. 1951. *Language and communication*. New York: McGraw Hill.

Mindell, D., J. Segal, and S. Gerovitch. 2003. Cybernetics and information theory in the United States, France and the Soviet Union. In *Science and ideology: A comparative history*, ed. M. Walker, 66–95. London: Routledge.

Moulton, W.G. 1961. Linguistics and language teaching in the United States 1940–1960. In *Trends in European and American Linguistics 1930–1960*, ed. C. Mohrmann, A. Sommerfelt, and J. Whatmough, 82–109. Utrecht/Antwerp: Spectrum Publishers.

Mounier-Kuhn, P.-E. 2010. *L'informatique en France, de la seconde guerre mondiale au Plan Calcul. L'émergence d'une science*. Paris: PUPS.

Mounin, G. 1961. Compte-rendu de Chomsky Syntactic Structures 1957. *Bulletin de la Société de Linguistique* 56 (2): 38.

———. 1963. *Les problèmes théoriques de la traduction*. Paris: Gallimard.

———. 1964. *La machine à traduire. Histoire des problèmes linguistiques*. La Haye: Mouton.

Murray, S.O. 1993. *Theory groups and the study of language in North America*. Amsterdam: Benjamins (SiHoLS 69).

Nefdt, R. 2019. Infinity and the foundations of linguistics. *Synthese* 196: 1671–1711.

Nevin, B.E., ed. 2002. *The Legacy of Zellig Harris*. Amsterdam: Benjamins.

———. 2009. More concerning the roots of transformational generative grammar. *Historiographia Linguistica* 36 (2/3): 459–479.

Nirenburg, S., ed. 1993. *Progress in machine translation*. Amsterdam: IOS Press.

Oettinger, A.G. 1955. The design of an automatic Russian-English technical dictionary. In *Machine translation of languages, 14 essays.*, ed. W.N. Locke and A.D. Booth, 47–65. Cambridge MA/ New York: MIT/Wiley.

Pagès, R. 1959. L'analyse codée, technique documentaire en psychologie sociale et en sciences humaines: présentation et résumé de la grammaire. *Chiffres* 2: 102–122.

Panov, D.I. 1956. Avtomatičeskij perevod, Moskva, AN SSSR. English translation (1960) Automatic translation. Oxford/New York: Pergamon Press Inc.

Panov, D.I., and L.N. Korolev. eds. 1959. La machine à traduire de P.P. Trojanskij. Édition de l'Académie des sciences de Moscou. French translation CASDN, n° T/R/ -1059 [Archives HTAL].

Panov, D.I., A.A, Liapunov, and I.S. Mukhin. 1956. *Avtomatizatsja perevoda s odnogo jazyka na drugoi*. Moscow Academy of Sciences. English translation: Automatisation of translation from one language to another. JPRS/DC-379, novembre 1958. [Archives HTAL].

Partee Hall, B. 1978. *Fundamentals of mathematics for linguistics*. Dordrecht: D.Reidel Publishing Company.

Pêcheux, M. 1967a. Analyse de contenu et théorie du discours. *Bulletin du CERP* 16 (3): 211–227.

———. 1967b. Analyse automatique du discours. mimeo document, November 1967.

———. 1968. Vers une technique d'analyse de discours. *Psychologie Française* 13 (1): 113–117.

———. 1969. *Analyse Automatique du Discours*. Paris: Dunod.

———. 1975. Analyse du discours, langue et idéologies. Langages:37.

Pêcheux, M., S. Bonnafous, J. Léon, and J.-M. Marandin. 1982. Présentation de l'analyse automatique du discours (AAD69): théorie, procédures, résultats, perspectives. *Mots* 4: 95–124.

Pélissier, A., and A. Tête. 1995. *Sciences cognitives. Textes fondateurs (1943–1950)*. Paris: PUF.

Pereira, F. 2002. Formal grammar and Information Theory: Together again? In *The Legacy of Zellig Harris*, ed. E. Nevin Bruce, 13–32. Amsterdam: Benjamins.

Perrault, R.C. ed. 1984. Special issue on mathematical properties of grammatical formalisms. *Computational Linguistics*, *10*(3–4).

Peters, S., and Robert Ritchie. 1973. On the generative power of transformational grammars. *Information Science* 6: 49–83.

Petruszewycz, M. 1981. *Les Chaînes de Markov dans le domaine linguistique*. Genève/Paris: Éditions Slatkine.

Pierce, J.E. 1952. Dialect distance testing in Algonquian. *IJAL* 18 (4): 203–210.

Pike, K.L. 1943. Taxemes and Immediate Constituents. *Language* 19: 65–82.

Plutniak, S. 2017. L'innovation méthodologique, entre bifurcation personnelle et formation des disciplines: les entrées en archéologie de Georges Laplace et de Jean-Claude Gardin. *Revue d'histoire des sciences humaines* 31: 113–139.

Polguère, A. 1998. La théorie Sens-Texte. *Dialangue* 8–9. *Université du Québec à Chicoutimi*: 9–30.

Post, E.L. 1943. Formal Reductions of the General Combinatorial Decision Problem. *American Journal of Mathematics* 65 (2): 197–215.

Pottier, B. 1962a. Introduction à l'étude des structures grammaticales fondamentales. *La Traduction Automatique* 3 (3): 63–91.

———. 1962b. Les travaux lexicologiques préparatoires à la traduction automatique. *Cahiers de lexicologie* 3: 200–206.

Pratt, V. 1987. *Thinking Machines. The Evolution of Artificial Intelligence*. Oxford: Basil Blackwell.

Puech, C. 2008. Qu'est-ce que faire l'histoire du 'récent'? In *Congrès mondial de Linguistique Française – CMLF08*, ed. J. Durand, B. Habert, and B. Laks. Paris: Institut de Linguistique Française.

Pulgram, E. ed. 1954. Applied linguistics in language teaching monograph series on languages and linguistics: 6

Pullum, G.K. 2007. Ungrammaticality, rarity, and corpus use. *Corpus Linguistics and Linguistic Theory* 3: 33–47.

Pullum, G.K., and B. Scholz. 2007. Review article: Tracking the origins of transformational grammar Marcus Tomalin, 2006, *Linguistics and the formal sciences: The origins of generative grammar* (Cambridge Studies in Linguistics 110). Cambridge: Cambridge University Press. *Journal of Linguistics* 43 (3): 701–723.

Quirk, R. 1960. Towards a description of English usage. *Transactions of the Philological Society* 59: 40–61.

Quirk, R., and J. Mulholland. 1964. Complex prepositions and related sequences. *English Studies* 45: 148–160.

Quirk, R., and J. Svartvik. 1966. *Investigating linguistic acceptability.* The Hague: Mouton.

Ramunni, J. 1989. *La physique du calcul, Histoire de l'ordinateur.* Paris: Hachette.

Reifler, E. 1955. The mechanical determination of meaning. In *Machine translation of languages, 14 essays,* ed. W.N. Locke and A.D. Booth, 136–164. Cambridge MA/New York: MIT.

Richens, R.H. 1955. *A general programme for mechanical translation between any two languages via an algebraic interlingua* [Archives HTAL].

Richens, R.H., and A.D. Booth. 1955. Some methods of Mechanised translation. In *Machine translation of languages, 14 essays,* ed. W.N. Locke and A.D. Booth, 24–46. Cambridge, MA/New York: MIT/Wiley.

Riemer, N. 2009. Grammaticality as evidence and as prediction in a Galilean linguistics. *Language Sciences* 31: 612–633.

Romashko, S. 2000. Vers l'analyse du dialogue en Russie. *Histoire Épistémologie Langage* 22 (1): 83–98.

Rorty, R., ed. 1967. *The Linguistic Turn. Recent Essays in Philosophical Method.* Chicago: The University of Chicago Press.

Rumelhart, D.E., J.L. McClelland, The PDP Research Group. 1986. *Parallel distributed processing: Explorations in the microstructure of cognition,* vol. 1 & 2. Cambridge, MA: MIT Press.

Salkoff, M. 2002. Some new results on transfer grammar. In *The Legacy of Zellig Harris,* ed. B. Nevin, 167–178. Amsterdam: Benjamins.

Salmon, V. 1979. *John Wilkins' Essay (1668): Critics and continuators. The study of language in 17th century England,* 97–126. Amsterdam: Benjamins.

Sampson, G. 2001. *Empirical linguistics.* London/New York: Continuum.

Sapir, E. 1949. *Selected writings of Edward Sapir in language, culture and personality.* David G. Mandelbaum ed. Berkeley: University of California Press.

Savitch, W.J., E. Bach, W. Marsh, and N.G. Safran, eds. 1987. *The formal complexity of natural language.* Dordrecht: D. Reidel.

Schütze, C.T. 1996. *The empirical base of linguistics: Grammaticality judgments and linguistic methodology.* Chicago: University of Chicago Press.

Segal, J. 2003. *Le Zéro et le Un. Histoire de la notion scientifique d'information au XXe siècle.* Paris: Éditions Syllepse.

Sériot, P., ed. 2006. *Nicolaï Troubetzkoy, Correspondance avec Roman Jakobson et autres écrits (traduction du russe par Patrick Sériot et Margarita Schoenenberger).* Lausanne: Payot Lausanne.

Seuren, P. 1998. *Western linguistics: An historical introduction.* Oxford: Blackwell.

———. 2006. Early formalisation tendencies in 20th-century American linguistics. In *History of the language sciences – An international handbook on the evolution of the study of language from the beginnings to the present. Handbooks of linguistics and communication sciences 18(3),* ed. E.F.K. Koerner, S. Auroux, H.J. Niederehe, and K. Versteegh, 2026–2034. Berlin: Walter de Gruyter.

———. 2009. Concerning the roots of transformational generative grammar. *Historiographia Linguistica* 36 (1): 97–115.

Shannon, C.E. 1950. A chess-playing machine. *Scientific American* 182 (2): 48–51.

———. 1956. *The Bandwagon.* Institute of Radio Engineers, Transactions on Information Theory, IT-2: 3.

Shannon, C.E., and W. Weaver. 1949. *The mathematical theory of communication, Urbana-Champaign.* Urbana: University of Illinois Press.

Sinclair, J. McH. 1965. When is a poem like a sunset? *A review of English literature* 6 (2): 76–91.

———. 1991. *Corpus, concordance, collocation.* Oxford: Oxford University Press.

Sinclair, J. McH, S. Jones, R. Daley, and R. Krishnamurthy, eds. 2004. *English collocation studies: The OSTI report*. London/New York: Continuum.

Stone, P.J., D.C. Dunphy, M.S. Smith, and D.M. Ogilvie. 1966. *The general inquirer: A computer approach to content analysis*. Cambridge: Cambridge Computer Associates/MIT Press.

Sweet, H. 1884. Practical study of language. *Transactions of the Philological Society* 4: 577–599.

Swiggers, P. 2008. Introduction: The problem of an international auxiliary language. In *The collected works of Edward Sapir*, ed. P. Swiggers, 245–250. Berlin/New York: Mouton de Gruyter.

Tesnière, L. 1953. *Esquisse d'une syntaxe structurale*. Paris: Klincksieck.

———. 1959. *Éléments de syntaxe structurale*. Paris: Klincksieck.

Togeby, K. 1951. Structure immanente de la langue française. *Travaux du cercle linguistique de Copenhague* 10: 1–89.

Toma, P. 2000. From Serna to Systran. In *Early years in machine translation*, ed. W. Hutchins, 135–145. Amsterdam/Philadelphia: John Benjamins.

Tomalin, M. 2006. *Linguistics and the formal sciences: The origins of generative grammar*. Cambridge: CUP.

Trubetzkoy. N.S. 1949 [1939]. *Principes de phonologie*. French translation J. Cantineau. Paris: Klincksieck.

Turing, A.M. 1950. Computing machinery and intelligence. *Mind* 59: 433–460.

Van de Walle, J. 2008. Roman Jakobson, cybernetics and information theory: A critical assessment. *Folia Linguistica Historica* 29 (1): 87–124.

Varela, F. 1989. *Invitation aux sciences cognitives*. Paris: Éditions du Seuil.

Velleman, B.L. 2008. The scientific Linguist' goes to war. *Historiographia Linguistica* 35 (3): 385–416.

Verleyen, S. 2007. Le fonctionnalisme entre système linguistique et sujet parlant: Jakobson et Troubetzkoy face à Martinet. *Cahiers Ferdinand de Saussure* 60: 163–188.

Verleyen, S., and P. Swiggers. 2006. Causalité et conditionnement dans le fonctionnalisme diachronique. *Folia Linguistica Historica* 27 (1–2): 171–195.

Victorri, B. 1995. Les enjeux de l'implémentation informatique de modèles linguistiques. In *Langage et sciences humaines: propos croisés*, ed. S. Robert, 79–95. Berne: Peter Lang.

Voegelin, C.F. 1951. Culture, language, and the human organism. *Southwestern Journal of Anthropology* 7: 352–373.

———. 1953. From FL (Shawnee) to TL (English), autobiography of a woman. *International Journal of American Linguistics* 19: 1–25.

———. 1954. Multiple stage translation. *International Journal of American Linguistics* 20 (4): 271–280.

Voegelin, C.F., and Z.S. Harris. 1951. Methods of determining intelligibility among dialects of natural languages. *Proceedings of the American Philosophical Society* 95 (3): 322–329.

Waltz, D.L., and J.B. Pollack. 1985. Massively parallel parsing: A strongly interactive model of natural language interpretation. *Cognitive Science* 9 (1): 51–74.

Waugh, L.R., and M. Monville-Burston. 1990. *On language. Roman Jakobson*. Cambridge: Harvard University Press.

Weaver, W. 1955. Translation. In *Machine translation of languages, 14 essays*, ed. W.N. Locke and A.D. Booth, 15–23. Cambridge MA/New York: MIT/Wiley.

———. 1970. *Scene of change. A lifetime in American Science*. New York: Charles Scribner's Sons.

Wells, R.S. 1947. Immediate constituents. *Language* 23: 81–117.

Whatmough, J. 1952. Natural selection in language. *Scientific American* 186: 82–86.

Wiener, N. 1948. *Cybernetics, or control and communication in the animal and the machine*. Paris/New York: Hermann & Cie/The MIT Press/Wiley.

———. 1950. *The human use of human beings*. Boston: Houghton Mifflin.

Wildgen, W. 2009. La rivalité historique entre une modélisation statique et dynamique des faits linguistiques. *Histoire Épistémologie Langage* 31 (1): 99–126.

Wilkins, J. 1668. *An essay towards a real character and a philosophical language*. London: The Royal Society.

Wilks, Y. 1968. On-line semantic analysis of English texts. *Mechanical Translation* 11 (3/4): 59–72.

Winograd, T. 1972. *Understanding natural language*. New York: Academic.

Wittgenstein, L. 1961 [1953]. *Tractatus logico-philosophicus suivi de Investigations philos-ophiques*. French Translation Pierre Klossowski. Paris: Gallimard.

Yngve, V.H. 1955. Syntax and the problem of multiple meaning. In *Machine translation of lan-guages, 14 essays*, ed. W.N. Locke and A.D. Booth, 208–226. Cambridge, MA/New York: MIT/Wiley.

———. 1959. The COMIT system for mechanical translation, 183–187. *IFIP Congress 1959*. Paris France.

———. 1960. A model and an hypothesis for language structure. *Proceedings of the American Philosophical Society* 104 (5): 444–466.

———. 1964. Implications of mechanical translation research. *Proceedings of the American Philosophical Society* 108 (5): 275–281.

Zipf, G.K. 1949. *Human behavior and the principle of least effort*. Cambridge: Addison Wesley.

Žolkovskij, A.K. 1961. Essays on and in MT by the Cambridge research unit, Cambridge, England, June 1959. *Masinnyj Perevod i Prikladnaja Linguistika* 5: 81–89. English translation JPRS 13761 mai 1962, pp 102–115 [Archives HTAL].

Archives

archives de l'EPRASS (EHESS)

archives du CNRS

archives Histoire du Traitement Automatique des Langues HTAL (UMR7597, Histoire des Théories Linguistiques).

Data Base

Corpus de Textes Linguistiques Fondamentaux (CTLF) http://ctlf.ens-lyon.fr/ Bernard Colombat, Arnaud Pelfrêne

Printed in the United States
by Baker & Taylor Publisher Services